TRADE ISSUES, POLICIES AND LAWS

DISPUTED WTO CASES INVOLVING THE UNITED STATES

Trade Issues, Policies and Laws

Additional books in this series can be found on Nova's website under the Series tab.

Additional E-books in this series can be found on Nova's website under the E-books tab.

Economic Issues, Problems and Perspectives

Additional books in this series can be found on Nova's website under the Series tab.

Additional E-books in this series can be found on Nova's website under the E-books tab.

TRADE ISSUES, POLICIES AND LAWS

DISPUTED WTO CASES INVOLVING THE UNITED STATES

JACQUELINE P. DANIELS
EDITOR

Nova Science Publishers, Inc.
New York

For permission to use material from this book please contact us:
Telephone 631-231-7269; Fax 631-231-8175
Web Site: http://www.novapublishers.com

NOTICE TO THE READER

LIBRARY OF CONGRESS CATALOGING-IN-PUBLICATION DATA
Disputed WTO cases involving the United States / editors, Jacqueline P. Daniels.
p. cm.
Includes index.
ISBN 978-1-61761-433-0 (hardcover)
1. World Trade Organization--United States. 2. Dispute resolution (Law)--Cases. 3. Foreign trade regulation--Cases. 4. United States--Trials, litigation, etc. I. Daniels, Jacqueline P.
K4610.D578 2010
382'.920973--dc22
2010028631

Published by Nova Science Publishers, Inc. † New York

CONTENTS

PREFACE

Although the United States has complied with adverse rulings in many past World Trade Organization (WTO) disputes, there are currently 10 cases in which rulings have not yet been implemented or the United States has taken action and the dispute has not been fully resolved. Under WTO dispute settlement rules, a WTO Member will generally be given a reasonable period of time to comply with an adverse WTO decision. While the Member is expected to remove the offending measure by the end of this period, compensation and temporary retaliation are available if the Member has not acted or taken sufficient action by this time. This book provides an overview of WTO dispute settlement procedures, focusing on the compliance phase of the process, followed by a discussion of U.S. laws relating to WTO dispute proceedings; and then lists pending WTO disputes in the compliance phase with a discussion of major issues and the U.S. compliance history in each.

Chapter 1- Although the United States has complied with adverse rulings in many past World Trade Organization (WTO) disputes, there are currently 10 cases in which rulings have not yet been implemented or the United States has taken action and the dispute has not been fully resolved. Under WTO dispute settlement rules, a WTO Member will generally be given a reasonable period of time to comply with an adverse WTO decision. While the Member is expected to remove the offending measure by the end of this period, compensation and temporary retaliation are available if the Member has not acted or taken sufficient action by this time. Either disputing party may request a compliance panel if there is disagreement over whether a Member has complied.

Chapter 2- On April 5, 2010, Brazil's Foreign Trade Council (CAMEX) approved a resolution that would postpone until April 22 the implementation of WTO-approved countermeasures by Brazil against U.S. imports in relation to a long-running dispute over U.S. cotton subsidies. Earlier, on March 10, 2010, Brazil had released a list of 102 goods of U.S. origin valued at $561 million that would be subject to import tariffs of up to 100% within 30 days unless a last-minute agreement was reached. Five days later, on March 15, Brazil released a preliminary list of U.S. patents and intellectual property rights it could restrict, barring a joint settlement. In light of the temporary suspension of countermeasures, negotiations between the United States and Brazil on a proposed settlement continue. If preliminary objectives (discussed in the report) are achieved, it may result in the permanent suspension of any countermeasures related to this case.

Chapter 3- In 2007, Brazil and Canada, independently of each other, requested consultations with the United States under the auspices of the World Trade Organization's (WTO's) Dispute Settlement process concerning similar grievances regarding U.S. domestic agricultural support programs and the U.S. export credit guarantee program. After consultations failed to resolve their concerns, both countries (again acting independently) requested the establishment of a WTO panel to rule on their complaints. The WTO's Dispute Settlement Body, on December 17, 2007, established a single panel to consider both cases. In late April 2008, Brazil and Canada informally agreed to postpone proceeding with their joint World Trade Organization (WTO) dispute settlement case challenging certain U.S. agricultural subsidies. At the time of the postponement, the three parties involved in the dispute had been unable to agree on panel membership.

Chapter 4- Dispute settlement in the World Trade Organization (WTO) is carried out under the WTO Understanding on Rules and Procedures Governing the Settlement of Disputes (DSU). In effect since January 1995, the DSU provides for consultations between disputing parties, panels and appeals, and possible retaliation if a defending party fails to comply with a WTO decision by an established deadline. Automatic establishment of panels, adoption of panel and appellate reports, and authorization of requests to retaliate, along with deadlines and improved multilateral oversight of compliance, are aimed at producing a more expeditious and effective system than had existed under the General Agreement on Tariffs and Trade (GATT). To date, 405 complaints have been filed, approximately half involving the United States as complainant or defendant.

In: Disputed WTO Cases Involving the United... ISBN: 978-1-61761-433-0
Editors: Jacqueline P. Daniels

Chapter 1

WTO DISPUTE SETTLEMENT: STATUS OF U.S. COMPLIANCE IN PENDING CASES*

Jeanne J. Grimmet

SUMMARY

Although the United States has complied with adverse rulings in many past World Trade Organization (WTO) disputes, there are currently 10 cases in which rulings have not yet been implemented or the United States has taken action and the dispute has not been fully resolved. Under WTO dispute settlement rules, a WTO Member will generally be given a reasonable period of time to comply with an adverse WTO decision. While the Member is expected to remove the offending measure by the end of this period, compensation and temporary retaliation are available if the Member has not acted or taken sufficient action by this time. Either disputing party may request a compliance panel if there is disagreement over whether a Member has complied.

The United States has not yet settled long-standing disputes with the European Union (EU) regarding a music copyright statute and a statutory trademark provision affecting property confiscated by Cuba. H.R. 1530, H.R. 1531, H.R. 2272, and S. 1189 would repeal the trademark statute, while H.R.

---

* This is an edited, reformatted and augmented edition of a United States Congressional Research Service publication, Report RL32014, dated January 29, 2010.

1103 and S. 1234 would amend the provision. Also unresolved is a dispute with Japan, initiated in 1999, over a provision of U.S. antidumping law. The Continued Dumping and Subsidy Offset Act of 2000 (CDSOA), which was held WTO-inconsistent in January 2003 and repealed, effective October 2005, by P.L. 109-171, remains the target of sanctions by complainants EU and Japan due to continued payments to U.S firms under the CDSOA program. In addition, the United States and Antigua have been consulting on the resolution of outstanding issues in Antigua's challenge of U.S. online gambling restrictions.

P.L. 109-171 also repealed a WTO-inconsistent cotton program at issue in Brazil's 2002 complaint over U.S. cotton subsidies, but other programs were also successfully challenged and the United States was later found not to have fully complied. The United States has since made statutory and administrative changes affecting the export credit guarantee programs faulted in the case. At the same time, Brazil has continued to pursue sanctions and on November 19, 2009, the WTO authorized Brazil to suspend tariff concessions on U.S. goods in an amount of $294.7 million a year, a figure that may vary annually based on actual U.S. export subsidization. In addition, if a variable threshold based on U.S. trade in goods with Brazil is exceeded, Brazil may suspend WTO obligations involving U.S. intellectual property and services. Brazil has published a list of U.S. goods potentially subject to increased tariffs, but will not announce until February 2010 the final list of products and the total value of sanctions that would be imposed. On December 21, 2009, Brazil announced that, based on 2008 data provided by the United States, it is entitled to annual retaliation of $829.3 million.

Four pending cases involve the U.S. practice of "zeroing," under which the Department of Commerce (DOC), in calculating dumping margins, disregards non-dumped sales. The practice was successfully challenged by the EU in two cases (EU I and II), Japan, and Mexico. In response to EU I, DOC discontinued the use of zeroing in the price comparison employed most often in original antidumping investigations and recalculated dumping margins in the cases cited by the EU. The United States has yet to fully comply in EU I and in the challenges by Japan and Mexico to the extent that the WTO decisions affect the use of zeroing in other phases of U.S. antidumping proceedings. Compliance proceedings in EU I and Japan's challenge, completed in 2009, found against the United States, permitting complainants to pursue sanctions requests. Also, Mexico initiated compliance proceedings in August 2009, and a compliance deadline of December 19, 2009, was established in EU II. The United States stated that it will recalculate dumping margins in four original antidumping investigations cited in EU II and that it is discussing outstanding issues with interested parties. With other facets of EU II remaining unaddressed, however, the EU has indicated that it may request a compliance panel in the proceeding.

This chapter provides a summary of the status of U.S. compliance efforts in pending World Trade Organization (WTO) disputes that have resulted in adverse rulings against the United States. Although the United States has complied with adverse rulings in many past WTO disputes,[1] there are 10 pending cases in which the United States has not fully implemented adopted WTO panel and Appellate Body reports or the United States has taken action, including the enactment of legislation, but the prevailing parties in the dispute continue to question whether the United States has fully complied and, in one case, continue to impose WTO-authorized trade sanctions. In all of these disputes, original or subsequently extended compliance deadlines have expired. Compliance in these cases may implicate either legislative or administrative action by the United States.

The report begins with an overview of WTO dispute settlement procedures, focusing on the compliance phase of the process, followed by a discussion of U.S. laws relating to WTO dispute proceedings. The report then lists pending WTO disputes in the compliance phase, with a discussion of major issues and the U.S. compliance history in each. Each entry contains a section titled "Recent Developments," which discusses the latest activity in the case.

WTO Dispute Settlement Procedures

WTO disputes are conducted under the terms of the WTO Understanding on the Rules and Procedures Governing the Settlement of Disputes (Dispute Settlement Understanding or DSU).[2] The DSU, which entered into force with the establishment of the World Trade Organization on January 1, 1995, carries forward and expands upon dispute settlement practices developed under the General Agreement on Tariffs and Trade (GATT). The DSU is administered by the WTO Dispute Settlement Body (DSB), which is composed of all WTO Members. Where individual WTO agreements contain special or additional dispute settlement rules that differ from those in the DSU (e.g., expedited timelines for subsidy disputes in the Agreement on Subsidies and Countervailing Measures), the former will prevail. A list of these agreements and rules is contained in Appendix 2 of the DSU. The Office of the United States Trade Representative (USTR) represents the United States in the WTO and in WTO disputes.

WTO dispute settlement may be characterized as a three-stage process: (1) consultations; (2) panel and, if requested, Appellate Body (AB) proceedings; and (3) implementation. Within this framework, the DSB establishes panels; adopts panel and appellate reports; authorizes countermeasures when requested; and monitors the implementation of dispute settlement results. The establishment of panels, adoption of panel and AB reports, and authorization of countermeasures are decisions that are subject to a "reverse consensus" rule under which the DSB agrees to these actions unless all DSB Members object. In effect, these decisions are virtually automatic. Article 23 of the DSU requires a complaining Member to act in accordance with the DSU when it initiates a dispute, including making any internal determination that another Member has violated a WTO obligation consistent with the WTO decision in the case and following DSU procedures to set a deadline by which the defending Member must comply, determining the level of sanctions for non-compliance, and obtaining authorization from the DSB to impose any such sanctions.

After the DSB adopts an adverse panel and any Appellate Body report, the defending Member must inform the DSB of its compliance plans. If it is impracticable for the Member to comply immediately, the Member will be allowed a "reasonable period of time" to do so. If the Member proposes a compliance period and it is not approved by the DSB, the disputing parties may negotiate a deadline themselves. If this fails, the length of the period will be arbitrated. A WTO Member found to have violated WTO obligations is expected to comply by withdrawing the offending measure by the end of the established compliance period, with compensation and temporary retaliation available to the prevailing party as alternative remedies. Full compliance is the preferred outcome, however, so as to ensure that negotiated rights and obligations are preserved and maintained.

Article 22 of the DSU provides that if the prevailing Member in a dispute believes that the defending Member has not implemented the WTO rulings and recommendations by the end of the established compliance period, it may request the other Member to negotiate a compensation agreement or it may ask the DSB for authorization to suspend WTO concessions, usually to impose higher tariffs on selected imports from the defending country. The Member may choose the latter option without first requesting compensation. In some cases, the prevailing party may agree to extend the original compliance deadline instead of immediately seeking a remedy.

If a prevailing Member does choose to suspend concessions, it is expected to do so in the same sector in which the WTO violation was found, but if the Member finds that this is not "practicable or effective," it may seek to suspend concessions in other sectors in the same agreement. If, however, the Member finds that this alternative would also be impracticable or ineffective and that "the circumstances are serious enough," it may seek to suspend obligations under another WTO agreement, referred to as "cross-retaliation." A prevailing Member may seek to cross- retaliate if, for example, in a dispute involving trade in goods, the Member does not import a sufficient amount of goods from the defending Member to remedy the trade injury involved or the Member believes that placing tariff surcharges on goods imported from the defending Member would be unreasonably costly for the prevailing Member's economy.

Under the DSU, the DSB is to authorize the retaliation request under the reverse consensus rule within 30 days after the compliance period expires. If the defending Member objects to the request, however, the proposed retaliation will be arbitrated and the 30-day deadline for approving the retaliation request effectively extended. The objection may relate to the level of nullification or impairment of benefits involved or whether DSU cross-retaliation rules have been followed. The arbitration, which may be carried out by the original panel if members are available, or by an arbitrator appointed by the WTO Director General, is ordinarily to be completed within 60 days after the compliance period expires. The DSB then meets to authorize the retaliation request, subject to any modification by the arbitrator.

In addition, Article 21.5 of the DSU provides for further dispute settlement proceedings in the event the disputing parties disagree as to whether the defending Member has implemented the WTO rulings and recommendations in a particular case. Once a compliance panel is convened, it is expected to issue its report within 90 days; the report may then be appealed. In practice, compliance panels may require a considerably longer period of time to complete their work where a complicated case is involved. For example, in the European Union's challenge to the U.S. use of "zeroing" in antidumping proceedings (DS294), the EU made its compliance panel request in September 2007, panelists were appointed in November 2007, and the panel report was not publicly circulated until December 2008.

Because the DSU fails to incorporate Article 21.5 proceedings into the 30-day period for approving countermeasures and the timeframe for any subsequent arbitration, a procedural problem, referred to as "sequencing," has resulted. Disputing Members have often filled the gap by entering into ad hoc bilateral procedural agreements setting out timelines for any requested compliance-related proceedings and reserving Members' rights in the unfolding of these proceedings.[3] Such agreements have been entered into in many of the cases discussed below.

The DSU provides that any suspension of concessions or other obligations is temporary and may only be applied by the prevailing Member until the WTO-inconsistent measure is removed, the defending Member provides a solution to any trade injury at issue, or a mutually satisfactory resolution of the dispute is reached.[4] Moreover, if a prevailing Member is ultimately authorized to impose countermeasures, the Member is not required to implement them. As evident from some of the cases discussed in this chapter, WTO Members may manage disputes in a variety of ways at the compliance phase, short of imposing sanctions.

Uruguay Round Agreements Act (URAA): Statutory Requirements for Implementing WTO Decisions

The legal effect of Uruguay Round agreements and WTO dispute settlement results in the United States is comprehensively dealt with in the Uruguay Round Agreements Act (URAA), P.L. 103- 465, which addresses the relationship of WTO agreements to federal and state law and prohibits private remedies based on alleged violations of WTO agreements.[5] The statute also requires the United States Trade Representative (USTR) to keep Congress informed of disputes challenging U.S. laws once a dispute panel is established, any U.S. appeal is filed, and a panel or Appellate Body report is circulated to WTO Members.[6] In addition, the URAA places requirements on regulatory action taken to implement WTO decisions and contains provisions specific to the implementation of panel and appellate reports that fault U.S. actions in trade remedy proceedings.

Section 102: Domestic Legal Effect of WTO Decisions

Section 102 of the URAA and its legislative history establish that domestic law supersedes any inconsistent provisions of the Uruguay Round agreements and that congressional or administrative action, as the case may be, is required to implement adverse decisions in WTO dispute settlement proceedings.

Federal Law

Section 102(a)(1), 19 U.S.C. § 3512(a)(1), provides that "[n]o provision of any of the Uruguay Round Agreements, nor the application of any such provision to any person or circumstance, that is inconsistent with any law of the United States shall have effect." The URAA further provides, at § 102(a)(2), 19 U.S.C. § 35 12(a)(2), that nothing in the statute "shall be construed ... to amend or modify any law of the United States ... or ... to limit any authority conferred under any law of the United States ... unless specifically provided for in this act."

As explained in Statement of Administrative Action (SAA) accompanying the Uruguay Round agreements when they were submitted to Congress in 1994, "[i]f there is a conflict between U.S. law and any of the Uruguay Round agreements, section 102(a) of the implementing bill makes clear that U.S. law will take precedence."[7] Moreover, section 102 is further intended to clarify that all changes to U.S. law "known to be necessary or appropriate" to implement the WTO agreements are incorporated in the URAA and that any unforeseen conflicts between U.S. law and the WTO agreements "can be enacted in subsequent legislation"[8] Congress has traditionally treated potential conflicts with prior GATT agreements and free trade agreements in this way, treatment that it also deems to be "consistent with the Congressional view that necessary changes in Federal statutes should be specifically enacted, not preempted by international agreements."[9]

This approach carries over into the implementation of WTO dispute settlement results, a situation explained as follows in URAA legislative history:

> Since the Uruguay Round agreements as approved by the Congress, or any subsequent amendments to those agreements, are non-self-executing, any dispute settlement findings that a U.S. statute is inconsistent with an agreement also cannot be implemented except by legislation approved by the Congress unless consistent implementation is permissible under the terms of the statute.[10]

State Law

Where a state law is at issue in a WTO dispute, the URAA provides for federal-state cooperation in the proceeding and limits any domestic legal challenges to the law to the United States.[11] The act's general preclusion of private remedies (discussed below) further centralizes the response to adverse WTO decisions involving state law in the federal government.[12]

Section 102(b) provides as follows:

> No State law, or the application of a such a State law, may be declared invalid as to any person or circumstance on the ground that the provision or its application is inconsistent with any of the Uruguay Round Agreements, except in an action brought by the United States for the purposes of declaring such law or application invalid.[13]

According to legislative history, the provision "makes clear that the Uruguay Round agreements do not automatically preempt State laws that do not conform to their provisions, even if a WTO dispute settlement panel or the Appellate Body were to determine that a particular State measure was inconsistent with one or more of the Uruguay Round agreements."[14] The statute also contains certain restrictions in any such legal action brought by the United States, including that the report of the WTO dispute settlement panel or the Appellate Body may not be considered binding or otherwise accorded deference.[15] Any such suit by the United States is expected to be a rarity.[16]

Preclusion of Private Remedies

Private remedies are prohibited under § 102(c)(1) of the URAA, 19 U.S.C. § 351 2(c)(1), which provides that "[n]o person other than the United States ... shall have a cause of action or defense under any of the Uruguay Round Agreements or by virtue of congressional approval of such an agreements" or "may challenge, in any action brought under any provision of law, any action or inaction by any department, agency, or other instrumentality of the United States, any State, or any political subdivision of a State, on the ground that such action or inaction is inconsistent with such agreement."

Congress has additionally stated in § 102(c)(2) of the URAA, 19 U.S.C. § 3512(c)(2), that it intends, through the prohibition on private remedies:

> to occupy the field with respect to any cause of action or defense under or in connection with any of the Uruguay Round Agreements, including by precluding any person other than the United States from bringing any action

against any State or political subdivision thereof or raising any defense to the application of State law under or in connection with any of the Uruguay Round Agreements—

(A) on the basis of a judgment obtained by the United States in an action brought under any such agreement; or

(B) on any other basis.

The House Ways and Means Committee report on the URAA discusses the rationale and implications of § 102(c) as follows:

> For example, a private party cannot bring an action to require, preclude, or modify government exercise of discretionary or general "public interest" authorities under other provisions of law. These prohibitions are based on the premise that it is the responsibility of the Federal Government, and not private citizens, to ensure that Federal or State laws are consistent with U.S. obligations under international agreements such as the Uruguay Round agreements.[17]

The SAA notes, however, that § 102(c) "does not preclude any agency of government from considering, or entertaining argument on, whether its action or proposed action is consistent with the Uruguay Round agreements, although any change in agency action would have to be authorized by domestic law."[18]

Domestic Implementation of WTO Decisions Involving Administrative Action

In addition to the URAA provisions that limit the direct effect of WTO rules and decisions in U.S. law, the URAA also places requirements on agencies in their implementation of WTO panel and Appellate Body reports. These provisions apply to regulatory action in general and to new agency determinations in response to WTO decisions involving trade remedy proceedings.

Section 123: Regulatory Action Generally

Section 123(g) of the URAA, 19 U.S.C. § 3533(g), provides that in any WTO case in which a departmental or agency regulation or practice has been found to be inconsistent with a WTO agreement, the regulation or practice may not be rescinded or modified in implementation of the decision "unless and until" the United States Trade Representative and relevant agencies meet congressional consultation and private sector advice requirements, the proposal has been published in the *Federal Register* with a request for public comment, and the final rule or other modification has been published in the *Federal Register*.[19] Section 123(g) does not apply to any regulation or practice of the U.S. International Trade Commission.

The statute requires the USTR to consult with "the appropriate congressional committees" regarding the proposed contents of the final rule or other modification. These committees include the House Ways and Means Committee, the Senate Finance Committee, and any other congressional committees that have jurisdiction over matter at hand.[20] In addition, the final rule or other modification may not take effect until 60 days after the USTR has begun committee consultations, unless the President determines that an earlier effective date is in the national interest. The House Ways and Means Committee and the Senate Finance Committee may vote to indicate the disagreement of the committee with the proposed action during the 60-day period. Any such vote is not binding on the agency or department involved.[21]

Section 129: Agency Determinations in Trade Remedy Proceedings

Section 129 of the URAA, 19 U.S.C. § 3538, sets forth authorities and procedures under which the Department of Commerce (DOC) and the U.S. International Trade Commission (ITC) may issue new subsidy, dumping and injury determinations, referred to as Section 129 Determinations, in implementation of adverse WTO decisions involving U.S. safeguards, antidumping, and countervailing duty proceedings. Section 129 does not authorize the Commerce Department or the ITC to issue new determinations on their own motion, but instead grants the USTR the discretion to direct the agency to do so in a given case.

In antidumping and countervailing duty investigations, which are carried out under authorities in Title VII of the Tariff Act of 1930, 19 U.S.C. §§ 1671-1677n, the Commerce Department determines the existence and level of dumping or subsidization, as the case may be, and the ITC determines whether the dumped or subsidized imports cause material injury, or a threat of material injury, to a domestic industry. Under U.S. safeguards law, set forth in Title II of the Trade Act of 1974, 19 U.S.C. §§ 2251-2254, the ITC conducts investigations to determine if increased imports, whether or not they are fairly traded, are a substantial cause of serious injury to a domestic industry. If the ITC makes an affirmative injury determination, it recommends remedial measures (e.g., a tariff surcharge or import quota) to the President, who ultimately determines whether or not to take action.

Implemented Section 129 Determinations in antidumping and countervailing duty cases are reviewable in the U.S. Court of International Trade and by binational panels established under Chapter 19 of the North American Free Trade Agreement (NAFTA).[22] Chapter 19 panels are available to review final agency determinations in antidumping and countervailing duty investigations involving NAFTA countries in lieu of judicial review in the country in which the determination is made.

U.S. International Trade Commission

If an interim WTO panel report or a WTO Appellate Body report concludes that an action by the ITC in connection with a trade remedy proceeding is inconsistent with U.S. obligations under the WTO Antidumping Agreement, the Agreement on Subsidies and Countervailing Measures, or the Agreement on Safeguards, the USTR may request the ITC to issue an advisory report on whether U.S. antidumping, countervailing duty, or safeguards law, as appropriate, allows the ITC to take steps with respect to the proceeding at issue that would render its action "not inconsistent with" the panel or AB findings.[23]

The ITC is to report to the USTR within 30 calendar days of the USTR's request where an interim report is involved, and within 21 calendar days in case of an AB report.[24] These deadlines are aimed at ensuring that the USTR will receive the requested advice in time to decide whether to appeal a panel's interim report or to implement an adverse report, and to estimate the period of time that may be needed to implementing the WTO decision.[25]

If a majority of the ITC Commissioners have found that action may be taken under existing law, the USTR must consult with the House Ways and Means Committee and the Senate Finance Committee and may request the ITC in writing to issue a new determination in the underlying proceeding that would render the ITC action "not inconsistent with" the WTO findings.[26] The new determination must be issued within 120 days of the USTR's request.[27] The 120-day limit is intended to allow the USTR to propose a reasonable period of time for implementation to the WTO Dispute Settlement Body once the DSB adopts a WTO panel and any Appellate Body report in a case.[28]

In the event the ITC issues a new negative injury or threat of injury determination, the imports subject to antidumping or countervailing duty order at issue, or a least a portion of them, would no longer be considered to have caused a harmful effect, even though they may in fact be dumped or subsidized. The Tariff Act requires that the imposition of antidumping or countervailing duties on dumped or subsidized imports be supported by an affirmative injury determination and thus, absent such a determination, the antidumping or countervailing duty order would need to be revoked in whole or in part. Section 129(a)(6) authorizes the USTR to direct the Commerce Department to take this action.[29] The USTR must consult with the House Ways and Means and Senate Finance Committees before the ITC's new determination is implemented.[30]

Where a safeguard proceeding is involved, section 129 authorizes the President, after receiving a new ITC determination, to reduce, modify, or terminate the safeguard notwithstanding other statutory requirements governing changes in existing safeguard measures.[31] The President must consult with the House Ways and Means Committee and Senate Finance Committee before acting under this authority. The USTR is required to publish a notice of the implementation of any ITC determination in the *Federal Register*.[32]

Department of Commerce

Section 129 also sets out a procedure for new Department of Commerce determinations in antidumping and countervailing duty proceedings, though without the requirement for an initial agency advisory report regarding the scope of the agency's statutory discretion. Instead, promptly after the issuance of a WTO panel or Appellate Body report finding that a DOC determination in an antidumping or countervailing duty proceeds is inconsistent with U.S. obligations under the WTO Antidumping Agreement or the Agreement on Subsidies and Countervailing Measures, the USTR is to consult with the Commerce Department and the House Ways and Means and Senate Finance Committees, and may request the Department, in writing, to issue a determination in connection with the underlying antidumping or countervailing duty proceeding that would render its action "not inconsistent with" the panel or appellate findings.[33] The Commerce Department must issue its Section 129 Determination within 180 days of the request.[34] A new determination may, for example, reduce the dumping margin or net subsidy and thus result in a reduction of existing duties. After consulting with DOC and the above-named congressional committees, USTR may direct DOC to implement its determination in whole or in part.[35]

Prospective Implementation of Section 129 Determinations

Section 129(c)(1) of the URAA provides that Section 129 Determinations, whether issued by the ITC or the Commerce Department, apply prospectively, that is, the full or partial revocation of the antidumping or countervailing duty order or the implementation of the DOC determination, as the case may be, applies to unliquidated entries of the subject merchandise that are entered, or withdrawn from warehouse for consumption, *on or after* the date on which the USTR directs the Commerce Department to revoke the order or implement the determination.[36] Unliquidated entries are those for which the U.S. Customs and Border Protection has not ascertained a final rate and amount of duty.[37] Notices of the implementation of Section 129 Determinations must be published in the *Federal Register*.

The Uruguay Round SAA explains the operation of § 129(c)(1) as follows:

> Consistent with the principle that GATT panel recommendations apply only prospectively, subsection 129(c)(1) provides that where determinations by the ITC or Commerce are implemented under subsections (a) or (b), such determinations have prospective effect only. That is, they apply to unliquidated entries of merchandise entered, or withdrawn from warehouse, for consumption on or after the date on which the Trade Representative directs implementation. Thus, relief available under subsection 129(c)(1) is distinguishable from relief available in an action brought before a court or a NAFTA binational panel, where, depending on the circumstances of the case, retroactive relief may be available. Under 129(c)(1), if implementation of a WTO report should result in the revocation of an antidumping or countervailing duty order, entries made prior to the date of Trade Representative's direction would remain subject to potential duty liability.[38]

Canada unsuccessfully challenged § 129(c)(1) in a WTO dispute settlement proceeding in 2001 on the ground that the provision violated the WTO Dispute Settlement Understanding and various WTO antidumping and countervailing duty obligations. Under the retrospective U.S. antidumping and countervailing duty system, DOC ordinarily makes a final assessment of the duties owed on dumped or subsidized goods in an administrative review conducted after the goods are imported. The review covers goods that enter the United States during a specified prior 12-month period. Until this final duty assessment is made for particular goods, importers must deposit estimated duties with U.S. Customs and Border Protection (CBP) on entry.[39] Canada argued that, where a DOC or ITC determination in an antidumping or countervailing duty proceeding is found to violate a WTO obligation, § 129(c)(1) effectively prohibits the United States from fully complying with the WTO decision by preventing it from refunding estimated duties deposited with CBP before the date that the Section 129 Determination is implemented. In other words, because the duty deposits supported by the challenged determination would no longer have a WTO-consistent basis, Canada argued that they must be returned.[40]

In response to Canada's claim, the United States maintained that § 129(c)(1) addresses only the treatment of imports entered after the implementation date and does not govern the treatment of prior entries for which final duties have not yet been calculated. The United States further argued that the statute does not mandate any particular treatment of these prior unliquidated entries and that the United States has other legal options for dealing with them, including establishing a new dumping or subsidy margin by using a WTO-consistent methodology in an administrative review of the entries or, in the event the duty order or orders were revoked as a result of the WTO proceeding, revising the duty rate in response to a domestic court decision involving the earlier entries.[41]

In a report issued in July 2002, the WTO panel concluded that Canada failed to establish that the statute either required WTO-inconsistent action on the part of the United States or precluded the United States from taking action in accordance with its WTO obligations.[42] Canada did not appeal, and the panel report was adopted by the DSB in August 2002.

Judicial Responses

Although private rights of action based on Uruguay Round agreements are precluded under § 102(c) of the Uruguay Round Agreements Act, WTO panel findings have at times been brought to the attention of federal courts, most often in challenges to agency determinations in antidumping and countervailing duty proceedings initiated under judicial review provisions contained in § 51 6A of the Tariff Act of 1930, 19 U.S.C. § 151 6a. Section 129 determinations issued by the ITC and the Commerce Department to comply with WTO decisions are also reviewable under this statute. These cases are heard in the U.S. Court of International Trade (USCIT), which has exclusive jurisdiction over civil actions brought under § 51 6A.[43] The USCIT's decisions may be appealed to the U.S. Court of Appeals for the Federal Circuit, whose decisions are reviewable by the U.S. Supreme Court.

Federal courts must hold a final agency determination in an antidumping or countervailing duty proceeding or a Section 129 Determination unlawful if it is found to be "unsupported by substantial evidence on the record, or otherwise not in accordance with law."[44] To determine whether an agency legal interpretation applied in an agency determination is in accordance with law, the court employs the two-step analysis set out by the U.S. Supreme Court in *Chevron, U.S.A., Inc. v. Natural Resources Defense Council,* 467 U.S. 837 (1984).[45] First, the court, using tools of statutory construction, determines whether Congress has clearly spoken to the issue at hand. Second, if the underlying statute is silent or ambiguous, the court decides whether the agency's construction of the statute is permissible and will defer to an agency's interpretation of a statute provided it is reasonable. It has also been argued that, in considering whether an agency construction is reasonable for purposes of the second prong of the *Chevron* test, the court should apply the canon of construction articulated by the Supreme Court in 1804 in *Murray v. Schooner Charming Betsy,* 6 U.S. (2 Cranch) 64, 118 (1804). This canon holds that where a statute does not require a specific interpretation, i.e., it permits more than one interpretation, it should be interpreted consistently with U.S international obligations.[46] In the current context, the international obligation would be that contained in a WTO agreement, either by itself or as interpreted in one or more WTO decisions.[47] Plaintiffs thus argue, on the basis of the *Charming Betsy* canon, that an agency interpretation that violates a WTO obligation is unreasonable under *Chevron* step two.

Because the underlying cause of action in domestic legal challenges to the agency actions described above is based in the Tariff Act and not on a provision of a WTO agreement, courts have not viewed § 102(c) of the URAA as preventing them from hearing a WTO-based argument in these challenges.[48] When faced with such arguments, courts may deem WTO decisions to be "persuasive"[49] or a source of useful reasoning, "if sound" to inform a court's decision,[50] but state that WTO decisions are not binding on the United States, U.S. agencies, or the judiciary.[51] Most recently, courts have made clear that, given the statutory scheme established in the URAA for implementing adverse WTO decisions, questions as to whether the United States should comply with an adverse WTO decision, and what the extent of U.S. compliance should be, are matters falling within the province of the executive branch. [52] As a result, in ruling on whether an agency's interpretation of a statute is reasonable, courts have rejected *Charming Betsy* arguments and declined to base their decision making on a WTO decision adverse to the United States where the executive branch has not taken the necessary domestic action to comply.[53]

PENDING CASES INVOLVING LEGISLATIVE ACTION

Six WTO dispute proceedings that involve federal statutes remain pending—that is, panel and Appellate Body reports adverse to the United States have been adopted by the WTO Dispute Settlement Body (DSB) and compliance issues have not yet been fully resolved. Among these are two long-standing disputes with the European Union (EU),[54] one involving § 110(5)(B) of the Copyright Act, a statute affecting music licensing, and the other, § 211 of the Omnibus Appropriations Act of 1998, a statute addressing trademarks that involve property confiscated by Cuba. Another is a long-standing dispute with Japan involving a provision of the U.S. antidumping statute governing the calculation of dumping rates for producers and exporters who are not individually investigated by the Commerce Department.

While Congress repealed the Continued Dumping and Subsidy Offset Act of 2000, a statute which required the distribution of collected antidumping and countervailing duties to petitioners and interested parties in the underlying trade remedy proceedings, the repeal legislation mandates the distribution to U.S. firms of duties collected on goods entered through September 30, 2007, two years after the statutory repeal date of October 1, 2005. The European Union and Japan, two complainants who have objected to these continued distributions, are continuing to retaliate with tariff surcharges on U.S. goods.

As the result of a completed compliance panel proceeding, the United States has been found not to have fully complied in Brazil's challenge to U.S. cotton subsidies and faces the possibility of retaliation by Brazil against U.S. goods and possibly U.S. services or intellectual property interests. While Congress repealed or made statutory changes to U.S. export credit guarantee programs that were found by the WTO to be prohibited subsidies and the Executive Branch made administrative changes to one of these programs under revised statutory authority, Congress also reauthorized payments under two domestic support programs that Brazil successfully challenged as actionable subsidies. Payments under these programs were found to cause serious prejudice to Brazil in the form of significant price suppression in the world upland cotton market. Brazil is currently authorized to impose sanctions to remedy both prohibited and actionable subsidy measures at issue in the case.

Antigua's challenge to federal laws governing the remote supply of gambling services, while only partially successful, left certain issues unresolved and resulted in the United States withdrawing its market access commitments for gambling services under the General Agreement on Trade in Services (GATS). Antigua sought both retaliation in the WTO dispute and compensation under the GATS for the negative effects of the change in the U.S. GATS commitments. Outstanding issues still remain subject to discussion by the two parties.

Section 110(5)(B) of the Copyright Act (Music Copyrights)(DS160)

This case, sometimes referred to as the "Irish music" dispute, involves legislation enacted in 1998 (17 U.S.C. § 110(5)(b), as added by P.L. 105-298, § 202(a)), which provides that it is not a copyright infringement for bars and restaurants and other retail outlets to play radio and television music without authorization from the copyright holder or the payment of fees so long as the establishments meet certain size limitations or equipment requirements.[55] Challenged by the European Union (EU) in 1999, this so-called "small business" exemption was found to be an improper rights limitation in violation of Article 13 of the Agreement on Trade-Related Intellectual Property Rights (TRIPS).

In the absence of U.S. legislative action by the end of the initial compliance period (July 27, 2001), complainant EU agreed to extend the period to the end of 2001, and to consider U.S. compensation for the EU music industry based on an amount of trade injury determined by arbitration under Article 25 of the DSU, a free-standing arbitration provision. A November 9, 2001, arbitral award determined that some $1.1 million in EU trade benefits are affected annually.

Notwithstanding the arbitration, the EU on January 7, 2002, requested authorization to impose countermeasures on the ground that the United States had not fully complied by the extended deadline, proposing to suspend concessions under the TRIPS Agreement by "levying a special fee from US nationals in connection with border measures concerning copyright goods." While the United States asked for arbitration of the proposal, the United States and the EU on February 26, 2002, asked that the arbitration be suspended, with the understanding that it could be reactivated by either party after March 1, 2002.

In April 2003, Congress appropriated $3.3 million for a "one-time only, lump-sum payment" to the EU to cover a three-year period of nullification and impairment of benefits in the dispute (P.L. 108-11).[56] The parties notified the WTO in late June 2003 that the payment, which will be made into a fund for EU performers, constitutes a temporary settlement of the dispute.[57] They also agreed that the EU may request that the suspended arbitration be resumed any time after December 20, 2004, or if the United States fails to pay within 45 days after being notified that the fund has been established.

Recent Developments

In late November 2004, shortly before the three-year U.S.-EU agreement expired, the EU complained to the DSB that the United States had taken only minimal steps to secure the passage of legislation that would bring the United States into full compliance in the case.[58] The EU has regularly raised the issue of U.S. noncompliance at DSB meetings, with the United States continuing to report to the DSB that it will work with Congress on the matter.[59] While the EU has stated that it has reserved the right to reactivate the arbitration on its retaliation request at any time,[60] the disputing parties have also indicated interest in possible discussions on a mutually satisfactory resolution of the matter.[61] During a July 2009 meeting on bilateral trade relations held in Washington, D.C., USTR Kirk and European Union Trade Commissioner Ashton "exchanged ideas on potential steps to address" this dispute, and "directed ... [their] staffs to explore new options on this dispute in the coming weeks."[62]

Section 211 of the Omnibus Appropriations Act of 1998 (Trademark Exclusion Involving Property Confiscated by Cuba)(DS176)

This dispute, at time referred to as the "Havana Club" case, involves a statute (P.L. 105-277, 112 Stat. 2681-88), which prohibits the registration or enforcement in the United States, without the consent of the original owner or successors, of a trademark that is the same or substantially the same as one used in connection with a business or assets confiscated by the Cuban government. Challenged by the European Union (EU) in 1999, the law was ultimately found to violate national treatment and most-favored-nation obligations in the TRIPS Agreement in that it limited the prohibition on registration and enforcement of rights to rights asserted by Cuba and Cuban nationals or their successors-in-interest. Panel and Appellate Body reports in the case were adopted January 2, 2002.[63]

The original compliance period, as agreed upon by the United States and the EU, expired December 31, 2002; it was extended four times, also by agreement, most recently to June 30, 2005.[64] The United States did not comply by this date. Instead of agreeing to an extension of the deadline or, alternatively, requesting authorization to retaliate, the EU entered into an agreement with the United States regarding rights and procedures involving any future EU retaliation request.[65] The EU agreed not to request authorization from the DSB to suspend concessions for the time being, but pledged to notify and consult with the United States before making any such request in the future. For its part, the United States agreed not to block any retaliation request by the EU on the ground that the request is outside the 30-day window provided for in Article 22.6 of the DSU. The United States also retained the right to object to a proposed retaliation request and to refer the matter to arbitration.

Recent Developments

As the EU, Cuba, and other WTO Members continue to raise the issue of U.S. noncompliance at DSB meetings,[66] the United States has been reporting to the DSB that legislative proposals that would implement the WTO ruling have been introduced in the House and Senate and that it will work with the Congress on legislative vehicles to resolve this matter.[67]

Various 111th Congress bills would either repeal or amend § 211. H.R. 1103 (Wexler) and S. 1234 (Lieberman) would amend § 211 to apply to all persons claiming rights in trademarks confiscated by Cuba, whatever their nationality. H.R. 1530 (Rangel) and H.R. 2272 (Rush) would repeal § 211, remove the current trade embargo on Cuba, and make other statutory changes involving U.S.-Cuba commercial relations. H.R. 1531 (Rangel) and S. 1089 (Baucus) would repeal § 211, require related regulatory changes, and remove statutory restrictions on U.S.-Cuba trade in agricultural and medical goods.

Antidumping Measures on Hot-Rolled Steel Products from Japan (DS184)

This case involves a challenge to preliminary and final agency determinations issued in 1998 and 1999 in an antidumping investigation of hot-rolled steel products from Japan. The panel, as upheld by the Appellate Body, found that the United States was in violation of the WTO Antidumping Agreement because (1) U.S. law, specifically § 735(c)(5)(A) of the Tariff Act of 1930, requires the Commerce Department to include dumping margins based in part on "facts available," including those contained in petitions, in calculating the antidumping duty rate for companies not investigated individually in a case ("all others" rate); (2) the Commerce Department improperly applied facts available in calculating dumping margins for specific producers; and (3) the Department had improperly excluded from the calculation of the normal value of the products under investigation certain home market sales to parties affiliated with the exporter involved. [68]

The Appellate Body also ruled against the United States with respect to the ITC's injury determination, reversing panel findings that the ITC had properly applied a captive production provision and that the agency had found a causal link between the dumped imports and material injury to the industry involved. With regard to Japan's causation claim, however, the AB found that there was an insufficient factual record to allow completion of the required analysis.[69]

The arbitrated compliance period in the case expired November 23, 2002. While Japan had threatened trade retaliation earlier in the month because it found it unlikely that the United States would comply with each element of the ruling by this date, the deadline was extended until December 31, 2003, or the end of the 108th Congress, 1st Session (whichever was earlier), to permit the United States to comply fully with the panel and appellate reports in the case.[70]

Administrative Compliance

In partial implementation of the WTO rulings, the Commerce Department modified the test that it uses to determine which transactions are made by an exporter or producer to an affiliate at arm's length and are therefore "in the ordinary course of trade."[71] The panel, as upheld by the Appellate Body, found that the test that the United States had applied in the dumping investigation at issue violated Article 2.1 of the Antidumping Agreement, which provides that a product "is to be considered dumped, i.e. introduced into the commerce of another country at less than its normal value, if the export price of the product exported from one country to another is less than the comparable price, in the ordinary course of trade, for the like product when destined for consumption in the exporting country."[72] Sales that are outside the "ordinary course of trade" are thus to be excluded by national authorities when calculating normal value.

Under past practice, the Department considered sales of a product to an affiliate to be at arm's length if the prices charged were on average at least 99.5% of the prices charged to unaffiliated comparison market customers. The Department's new test provides that for affiliate sales to be considered, the sales prices "must fall, on average, within a defined range, or band, around sales prices of the same or comparable merchandise sold by that exporter or producer to all unaffiliated customer's. The band applied for this purpose will provide that the overall ratio calculated for an affiliate be between 98 percent and 102 percent, inclusive, of prices to unaffiliated customers...."[73]

According to the Department, the regulatory revision "is consistent with the view, expressed by the WTO Appellate Body, that rules aimed at preventing the distortion of normal value through sales between affiliates should reflect, 'even-handedly,' that 'both high and low-price sales between affiliates might not be 'in the ordinary course of trade.''"[74] The Department stated that the new methodology would be used to implement the WTO findings regarding the Japan hot-rolled steel AD proceeding, and applied in all investigations and reviews initiated on or after November 23, 2002.[75]

On December 3, 2002, the Department announced a new dumping determination in the AD proceeding at issue, stating that in implementation of the WTO rulings and recommendations, it had recalculated dumping margins for three affected Japanese producers using the new methodology; addressed issues related to the use of adverse facts available; and recalculated the all-others rate based on the new rates for the respondent companies.[76] The recalculations resulted in reduced dumping margins for the three companies as well for all other exporters.

Legislative Compliance

As noted earlier, the dispute panel, as upheld by the Appellate Body, concluded that the United States was in violation of its WTO obligations because it used dumping margins based in part on facts available in determining the "all others" rate in antidumping proceedings. Article 9.4 of the WTO Antidumping Agreement provides, in pertinent part, that the "all others" rate may not exceed the weighted average margin established with respect to individually investigated producers or exporters, excluding any zero and de minimis margin and margins established on the basis of facts available.[77] Section 735(c)(5)(A) of the Tariff Act of 1930 states that, for purposes of preliminary and final dumping determinations, the estimated dumping margin for producers that are not investigated individually "shall be an amount equal to the weighted average of the estimated weighted average dumping margins established for exporters and producers individually investigated, excluding any zero and de minimis margins, and any margins determined *entirely* under section 776."[78] Section 776 of the Tariff Act governs the use of facts available by the DOC and ITC in making dumping, subsidy, and injury determinations.[79] The WTO panel, as affirmed on appeal, concluded that §

735(c)(5)(A) is inconsistent with Article 9.4 because it requires DOC to consider dumping margins based *in part* on facts available in determining the all-others rate, while the cited WTO article was found to require the *exclusion* of dumping margins based either in whole *or* in part on such facts.[80]

Absent legislative compliance by the United States, the December 2003 deadline referred to earlier was extended twice, most recently to July 31, 2005.[81] The deadline lapsed without U.S. action. In an understanding between the disputing parties reached earlier in July 2005, Japan stated that it would not request authorization to retaliate at the time but might choose to do so in the future.[82]

Recent Developments

No legislation has been introduced to amend § 735(c)(5) of the Tariff Act of 1930 since the 109th Congress. H.R. 2473 (Shaw), 109th Cong., 1st Sess., would have amended § 735(c)(5) to remove the word "entirely" each time it appears in the provision, thus enabling the Department of Commerce to exclude dumping margins based in whole or in part on facts available in determining the "all others" rate, as called for by the WTO decision. Although the text of H.R. 2473 was listed for possible inclusion in 109th Congress miscellaneous tariff legislation,[83] the bill was not made part of the tariff legislation nor was it acted upon as stand-alone legislation.

Japan continues to seek legislative action,[84] as the United States continues to state its support for legislative amendments that would achieve full compliance in the case.[85] The United States has also submitted a proposal to the Doha Round Negotiating Group on Rules that Article 9.4 of the Antidumping Agreement be clarified to allow the invalidated practice.[86] No revisions or clarifications of Article 9.4, however, were included in the draft texts of proposed revisions to the Antidumping Agreement circulated by the Chair of the Negotiating Group in November 2007 and December 2008.[87]

Continued Dumping and Subsidy Offset Act (DS217/DS234)

The Continued Dumping and Subsidy Offset Act (CDSOA) of 2000, also known as the Byrd Amendment, required that duties collected under an existing antidumping or countervailing duty order be distributed annually to petitioners and interested parties in the underlying antidumping or countervailing duty proceeding.[88] Payments were available for "qualifying expenditures" in specified categories (e.g., manufacturing facilities or equipment) incurred by the petitioners and interested parties after the applicable antidumping or countervailing duty order was issued. To be eligible, petitioners and interested parties, referred to in the statute as "affected domestic producers," must also have remained in operation. Although the statute was held WTOinconsistent in January 2003 and repealed, effective October 2005, by P.L. 109-171, it remains the target of authorized sanctions by complainants European Union and Japan due to continued payments to U.S firms under the CDSOA program.

Original WTO Complaints

Eleven WTO members challenged CDSOA shortly after its enactment in October 2000 as violative of the WTO Antidumping Agreement, the WTO Agreement on Subsidies and Countervailing Measures (SCM Agreement), and other WTO obligations. The complainants based their argument in part on the prohibitions in Article 18.1 of the Antidumping Agreement and Article 32.1 of the SCM Agreement against Members' taking any "specific action against" dumping and subsidization, respectively, except for action taken in accordance with the GATT 1994 as interpreted by, as appropriate, the Antidumping or SCM Agreement.[89] Two complaints were filed: DS217, filed jointly by Australia, Brazil, Chile, the European Union (EU), India, Indonesia, Japan, Korea and Thailand, and DS234, filed jointly by Canada and Mexico.

The WTO panel, which considered both complaints at the same time, found that the CDSOA did create an impermissible "specific action against" dumping and subsidization and that it provided a financial incentive for domestic producers to file or support antidumping and countervailing duty petitions, thereby undermining the industry support requirements in the Antidumping and SCM Agreements. At the same time, the panel rejected complainants' argument that the act would make it more difficult for the United States to enter into subsidy and price undertakings with foreign governments allowing the suspension of investigations ("suspension agreements"), along with Mexico's claim that the act constituted a subsidy in and of itself.[90] The Appellate Body upheld the panel's finding that the statute created a "specific action against" dumping and subsidization not allowed under WTO agreements, but reversed the panel on its conclusion regarding industry support requirements.[91] The reports were adopted January 27, 2003, and the compliance period was subsequently determined by arbitration to expire December 27, 2003.[92]

Requests to Impose Sanctions

Because the United States did not comply by the December 2003 deadline, eight complaining Members—Brazil, Chile, EU, India, Japan, Korea, Canada, and Mexico—asked the WTO in January 2004 for authorization to impose retaliatory measures.[93] The United States objected to the requests, sending them to arbitration.[94] The remaining three complainants—Australia, Indonesia, and Thailand—agreed to give the United States until December 27, 2004, to comply.[95]

In awards issued August 31, 2004, the WTO Arbitrator (a panel of three) determined that each of the eight Members could impose countermeasures on an annual basis in an amount equal to 72% of the CDSOA disbursements for the most recent year for which official U.S. data are available relating to antidumping and countervailing duties paid on imports from the Member at that time.[96] The Arbitrator stated that the disbursements "operate, in economic terms, as subsidies that may generate import substitution production"[97] and used an economic model to determine the level of nullification or impairment of benefits, or what the Arbitrator characterized as "a value of trade" affected by application of the CDSOA.[98] The Arbitrator also made clear that each Member would need to ensure that the total value of U.S. trade subject to the proposed duty increase does not exceed the total value of trade determined to constitute the level of nullification or impairment or else propose other forms of suspending concessions to the DSB that are less likely to have trade effects exceeding this level in terms of value of U.S. exports to the country involved.

The eight complainants received formal authorization from the DSB to impose retaliatory measures in late 2004.[99] The EU and Canada began to impose countermeasures in the form of higher tariffs and surcharges on selected U.S. products, respectively, as of May 1, 2005.[100] Mexico began to impose $20.9 million in retaliatory tariffs effective August 18, 2005.[101] In addition, Japan imposed additional tariffs of 15% on 15 categories of U.S. goods as of September 1, 2005.[102]

U.S. Judicial and Legislative Action

In April 2006, the U.S. Court of International Trade ruled that the CDSOA did not apply to imports from Canada or Mexico,[103] and on September 28, 2006, U.S. Customs and Border Protection announced that it was withholding FY2006 and subsequent years' distributions on imports from the two countries pending the outcome of any appeal.[104] Canada allowed its retaliatory tariffs to terminate as of April 30, 2006.[105] Mexico, after a month's lapse, imposed increased tariffs on U.S. dairy products from September 18 through October 31, 2006.[106] These tariffs surcharges have not been reimposed.

A provision repealing the CDSOA as of October 1, 2005, but providing for the distribution of "duties on entries of goods made and filed before October 1, 2007," was enacted in the Deficit Reduction Act of 2005, signed by the President on February 8, 2006.[107] While collection of antidumping and countervailing duties for purposes of CDSOA disbursal has thus ceased, duties will continue to be available for disbursement until all relevant customs entries before September 1, 2007, are liquidated, i.e., the final assessment of duties on these entries is made. On May 29, 2009, U.S. Customs and Border Protection issued its most recent annual notice of intent to distribute these funds.[108] In addition, Congress has routinely included provisions in annual appropriations legislation directing the Commerce Department and the Office of the USTR to conduct negotiations in the WTO "to recognize the right of members to distribute monies collected from antidumping and countervailing duties."[109]

Following the 2006 enactment, the United States informed the WTO Dispute Settlement Body (DSB) that it had taken the actions necessary to implement the WTO rulings.[110] Although complaining Members expressed support for the repeal, Members also stated their concerns that the requirement that duties be distributed through 2007 and possibly after this date would prevent the United States from complying fully with its WTO obligations in the case.[111]

Recent Developments

Although WTO Members have regularly called on the United States to cease payments under the CDSOA program,[112] no Member has formally challenged the compatibility of the 2006 statute with U.S. WTO obligations. The EU and Japan are continuing to impose retaliatory tariffs on U.S. products, albeit at lower levels than in the past due to reduced payments to affected U.S. producers under the CDSOA program. As noted earlier, authorized retaliation may not exceed 72 percent of the antidumping and countervailing duties collected on EU and Japanese products disbursed in the most recent year for which data is available. On May 1, 2009, the EU reduced its annual level of retaliation from $33.38 million to $16.31 million in trade and removed goods classified in 14 tariff categories from its retaliation list.[113] U.S. products currently subject to the EU's 15% tariff surcharge are diaries, various clothing items, sweet corn, metal frames and mountings for glasses and goggles, and crane lorries. In September 2008, Japan reduced its level of retaliation from $48.14 million to $16.49 million, imposing its 10.6%

additional duty on two U.S. products: ball bearings and tapered roller bearings.[114] Japan notified the WTO on August 14, 2009, that as of September 1, 2009, it was reducing its duty on these products to 9.6% ad valorem for the upcoming year, covering a total value of trade that does not exceed $16.54 million.[115]

Subsidies on Upland Cotton (DS267)

In September 2002, Brazil requested consultations with the United States regarding U.S. statutes and programs that Brazil claimed provided prohibited and actionable subsidies to U.S. producers, users, and exporters of upland cotton.[116] Brazil alleged violations of the WTO Agreement on Agriculture, the Agreement on Subsidies and Countervailing Measures (SCM Agreement), and national treatment obligations in the GATT. It requested a panel in February 2003, adding a claim based on subsidy obligations in GATT Article XVI.[117] The panel was established in March 2003; panelists were appointed in May of that year.

WTO Members have made commitments in the WTO Agreement on Agriculture to reduce, and in some cases eliminate, domestic support in favor of agricultural producers and export subsidies on agricultural products.[118] The commitments made by each Member to limit domestic support and export subsidization are contained in the Member's Schedule, which is attached to and considered an integral part of the Agreement.[119] "Scheduled products" are those products for which a WTO Member has made domestic support and export subsidy reduction commitments. The United States did not schedule any export subsidy reduction commitments regarding upland cotton.

The types of export subsidies for which reduction commitments are made are listed in Article 9.1 of the Agreement. Members may not provide any export subsidy listed in Article 9.1 to an "unscheduled product" or to a "scheduled" product in excess of the Member's scheduled reduction commitments. If the Member does so it is in violation of Articles 3.3 and 8 of the Agreement. In addition, Article 10.1 prohibits Members from applying any subsidy that is not listed in Article 9.1 "in a manner which results in, or which threatens to lead to, circumvention of export subsidy commitments."

Alleged violations of the Agriculture Agreement may be challenged under WTO dispute settlement procedures. Agricultural subsidies may also be challenged under the SCM Agreement, which defines the term "subsidy," prohibits export subsidies and subsidies contingent on the use of domestic over imported products "except as provided in the Agreement on Agriculture," and makes any subsidy fitting the Agreement definition "actionable" if the subsidy is specific to an industry and causes "adverse effects" to the interests of another WTO Member.[120] Among these adverse effects is what the Agreement refers to as "serious prejudice," an effect that will be found where there is, inter alia, "a significant price undercutting by the subsidized product as compared with the price of a like product of another Member in the same market or significant price suppression, price depression or lost sales in the same market."[121] The SCM Agreement contains timelines for dispute settlement proceedings that are shorter than those in the WTO Dispute Settlement Understanding and in general contemplates expedited compliance with adverse WTO decisions in disputes arising under the Agreement.

Resort to WTO dispute settlement had been temporarily limited by Article 13 of the Agriculture Agreement—the now-expired "Peace Clause"—which provided that certain domestic support measures and export subsidies that conformed fully with enumerated requirements in the Agriculture Agreement were "exempt from actions" under specified subsidy-related provisions in the GATT 1994 and the SCM Agreement through the end of the "implementation period," i.e., the end of the nine-year period following the date the Agriculture Agreement entered into force (January 1, 1995), or December 31, 2003. The United States unsuccessfully argued in the case that certain of its agricultural programs were covered by this provision.

Panel and Appellate Body Reports

In a report issued September 8, 2004, the WTO panel found that the United States was maintaining export subsidy programs and providing payments under domestic support programs in violation of the Agriculture Agreement and the SCM Agreement.[122]

First, the panel found that three U.S. export credit guarantee programs in effect at the time constituted export subsidies for purposes of WTO obligations because the programs were provided at premium rates that were "inadequate to cover the long-term operating costs and losses" of the programs.[123] The panel looked to the Illustrative List of Export Subsidies set out in Annex I of the SCM Agreement, which includes export credit guarantee programs fitting this description in item (j) of the List.[124] The cited programs were: (1) the Commodity Credit Corporation (CCC) Export Credit Guarantee Program (GSM-102), providing export credit guarantees for up to three years; (2) the CCC Intermediate Export Credit Guarantee Program (GSM-103), providing export credit guarantees for up to 10 years; and (3) the Supplier Credit

Guarantee Program (SCGP), allowing export guarantees for 180 days and in some cases up to 360 days.

The panel found that the premiums charged for the U.S. programs would not insure adequate financial coverage for several reasons: (1) the existence of a statutory 1% fee cap in connection with GSM-102 and SCGP transactions; (2) the fact that premiums were not risk-based either as to country risk or the creditworthiness of the borrower in individual transactions; and (3) even though the premiums charged offset the programs' long-term costs and losses "to some degree," coverage was "effectively ensure[d]" by the U.S. Government's subsidy estimates and re- estimates "and ultimately the availability of United States government funds to cover any costs to government."[125] The panel further found that, to the extent that these programs applied to exports of upland cotton and other unscheduled agricultural commodities supported under the programs, and to exports of rice (a scheduled commodity), the export subsidies were being applied in a manner that circumvented U.S. export subsidy commitments in the Agriculture Agreement in violation of Article 10 of the Agreement. As these programs did not conform fully to export subsidy obligations in the Agreement, they were found not to be covered by the Peace Clause and thus subject to challenge. The panel went on to find that these programs were prohibited export subsidies under Article 3.1(a) of the SCM Agreement.

Second, the panel faulted the "Step 2" program, authorized in § 1207(a) of the Farm Security and Rural Investment Act of 2002, P.L. 101-171 ("2002 farm bill"), 7 U.S.C. § 793 7(a), as it applied both to exporters and domestic users of upland cotton. To the extent that the program provided for payments to *exporters* for their purchase of higher priced upland cotton, it was found to constitute an export subsidy that was not scheduled by the United States in the Agreement on Agriculture and was therefore inconsistent with U.S. obligations under the Agreement. As such, this part of the Step 2 program was found not to be covered by the Peace Clause and thus also subject to challenge. The panel then found that the program constituted a prohibited export subsidy under the Article 3.1(a) of the SCM Agreement. In addition, the panel found that the Step 2 program, insofar as it provided for payments to domestic *users* of upland cotton, qualified as a subsidy contingent on the use of domestic over imported products and was thus prohibited under Article 3.1(b) of the SCM Agreement.

Third, the panel found that payments under various U.S. domestic support programs, including counter-cyclical payments (CCP), market loss assistance payments (MLA), marketing loan program payments, and Step 2 payments for

U.S. cotton producers, were measures that granted sufficient amounts of support to upland cotton to exempt them from the Peace Clause.[126] The panel then found that the payments under the four cited programs—which it characterized as "mandatory price-contingent subsidies"—caused serious prejudice to Brazil's interests in the form of significant price suppression in the world upland cotton market for purposes of Articles 5(c) and Article 6.3(c) of the SCM Agreement.

At the time, CCP payments, market loan program payments, and Step 2 payments were authorized in the 2002 farm bill, while the authority for the MLA payments had expired. Among other findings, however, the panel determined that an agricultural program could be challenged in the WTO even though it had expired so long as the program was in force during the Agriculture Agreement implementation period (*i.e.*, between 1995 and the end of 2003) and continued to have an adverse effect on the complaining Member. This finding allowed Brazil to challenge MLA payments and flexibility contract payments (FCP), the legislative basis of which had lapsed in 2002. Brazil was unable, however, to show serious prejudice from the FCP program.

The panel recommended that the prohibited subsidies be removed "without delay" and specified that this be done at the latest within six months of the date of adoption of the panel report or July 1, 2005, whichever was earlier.[127] The panel cited Article 4.7 of the SCM Agreement, which requires that where an export subsidy is found, the panel recommend expeditious removal and specify a time period for such action. The panel also recommended that the adverse effects of the actionable subsidies, or alternatively, the subsidies themselves, be removed, as provided in Article 7.8 of the SCM Agreement, i.e., upon adoption of the panel report.[128]

The panel's finding of serious prejudice for the actionable subsidies also implicated a deadline in Article 7.9 of the SCM Agreement affecting requests for authorization to impose retaliatory measures. Provided there is no agreement between the disputing parties on compensation, Article 7.9 accords a prevailing Member the right to make such a request in the event the defending Member "has not taken appropriate steps to remove the adverse effects of the subsidy or withdraw the subsidy within six months" after the date the panel or Appellate Body report is adopted.[129]

The United States and Brazil appealed the panel report, and the Appellate Body, in a March 5, 2005, report largely upheld the panel.[130] The reports were adopted on March 21, 2005.[131] This action effectively established a July 1, 2005, deadline for removal of the prohibited subsidies and an Article 7.9 deadline of September 21, 2005, with respect to the actionable subsidies.

The United States told the WTO Dispute Settlement Body, on April 20, 2005, that it would implement the WTO rulings, but that it would need a reasonable period to comply and that it had begun to consider its options for doing so.[132] Brazil complained that the U.S. statement was not sufficiently detailed and made reference to the panel's recommended time periods for compliance. [133] The European Union noted that because the subsidies at issue were found to infringe both the SCM Agreement and the Agreement on Agriculture, the United States was entitled to a "reasonable period of time" to comply with Agriculture Agreement, i.e., a compliance period determined on an *ad hoc* basis, as ordinarily available under the WTO Dispute Settlement Understanding.

Responses of the United States and Brazil

In response to the WTO finding that fees charged by the Commodity Credit Corporation (CCC) guarantee programs must be risk-based, the United States Department of Agriculture (USDA) announced on June 30, 2005, that, as of July 1, 2005, CCC would use a risk-based fee structure for both the GSM-102 and SCGP program. [134] USDA also announced that CCC would no longer accept applications for payment guarantees under the GSM- 103 program.

Because prohibited export subsidies had not been removed by July 1, 2005, Brazil requested that the DSB meet on July 15, 2005, to consider its request for authorization to impose countermeasures against the United States. Brazil sought to suspend tariff concessions as well as obligations under the WTO Agreement on Trade-Related Intellectual Property Rights (TRIPS) and the General Agreement on Trade in Services (GATS) until the United States withdrew the exports subsidies identified by the WTO. [135] Brazil proposed sanctions in an amount corresponding to: (1) the Step 2 payments made in the most recent concluded marketing year and (2) the total of exporter applications received under the GSM-102, GSM-103 and SGCP programs, for all unscheduled commodities and for rice, for the most recent concluded fiscal year, estimating the annual total for both to be $3 billion.[136]

On July 5, 2005, USDA announced that, to further comply with the WTO decision, it was sending proposed statutory changes to Congress to eliminate the Step 2 cotton program, remove the 1% cap on origination fees under the GSM- 102 program, and terminate the GSM- 103 program.[137] According to USDA:

> Repealing the Step 2 program would remove both the export subsidies and import substitution subsidies that the WTO cited and address issues related to suppression of cotton prices in world markets. Eliminating the one-percent fee cap would make the Export Credit Guarantee Program more risk-based. Terminating the GSM-103 program would reinforce the recent U.S. decision to stop using longer-term export credit guarantees.[138]

On the same day, Brazil and the United States notified the DSB that they had entered into a procedural agreement covering the implementation phase of the dispute.[139] The agreement also recognized both the changes to the CCC programs announced June 30, 2005, and the legislative proposal sent to Congress to repeal the Step 2 program. As provided in the agreement, the United States requested arbitration of Brazil's retaliation proposal; the DSB referred the matter to arbitration at its July 15, 2005, meeting; [140] and the two countries, on August 17, 2005, requested that the arbitration be suspended. [141] The agreement also provided that Brazil could request an Article 21.5 compliance panel at any time after the July 15, 2005, meeting.

In addition, because the United States had not complied with its WTO obligations regarding the actionable subsidies by September 21, 2005, Brazil shortly thereafter proposed to suspend tariff concessions as well as obligations under the TRIPS Agreement and the GATS in the annual amount of $1 .037 billion.[142] The United States objected to the proposal, and the matter was referred to arbitration. [143] On November 21, 2005, the parties requested that the arbitration be suspended, "noting that the United States reaffirmed" at the November 18, 2005, DSB meeting "its commitment to implement the recommendations and rulings of the DSB in this dispute, and in light of the preference for WTO-consistent solutions mutually acceptable to the parties to a dispute set out in DSU Article 3.7."[144]

Congress subsequently repealed the Step 2 program, effective August 1, 2006.[145]

Compliance Panel Proceeding

On August 21, 2006, Brazil requested an Article 21.5 compliance panel, claiming WTO violations stemming from the U.S. failure to repeal the Step 2 program as of end of the 6-month period set out in Article 7.9 of the SCM Agreement (i.e., by September 21, 2005), the continued payments under the marketing loan and counter-cyclical programs authorized in the 2002 farm bill, and continued WTO-related defects in the export credit guarantee programs at issue in the case.

In December 2007, the compliance issued a report adverse to the United States with respect to both the marketing loan and CCL payments and the GSM- 102 program.[146]

First, the panel found that payments under the marketing loan and counter-cyclical programs authorized in the 2002 farm bill resulted in significant price suppression, which constituted present serious prejudice to the interests of Brazil in violation of Articles 5(c) and 6.3(c) of the SCM Agreement. The panel thus found that the United States was in violation of its obligation under Article 7.8 of the SCM Agreement to take "appropriate steps to remove the adverse effects of ... or withdraw the subsidy."

Second, regarding GSM-102 export credit guarantees provided after July 1, 2005 (the deadline set by the original panel), the panel found that Brazil had established that the revised GSM-102 program constituted an export subsidy on the ground that the program continued to be provided against premiums that were inadequate to cover its long-term operating costs and losses and that the program thus qualified as such under item (j) of the Illustrative List.[147] The panel further found that United States was in violation of its obligations in the Agreement on Agriculture in applying export subsidies in a manner that circumvented its export subsidy commitments regarding various unscheduled products (e.g., cotton, oilseeds, protein meals) as well as three scheduled products (rice, poultry meat, and rice).[148] By providing export subsidies both to unscheduled products and to scheduled products in excess of its reduction commitments, the United States was also found to be granting prohibited subsidies in violation of the SCM Agreement.[149]

The panel based its conclusion that the GSM-102 program constituted an export subsidy on the following factors:

> (a) The US Government continues to project that new GSM 102 export credit guarantees issued under the new fee schedule will be provided at a net cost to the Government.
>
> (b) GSM 102 fees are well below the OECD MPR's [minimum premium rates], which we consider to provide an informed appraisal of the level of fees necessary to cover the longterm, operating costs and losses of an export credit guarantee programme;
>
> (c) Elements of the structure, design and operation of the GSM 102 programme indicate that the programme is not designed to cover the long term operating costs and losses of that programme.[150]

The compliance panel's conclusion in (c) resulted from the following considerations: "the CCC's access to funds from the US Treasury, which facilitates the functioning of the programme"; "the fact that GSM 102 fees do not vary with foreign obligor risk"; and "the fact that the one percent fee cap has not been repealed and in our view prevents the adoption of risk-based fees (notably due to the insufficient 'scaling' of GSM 102 fees [as risk increases])."[151] The panel ultimately found that the United States had failed to bring its measures into conformity with the Agreement on Agriculture and to "withdraw the subsidy without delay" as recommended by the WTO Dispute Settlement Body pursuant to Article 4.7 of the SCM Agreement.

Both the United States and Brazil appealed. In a report issued June 2, 2008, the Appellate Body largely upheld the compliance panel, though taking issues with an aspect of the panel's methodology regarding the existence of export subsidization.[152] The Appellate Body reversed the panel's intermediate conclusion that the GSM-102 program would be run at a net cost to the government on the ground that the panel had not accorded sufficient weight to data provided by the United States concerning re-estimates of initial subsidy estimates for the three challenged programs for 1992-2006.[153] The United States had argued that the re-estimates demonstrated that the programs "were in fact not provided at a net loss to the US Government even before the United States took any measures to comply with the DSB recommendations" in the case.[154] At the same time, the Appellate Body upheld the panel's ultimate conclusion that the revised program fell within the scope of item (j) and thus constituted an export subsidy, determining that the panel's findings on the structure, design, and operation of the revised GSM 102 program provided "a sufficient evidentiary basis for the conclusion that it is more likely than not that ... [it] operates at a loss."[155]

The WTO Dispute Settlement Body adopted the reports on June 25, 2008.

2008 Farm Bill Amendments

On June 18, 2008, a week before the compliance panel and appellate reports were adopted, President George W. Bush signed the Food, Conservation, and Energy Act of 2008, P.L. 110-246 ("2008 farm bill"), a statute containing several provisions relevant to the pending dispute. Section 3101 of the act made statutory changes affecting U.S. export credit guarantee programs, changes that the bill Managers believed "satisfy U.S. commitments to comply with the Brazil cotton case with regard to the export credit programs."[156] The act repealed the GSM-103 intermediate export credit guarantee program and the Supplier Credit Guarantee Program (SCGP)[157] and eliminated the 1% cap on origination fees under the GSM-102 program, a requirement contained in 7 U.S.C. § 5622(b).[158] While leaving the GSM-102 program intact, Congress placed new requirements on the Secretary of Agriculture in administering the program, including "work[ing] with industry to ensure, to the maximum extent practicable, that risk-based fees associated with the guarantees cover, but do not exceed, the operating costs of and losses over the long term."[159] The phrase "long term" is defined in the statute as "a period of 10 or more years."[160] In addition, Congress directed the Commodity Credit Corporation to make available for GSM-102 programs each year through FY2012 a maximum $5.5 billion, or "the amount of guarantees that can be supported by $40 billion in budget authority (plus any budget authority for prior years) – whichever amount is less."[161]

In addition, Congress reauthorized counter-cyclical payments and marketing assistance loans for cotton and other commodities for the 2008-20 12 crop years.[162] As discussed earlier, these two programs, as authorized in the 2002 farm bill, were successfully challenged by Brazil as actionable subsidies in the pending WTO case and are the basis of one of Brazil's retaliation requests.

Arbitration of Brazil's Retaliation Request

In August 2008, following the DSB 's adoption of the compliance panel and Appellate Body reports finding the U.S. not to be in full compliance in the case, Brazil requested that the arbitrations on its retaliation proposals be resumed. Brazil lowered its retaliation requests in March 2009 to approximately $2.5 billion consisting of three components: (1) a one-time countermeasure of $350 million based on payments made under the repealed Step 2 program during the 13-month period between the compliance deadline of July 1, 2005, set by the original panel, and August 1, 2006, the date that the statutory repeal entered into force; (2) an annual countermeasure of approximately $1.2 billion for prohibited subsidies resulting from the GSM-102 export credit guarantee program; and (3) an annual countermeasure of approximately $1 billion based on actionable subsidies resulting from marketing loan and countercyclical payments.[163]

In an arbitral proceeding involving prohibited subsidies, the Arbitrator determines whether the proposed countermeasures are "appropriate," that is, not "disproportionate in light of the fact that the subsidies ... are prohibited."[164] Where actionable subsidies are involved, the Arbitrator determines whether the proposed countermeasures are "commensurate with the degree and nature of the adverse effects determined to exist."[165]

On August 31, 2009, the Arbitrator issued two reports – the first addressing retaliation for prohibited subsidies, the second for actionable subsidies.[166] The Arbitrator rejected Brazil's request for a one-time payment based on the Step 2 program; lowered the other amounts proposed by Brazil to a total $ 297.4 million annually for both prohibited and actionable subsidies (based on the FY2006 figures); and set out conditions under which Brazil could suspend WTO obligations involving U.S. services and intellectual property, or "cross-retaliate." Among other findings, the Arbitrator rejected U.S. arguments that, with the expiration of the statutory authority for the marketing loan and countercyclical payments at issue in the underlying WTO proceedings, Brazil could not pursue countermeasures for serious prejudice resulting from payments under these programs. The Arbitrator's decisions are final and not subject to appeal.

Prohibited Subsidies

In examining Brazil's request for countermeasures for the prohibited subsidies, the Arbitrator first concluded that there was no legal basis for Brazil's request for a one-time payment based on past disbursements under the Step 2 program. The Arbitrator found that countermeasures are an exceptional temporary remedy aimed at inducing compliance and that the United States had in fact complied with respect to this program.[167]

Second, the Arbitrator determined that Brazil could suspend concessions amounting to $147.4 annually for the continued operation of the GSM- 102 export credit guarantee program, based on GSM-102 transactions in FY2006. As summarized by the Arbitrator, Brazil determined the trade-distorting impact of the program and thus the level of "appropriate" countermeasures for the prohibited subsidy by determining "the interest rate discounts secured by creditworthy and uncreditworthy foreign obligors backed by GSM- 102 guarantees and estimating the additional export sales obtained by US exporters as a result of these discounts."[168] Brazil referred to these two factors as the "interest rate subsidy" and "additionality." The Arbitrator modified Brazil's calculations, however, "in order to more accurately calculate the trade-distorting impact of the GSM- 102 programme on Brazil" and, taking into account other determinations it had made, reduced Brazil's original proposal to the figure stated above.[169]

The Arbitrator found that $147.4 figure was variable, however, and could change annually depending on the total of amount of GSM-102 transactions in the most recently concluded fiscal year. The Arbitrator set out a formula that Brazil would need to use to determine the amount of permissible sanctions for a given year due to these payments, noting that "the United States does not dispute that it would be permissible for the level of appropriate countermeasures to be determined through a formula, provided that this formula was sufficiently well defined so as to make it applicable in a transparent and predictable manner."[170]

Third, the Arbitrator determined that Brazil could cross-retaliate in order to remedy the prohibited subsidy resulting from the GSM- 102 payments, but set conditions on Brazil's use of this remedy. The Arbitrator stated that "Brazil has at its disposal a sufficient range of imports of goods, including consumer goods, from the United States so as to enable it to suspend concessions in the area of trade in goods alone, without causing itself such economic harm so as to render such suspension 'not practicable or effective,'" the standard set out in the Dispute Settlement Understanding, taking into account the cumulated $294.7 million in countermeasures the Arbitrator had determined Brazil could impose for both prohibited and actionable subsidies in this case.[171] Based on Brazil's imports of consumer goods for 2007, the Arbitrator identified at least $409.7 million of such goods that could be the subject of countermeasures.[172] For certain consumer goods (food, medical products, and arms), the Arbitrator adopted a benchmark of 20%, finding that a U.S. import share of the good of less than this amount "constitutes a reasonable threshold by which to estimate the extent to which Brazil may be able to find alternative sources of supply" for the product.[173] This annual goods "threshold" is to be updated, however, under a formula set out by the Arbitrator, to take into account any change in Brazil's total imports of U.S. consumer goods *for the same year* for which the annual countermeasures are determined.[174]

Under the decision, if the total level of countermeasures for prohibited and actionable subsidies that Brazil is entitled to for a given year exceeds the updated goods threshold for that year, Brazil may cross-retaliate, i.e., suspend WTO obligations involving U.S. services, intellectual property rights, or both, in excess of the goods threshold to the full amount of permissible sanctions for the year. If permissible sanctions do not exceed the goods threshold, however, Brazil may only suspend concessions on trade in goods.

Actionable Subsidies

The United States preliminarily argued in the arbitration involving actionable subsidies that, with the expiration of the 2002 farm bill, payments would no longer be made under the marketing loan and countercyclical payments programs at issue in Brazil's WTO challenge and that, because the challenged measures were removed, there was no longer a legal basis for Brazil to impose countermeasures with regard to these payments. Brazil argued that because these programs were reauthorized in the 2008 farm bill in a manner that did not materially change them as they applied to cotton, the problematic payments would continue under the same conditions and criteria as the payments subject to the earlier WTO proceedings. Until the United States achieved what the WTO Appellate Body deemed "substantial compliance," Brazil claimed that it had the right to pursue countermeasures for continuing present serious prejudice. The United States responded that Brazil's conclusions about payments that might be made under the 2008 farm bill and their price effect were speculative.

In assessing whether the United States had complied, the Arbitrator quoted from the Appellate Body report referred to by Brazil, in which the Appellate Body had stated that for purposes of determining whether a WTO Member has complied in a case, "substantive compliance is required, rather than formal removal of the inconsistent measure."[175] Informed by this principle, the Arbitrator compared the 2002 and 2008 farm bills and concluded that the replacement of the 2002 provisions with new measures that are "essentially the same" as those found to be WTOinconsistent was not a basis for finding that the United States had complied, if the United States had not shown that "the inconsistencies that were the object of the [prior WTO] proceedings have been remedied."[176] Seemingly alluding to possible activity under the reauthorized CCP and marketing loan provisions, the Arbitrator noted that "any uncertainty about what might happen in the future" could not dissuade the Arbitrator from "assessing the adverse effects determined to exist in relation to a measure which did exist and which, on the facts, continues to exist."[177] The Arbitrator thus stated that "although the legal basis for the granting of ML and CCPs has been modified, such payments continue to be offered and may continue to be made under a new legal basis."[178] The Arbitrator concluded that, to the extent that it was entitled to review whether compliance has been achieved in a case (a task it earlier admitted was not normally the task of arbitrators), it would not have adequate grounds to conclude that the United States had complied.[179] Further noting that the findings in the underlying WTO proceedings related to the payments under the 2002 farm bill and not to the farm bill as such, the Arbitrator concluded that the United States had failed to establish that Brazil no longer had a legal basis to seek countermeasures for payments under these two programs.[180]

The Arbitrator ultimately determined that Brazil could impose countermeasures for the actionable subsidies in an amount not to exceed $147.3 million annually.[181] The Arbitrator arrived at this figure by first determining that the world cotton price would have been 9.38 % higher but for the U.S programs, with adverse effects for the rest of the world of $2.905

billion in marketing year (MY) 2005. The Arbitrator further found that this overall amount needed to be apportioned to Brazil, basing this apportionment on Brazil's 5.1% share of worldwide cotton production for the same marketing year, or $147.3 million.

The Arbitrator also found that Brazil may cross-retaliate with regard to the actionable subsidies only if the total amount of permissible countermeasures for a given year (i.e., $284.7 million, as adjusted) exceeds the monetary import threshold (i.e., $409.7 million, as adjusted). [182] Since annual countermeasures for the actionable subsidies is fixed at $147.3 million, the use of cross-retaliation will depend on annual increases in countermeasures due to increased U.S. payments under the prohibited subsidy, i.e., the GSM-102 export credit guarantee program.

Recent Developments

After the August 2009 Arbitrator's reports on Brazil's retaliation requests were issued, Brazil requested that the United States provide it with data on GSM- 102 transactions for FY2008 and FY2009 and the most recent data on U.S. export prices of products for which the United States had made export subsidy reduction commitments ("scheduled" products), namely, pig meat, poultry meat, and rice, for 2008 and 2009.[183] Brazil's request was based on language in the Arbitrator's report directing the United States to provide such data to Brazil to enable it to calculate its annual countermeasures under the formula set out by the Arbitrator in Annex 4 of the arbitral report.

On November 9, 2009, Brazil published a preliminary list of over 200 U.S. products, primarily consumer and agricultural goods, that could potentially be subject to increased tariffs.[184] On November 19, 2009, Brazil received authorization from the WTO Dispute Settlement Body to suspend WTO tariff concessions and other obligations owed the United States in an amount, and with respect to types of trade, consistent with the August 2009 Arbitrator's decisions.[185] WTO dispute settlement rules do not require that Brazil impose these measures once authorized or that it do so by a given date. The United States stated at the DSB meeting that it intended to comply and hoped that a resolution of the dispute could be reached, obviating the need for Brazil to impose the authorized measures.[186]

As Brazil prepared for and pursued its retaliation request, the USDA made various administrative changes to the GSM-program for FY2010 that tightened prior program requirements. On September 21, 2009, the Commodity Credit Corporation and the Foreign Agricultural Service solicited comments from stakeholders on revisions to the GSM-102 fee rate schedule that were being proposed in order to implement requirements in the 2008 farm bill for the development of a risk-based fee structure for the program.[187] CCC's goals in proposing the revisions were "to create fees more commensurate with risk, generate additional program revenue in fiscal (FY) 2010 to offset program costs, and consider allowing program participation by riskier countries."[188] The fee rate schedule for GSM-102 program dated November 17, 2009, posts fees that exceed those originally proposed in September.[189] In addition, maximum credit terms for the FY2010 program will be based on the risk category of the obligor country associated with the CCC payment guarantees, with shorter repayment terms or "tenor" as country risk category increases.[190] Under the program, the maximum allowable tenor for the category of countries with the highest risk is currently one year.[191] The CCC has so far allocated $1.2 billion for the FY2010 program.[192]

As an additional option for resolving the cotton dispute, some have suggested that the United States request a ruling by a compliance panel that the objectionable elements of the prohibited subsidy, i.e., the GSM-102 program, have been eliminated.[193] To date, there has been no official indication that this option will be pursued[194] and, even were a compliance panel established, Brazil would not be precluded from imposing countermeasures during a compliance panel proceeding.

While Brazil has not definitively stated that it will impose retaliatory measures as of a given date, the Chamber of Foreign Trade of Brazil (CAMEX) stated on December 15, 2009, that a final decision regarding the products subject to retaliation and the total amount of retaliation to be imposed would be announced in February 2010.[195] Originally expected in December 2009, the announcement is reportedly being delayed because Brazil has yet to review full FY2009 data regarding the GSM-102 program being provided by the United States.[196] On December 21, 2009, Brazil reported to the WTO Dispute Settlement Body that, based on U.S.-supplied fiscal and calendar year data for 2008, it is entitled to annual retaliation of $829.3 million, with $561 million covering trade in goods and $268.3 million covering other sectors and agreements.[197]

If applied, Brazil's countermeasures would be subject to Article 22.8 of the WTO Dispute Settlement Understanding, which provides that the "suspension of concessions or other obligations shall be temporary and shall only be applied until such time as the measure found to be inconsistent with a covered agreement has been removed ... or a mutually satisfactory resolution is reached."[198] Given the variables affecting the actual level of countermeasures that may be imposed by Brazil in a particular year, the United States would have the option, albeit a time-consuming one, of challenging any such measures in a new WTO dispute settlement proceeding if it believed that they exceeded the levels that the Arbitrator deemed to be proper in this case.[199] For the present, it appears unlikely that a settlement will be reached in the case.[200]

Measures Affecting Cross-Border Supply of Gambling and Betting Services (DS285)

Antigua and Barbuda (Antigua) requested consultations with the United States in March 2003 regarding federal, state, and local laws affecting the remote supply of gambling and betting services, alleging that the overall effect of these laws was to prevent the supply of gambling and betting services from the territory of one WTO Member into the United States in violation of U.S. market access commitments in Article XVI of the General Agreement on Trade in Services (GATS).[201]

As part of their GATS obligations, WTO Members make specific commitments involving particular service sectors, subject to any terms, limitations, or conditions Members may add. Commitments are made with respect to four means or "modes" by which services may be supplied, including supply from the territory of one Member into the territory of any other Member, which is the mode of supply at issue in this case. Each Member's sectoral commitments are set out in a Schedule of Specific Commitments, which is attached to the GATS and considered an integral part of the agreement. GATS market access and national treatment apply only with respect to scheduled commitments. These obligations are set out in GATS Articles XVI and XVII, respectively. All GATS obligations are subject to various general exceptions set out in Article XIV.

Among other market access obligations, Article XVI(a) of the GATS prohibits a WTO Member, in sectors where it has scheduled a specific commitment, from maintaining or adopting, unless specified in its Schedule, "limitations on the number of service suppliers whether in the form of numerical quotas, monopolies, exclusive service suppliers or the requirements of an economic needs test." In addition, Article XVI(c) prohibits a Member, in any such sectors, from maintaining or adopting, unless specified in its Schedule, "limitations on the total number of service operations or on the total quantity of service output expressed in terms of designated numerical units in the form of quotas or the requirement of an economic needs test."

Panel and Appellate Body Reports

Although the United States did not expressly identify gambling and betting services in its Schedule of Specific Commitments to the GATS, the WTO panel, in its November 2004 report, interpreted the services sub-sector titled "Other Recreational Services (except sporting)" as including gambling and betting services, and concluded that the United States, by not placing any limitations on the supply of such services from the territory of one WTO Member into the United States, had made market access commitments in the area.[202] The panel then found that three federal statutes and provisions of four state laws conflicted with these obligations. The federal statutes were the Wire Act, the Travel Act, and the Illegal Gambling Business Act (IGBA);[203] the state laws were those of Louisiana, Massachusetts, South Dakota, and Utah. The panel found that by preventing one, several, or all means of delivering gambling and betting services, the statutes constituted impermissible market access limitations on the number of service suppliers for purposes of Article XVI:2(a) of the GATS or, alternatively, on the total number of total number or service operations or total quantity of service output for purposes of Article XVI:2(c).

The panel further found that, with regard to the federal laws, the United States could not successfully invoke exceptions in GATS Article XIV for "measures necessary to protect public morals or to maintain public order" (Article XIV(a)) or for "measures necessary to secure compliance with" GAT S-consistent laws and regulations (Article XIV(c)) because the United States had not shown that the measures were "necessary" to achieve the stated end or that they were consistent with the Article XIV proviso, which requires that measures justified under the exception not be applied "in a manner which would constitute a means of arbitrary or unjustifiable discrimination between countries where like conditions prevail." Under WTO jurisprudence, such discrimination may occur not only between the different exporting Members but also between an exporting Member and the importing Member and thus in this case between foreign and domestic providers of Internet gambling services.[204]

In an appeal by both parties to the dispute, the WTO Appellate Body, using a different mode of analysis than the panel, nonetheless determined that the United States had made sectoral commitments regarding gambling and betting services.[205] Though the AB upheld the panel's finding of a violation of GATS market access obligations,[206] it reversed the panel on its finding that the United States could not justify the federal measures under GATS exceptions. The AB also reversed the panel's finding that four state laws were inconsistent with the GATS, finding that because Antigua had not made a prima facie case that eight state measures violated the Agreement, the panel had improperly examined their GAT S-consistency.

With respect to the GATS exceptions, the AB found that the panel had erroneously concluded that the three federal statutes could not be considered "necessary" for purposes of Articles XIV(a) and XIV(c) because the United States had not entered into consultations with Antigua to find a less trade-restrictive alternative. The AB ultimately found that statutes were "necessary to protect public morals or to protect public order" for purposes of Article XVI(a) and that they thus fell within the scope of this exception.[207] At the same time, the AB also found that, in light of a provision in the Interstate Horseracing Act (IHA) that might facially continue to allow the remote supply of wagering on horseracing by domestic firms, the United States had not shown that the Wire Act, the Travel Act, and the IGBA were being applied consistently with the Article XVI proviso, that is, that they may possibly be used to prosecute foreign, but not domestic, providers of remote horserace gambling services.[208]

Antigua had based its argument that the United States was applying the three statutes inconsistently with the Article XIV proviso on two aspects of the IHA, a statute allowing the acceptance of interstate off-track wagers provided certain conditions are met, making violators civilly liable for damages to named entities, including the state in which the subject horserace takes place, and authorizing certain civil suits against violators.[209] First, Antigua cited § 5 of the act, which it characterized as expressly allowing an interstate off-track wager to be accepted by an off-track betting system, where consent is obtained from certain organizations.[210] Second, it cited the statutory definition of "interstate off-state wager," which, in pertinent part, includes pari- mutuel wagers "placed or transmitted by an individual in one State via telephone or other electronic media and accepted by an off-track betting system in the same or another State," provided the wagers are lawful in the States involved.[211] In the words of the AB, Antigua thus argued that:

> the IHA, on its face, authorizes *domestic* service suppliers, but not *foreign* service suppliers, to offer remote betting services in relation to certain horse races. To this extent, in Antigua's view, the IGHA "exempts" domestic service suppliers from the prohibitions of the Wire Act, the Travel Act, and the IGBA.[212]

As further described by the AB, "[t]he Panel found that the evidence provided by the United States was not sufficiently persuasive to conclude that, as regards wagering on horseracing, the remote supply of such services by *domestic* firms continues to be prohibited notwithstanding the plain language of the IHA."[213] The AB concluded that the panel did not err in making this finding.

The Appellate Body report and the panel report, as modified by the AB, were adopted April 20, 2005.

Responses of the United States and Antigua

The United States reported at the May 19, 2005, meeting of the DSB that it intended to implement the rulings and had begun to consider options for doing so, but that it would need a reasonable period to comply.[214] After the disputing parties had failed to agree on a reasonable period of time for compliance, Antigua requested that the compliance period be arbitrated.[215] In its submission to the Arbitrator, the United States stated that compliance would be achieved "by further clarifying the relationship between the IHA and preexisting federal criminal laws" and that "U.S. authorities intend to seek further clarification through legislation."[216]

The United States sought a 15-month compliance period, stressing that such legislative action would be "technically complex."[217] In an award made public August 19, 2005, the Arbitrator determined that the compliance period would last 11 months and two weeks from the date of adoption of the panel and AB reports, thus expiring April 3, 2006.[218]

Legislative action was not taken before the deadline; instead, the United States stated in a status report to the DSB that it had complied in the case based on the position of the Department of Justice (DOJ) regarding remote gambling on horse racing, articulated as follows in April 5 DOJ testimony before a House committee:

> The Department of Justice views the existing criminal statutes as prohibiting the interstate transmission of bets or wagers, including wagers on horse races. The Department is currently undertaking a civil investigation relating to a potential violation of law regarding this activity. We have previously stated that we do not believe that the Interstate Horse Racing Act, 15 U.S.C. §§ 3001-3007, amended the existing criminal statutes.[219]

Antigua disagreed that the United States was in compliance, and in May 2006, the parties entered into a procedural agreement regarding the possible seeking by Antigua of a compliance panel and countermeasures in the case.[220]

Compliance Proceedings

Antigua requested a compliance panel in July 2006, claiming that the United States had failed to bring the Wire Act, the Travel Act and the Illegal Gaming Business Act into conformity with U.S. GATS obligations and that then-pending legislation—H.R. 4777 and H.R. 4411—was "expressly contrary "to the WTO ruling in that each bill "would further institutionalise the discriminatory effect" of the three cited statutes. It also questioned whether the DOJ statement was a "measure" or a "measure taken to comply" for purposes of the DSU, noting that the same position had been maintained by the United States during the course of the dispute and was subsequently rejected by the panel and Appellate Body. Antigua further argued that regardless of the nature of the DOJ statement for purposes of the DSU, the United States remained out of compliance with the GATS because of, *inter alia*, the existence of reasonable technical alternatives to prohibitions on remote gambling and betting services and governmental enforcement problems regarding domestic and cross-border service providers.[221] The compliance panel was established July 19, 2006.

On March 30, 2007, the compliance panel issued a report adverse to the United States, finding that the United States had not taken any measures to comply in the case and thus left the statutory ambiguity cited by the panel unresolved.[222] The panel noted that legislation was not the only means of compliance in the proceeding and that "other forms of administrative action, or judicial action, [could be used] to bring the measures into conformity."[223] The United States did not appeal the report, which was adopted by the DSB on May 22, 2007.

In early May 2007, the Office of the USTR announced that the United States intended to invoke Article XXI of the GATS "in order to clarify its commitment involving 'recreational services,'" in order to bring the United States into compliance in the dispute and to resolve the dispute permanently.[224] The modification would explicitly exclude gambling and betting services from this broader services category. With Antigua's subsequent pursuit of retaliation in the underlying WTO dispute, the United States became engaged in two WTO proceedings, one involving negotiations with various WTO Members under Article XXI on compensation for changes in the U.S. GATS schedule, and the other involving arbitration of Antigua's request to impose countermeasures against the United States for non-compliance with the WTO decision.

Negotiations on Compensation under GATS Article XXI

Article XXI allows a WTO Member to modify or withdraw any commitment in its GATS Schedule, but any WTO Member whose GATS benefits may be affected by the proposed change has a right to negotiate a compensation agreement with the Member making the change. In negotiating an agreement, Members must try to maintain "a general level of mutually advantageous commitments" that are as favorable to trade as was the case with the Schedule in its original form. In its May 2007 announcement, USTR stated that in negotiating the GATS, the United States "did not make it clear" that its international commitments to open its market to recreational services did not extend to gambling and that since "no WTO Member either bargained for or reasonably could have expected the United States to undertake a commitment on gambling, there would be very little, if any basis for ... [compensation] claims."[225]

Antigua, Australia, Canada, Costa Rica, European Union (EU), India, Japan, and Macao requested consultations with the United States by June 22, 2007, the deadline for WTO Members to notify the United States that their interests may be affected by the U.S. Schedule modification,.[226] The following month USTR filed a notice in the *Federal Register* asking for public comment on the requested compensation negotiations.[227] As provided in GATS procedural rules, negotiations were expected to conclude within three months, i.e., toward the end of September 2007, but the parties agreed on two extensions with a final deadline of January 14, 2007.[228] On December 17, 2007, the United States and the EU announced that they had reached a bilateral compensation agreement providing EU service suppliers with improved market access in the U.S. postal and courier, research and development, warehouse and storage, and technical testing services sectors.[229] The United States also announced that it had reached agreement with Canada and Japan as well.[230] Australia had reportedly settled outstanding issues with the United States several months earlier and had withdrawn from the negotiations.[231]

Since the United States had not agreed on compensation with Antigua, Costa Rica, India, or Macao by the end of the negotiating period, these Members had a right to request that compensation be arbitrated, provided that they made their request within 45 days after deadline, i.e., by January 28, 2008. If none of these Members requested arbitration, the United States would then be free to implement its Schedule modification, as originally proposed.

Antigua and Costa Rica each filed timely arbitration requests.[232] India and Macao reportedly did not choose this option and thus effectively abandoned their claims.[233] In February 2008, Costa Rica reached agreement with the United States on compensation and as a result withdrew its request to arbitrate.[234] Antigua was thus the only remaining Member pursuing arbitration under Article XXI.

Under GATS rules, any arbitral panel established under Article XXI would be expected to issue its report within three months after the panel is appointed.[235] Once a report is issued, the United States would not be able to modify its GATS Schedule until it made compensatory adjustments in conformity with the arbitration. If the United States modified its Schedule without complying with the arbitral decision, Antigua could modify or withdraw substantially equivalent benefits in conformity with the arbitral findings. GATS rules would allow the Antigua to apply any such change only to the United States, notwithstanding the general most-favored-nation obligation in GATS Article II.

Antigua's Retaliation Request

In the WTO dispute itself, Antigua has requested authorization from the DSB to impose $ 3.4 billion in countermeasures against the United States for non-compliance, primarily by suspending obligations owed the United States under the Agreement on Trade-Related Intellectual Property Rights.[236] The United States objected to the request, challenging both the level of suspension of concessions and Antigua's compliance with DSU principles and procedures governing a WTO Member's consideration of which concessions to suspend.[237] Because of the U.S. objection, Antigua's proposal was sent to arbitration. In a ruling issued December 21, 2007, the Arbitrator determined that Antigua may request authorization from the DSB to suspend concessions under the TRIPS agreement at a level not to exceed $21 million annually.[238] The amount was based on the Arbitrator's assumption that the United States would have complied with the ruling by opening its market to Antiguan providers of remote gambling on horseracing.

Recent Developments

Although Antigua requested arbitration in January 2008 under GATS Article XXI on compensation owed by the United States because of the U.S. withdrawal of gambling commitments in its GATS Schedule, there have not been reports that panelists have been appointed to hear this claim. Moreover, Antigua has not yet requested the WTO Dispute Settlement Body to authorize its retaliation request as modified by the December 2007 Arbitrator's report in the original WTO dispute settlement proceeding. In a July 2009 government press release, the Minister of Finance of Antigua is quoted as stating that "'[w]hile we may in the future consider exercising the right to impose sanctions, as of this moment, I am instead looking forward to meeting with the United States government in the near future and focusing on a mutually beneficial resolution of the issues raised by the remote gambling case.'"[239] The USTR's annual report for 2008 also indicates that the parties have been consulting with a view to achieving "a mutually agreeable resolution" to the dispute.[240]

A June 10, 2009, European Commission staff report on an investigation under the European Union (EU) Trade Barriers Regulation, initiated as a result of a complaint submitted by the London-based Remote Gambling Association, indicates persistent EU concerns over U.S. Internet gambling regulation and its consistency with U.S. GATS obligations.[241] Regarding possible future action, a fact sheet accompanying the report states as follows: "The report concludes that WTO action would be justified. However, this is not an automatic consequence. The report does not include any recommendation for action and also suggests that the issue should be addressed with the US Administration, with a view to finding an amicable solution."[242] During their July 2009 meeting in Washington, USTR Kirk and EU Trade Ambassador Ashton discussed the EU report "and its implications for the WTO rights and obligations of the parties concerned."[243]

In November 2008, the Treasury Department and the Board of Governors of the Federal Reserve System issued a final rule implementing the provisions of the 2006 Unlawful Internet Gambling Enforcement Act (UIGEA), P.L. 109-347, Title VIII.[244] The statute prohibits gambling businesses from accepting checks, credit cards, electronic transfers and similar forms of payment in connection with illegal Internet gambling, while exempting intrastate and intratribal Internet gambling operations that include age and location verification requirements imposed as a matter of law. The rule became effective on January 19, 2009; the original compliance date of December 1, 2009, was recently extended, however, to June 1, 2010. Various bills have also been introduced in the 111th Congress to permit Internet gambling under a federal licensing program.[245]

Pending Cases Involving Administrative Action

Four pending WTO disputes in the compliance phase involve administrative action. These address the practice of "zeroing," a methodology used by the Department of Commerce (DOC) in antidumping proceedings under which, in calculating dumping margins for an imported product, it disregards non-dumped sales. Two of these cases were brought by the European Union (DS294 and DS350), one by Japan (DS322), and one by Mexico (DS344). These have a resulted in a broad prohibition on the use of this practice in U.S. antidumping investigations and related antidumping proceedings.

In response to the first EU challenge, the Commerce Department in early 2007 discontinued the use of zeroing in the price comparison employed most frequently in original antidumping investigations and recalculated dumping margins in the investigations cited by the EU under the revised methodology. The United States has yet to fully comply with the WTO decisions in this case and in the cases initiated by Japan and Mexico to the extent that the decisions affect the use of zeroing in other aspects of U.S. antidumping proceedings. WTO compliance proceedings in the first EU case and Japan's challenge, concluded in 2009, resulted in findings adverse to the United States and the complainants may now pursue requests to impose sanctions. In addition, Mexico initiated compliance proceedings against the United States on August 19, 2009, and a compliance deadline of December 19, 2009, was established in the second EU challenge. With the United States having taken limited action to comply with the WTO decision in the second EU challenge, the United States and the EU have entered into a "sequencing" agreement setting out a procedural framework for a compliance panel request by the EU.

The United States acted in 2009 to resolve two other disputes in which administrative action was needed to comply: *United States – Measures Related to Shrimp from Thailand* (DS343) and *United States – Customs Bond Directive for Merchandise Subject to Anti-Dumping/Countervailing Duties* (DS345).[246] Each of these involved a successful challenge to the U.S. enhanced customs bond requirement (EBR) for shrimp subject to antidumping duty orders, with the dispute with Thailand also involving a successful challenge to the U.S. use of zeroing in determining the original dumping margin for the subject shrimp imports. The United States was subject to an April 1, 2009, deadline in both disputes for all issues raised.

In January 2009, the United States implemented a Section 129 determination in which the Commerce Department recalculated the dumping margins for shrimp from Thailand without the use of zeroing using its modified methodology for original investigations (discussed below). The recalculation resulted in two de minimis margins, a lower margin for one exporter, and a lower rate for exporters that were not individually investigated ("all others"rate), effective January 16, 2009. Consequently, antidumping duties were no longer collected for the two exporters with de minimis rates. [247]

In a *Federal Register* notice published April 1, 2009, U.S. Customs and Border Protection (CBP) announced that, in response to the two WTO decisions, it was as of that date ending the designation of shrimp subject to antidumping duty or countervailing duty orders as a "special category" or "covered case" subject to the EBR and that importers subject to this requirement could request the termination of any existing continuous bonds and submit a new bond application.[248] CBP did not apply the new policy retroactively to all entries of subject merchandise calculated using the EBR, which some commenters had argued was necessary to fully comply with the WTO decision.[249] At the WTO Dispute Settlement Body meeting of April 20, 2009, the United States announced the revision of its policy and stated that, with this change, it had complied with its WTO obligations in each dispute.[250] While Thailand and India indicated at the time that they did not consider the issues raised in the case to be fully resolved and that they would thus monitor U.S. implementation,[251] neither WTO Member appears to have raised the issue of U.S compliance at subsequent DSB meetings. In August 2009, the U.S. Court of International Trade ruled that the EBR, in applying only to importers of shrimp subject to antidumping duties, was arbitrarily and capriciously applied, that it was unreasonable in amount, and that, thus, individual bond determinations were not in accordance with law. [252] The court ordered broad relief for shrimp importers, including the recalculation of bonds for earlier time periods on which plaintiffs may remain liable as principal until all goods entered during the period are liquidated.

Use of "Zeroing" in Antidumping Proceedings: Background

Under U.S. law, antidumping duties will be applied to an imported product if the Department of Commerce (DOC) determines that the product is being, or is likely to be sold, in the United States at less than its fair value and the U.S. International Trade Commission (ITC) determines that a U.S. industry is materially injured or threatened with material injury by reason of either imports of dumped goods, or sales or likely sales of such goods for importation.[253] Antidumping duties are imposed in the amount of the dumping margin calculated by DOC. The dumping margin is the amount by which the normal value of the product, i.e., the price at which the product is sold in the exporting country, exceeds the export price or constructed export price.[254] Antidumping duties will not be imposed if the weighted average dumping margin is de minimis, i.e., less than two percent ad valorem.[255]

Under the practice of zeroing, the Department assigns a zero value to non-dumped sales—that is, sales at prices that are equal to or greater than normal value—and disregards these sales in calculating a dumping margin for the product under investigation. The practice of zeroing is said to inflate dumping margins by not allowing dumped sales to be weighed against non-dumped sales, whereas others argue that the practice combats masked dumping—i.e., the situation where an exporter masks sales of goods at less than normal value by sales at prices above normal value—and that actual dumping may be remedied even though exporters may not sell all products at dumped prices in a national market.[256] The United States has applied zeroing or relied on zeroing-based dumping margins in all phases of U.S. antidumping duty proceedings.

Original Antidumping Investigations

The United States uses a "retrospective" system of duty assessment under which the final liability for antidumping duties is determined after the goods are imported.[257] The Commerce Department, ordinarily on the basis of an industry petition, first conducts an original investigation of the allegedly dumped product. It investigates merchandise sold for a specified annual period, usually the four most recently completed fiscal quarters as of the month preceding the month in which the petition was filed.[258] DOC ultimately makes a final determination as to whether dumping has occurred during the period of investigation and, if so, calculates an estimated weighted-average dumping margin for each known exporter of the subject merchandise.[259] It also calculates an "all others" rate for exporters that are not investigated individually.[260] If the ITC makes a final determination that domestic industry is materially injured by reason of the dumped imports, DOC will issue an antidumping order under which estimated duties are assessed and importers make cash deposits in this amount on the subject goods. DOC also orders the suspension of liquidation, i.e., the final assessment of duties, for the imported items.

Annual Administrative Reviews

One year after the antidumping order is published, an interested party may petition DOC for an administrative review of the order. In an administrative review, DOC examines entries or sales of the subject merchandise during the 12 months immediately preceding the anniversary month of the order, and calculates dumping margins for these goods.[261] The Department considers this the final antidumping duty and the goods are liquidated in this amount. The rate calculated in the administrative review also serves as the cash deposit rate for goods entering the United States under the antidumping order during the upcoming year. If requested, administrative reviews are conducted annually. If no review is requested for the first anniversary, DOC will apply the cash deposit rate applicable at the time the merchandise was entered and liquidate the entries at this amount.[262] If there is an initial administrative review and a review is not requested for the following year, duties will be assessed at the rate established in the completed review covering the most recent prior period.

Other Reviews of Antidumping Orders

DOC also conducts other types of reviews of antidumping duty orders, including: (1) "new shipper reviews," in which exporters that did not export goods during the period of investigation or that were not affiliated with an exporter that did export, may obtain their own individual dumping margins on an expedited basis;[263] (2) "changed circumstances reviews," under which interested parties may seek revocation of an AD order on the ground that changed circumstances (e.g., the cessation of material injury to the U.S. industry) are sufficient to warrant revocation;[264] and (3) mandatory five-year "sunset reviews" of existing AD orders, under which DOC and the ITC determine whether revocation of the order would be likely to lead to continuation or recurrence of dumping and material injury and DOC must revoke the order if negative determinations are made.[265]

Calculating Dumping Margins with Use of Zeroing

In calculating dumping margins in original investigations, the Department of Commerce is authorized under U.S. law to make three types of price comparisons, each of which is recognized in Article 2.4.2 of the Antidumping Agreement.[266] These comparisons are: (1) weighted average of normal values to weighted average of export prices for comparable merchandise (average-to-average); (2) normal values of individual transactions to export prices of individual transactions for comparable merchandise (transaction-to-transaction); and (3) where there is a pattern of prices that differs significantly among purchasers, regions or time periods, or so-called "targeted dumping," weighted average of normal values to export prices of individual transactions for comparable merchandise (average-to-transaction).[267]

The DOC ordinarily uses average-to-average comparisons in original investigations,[268] as was the case in the original investigations cited in the EU's complaint in DS294, discussed below. In applying the average-to-average method to a product under investigation, DOC ordinarily divides export transactions into sub-groups of the product.[269] Considering sales of the products in a subgroup to be comparable, DOC compares an average of the export prices or constructed export prices of the sales in the group to the weighted average of the normal values of such sales and determines a dumping margin for the group.[270] Once DOC determines the dumping margin for each such group, DOC calculates a weighted average dumping margin for each individual exporter or producer by aggregating the results of the comparisons. The term "weighted average dumping margin" is defined in statute as "the percentage determined by dividing the aggregate dumping margins determined for a specific exporter or producer by the aggregate export or constructed export prices of such exporter or producer."[271]

Before the Department discontinued the use of zeroing (sometimes referred to as "model zeroing") in average-to-average comparisons in original investigations, an action it announced in late 2006 in response to the adverse decision in DS294, it would have assigned a dumping margin of zero to any subgroup for which the export price was equal to or exceeded the normal value, i.e., where there was no dumping. As a result, when the results of the averaging groups were aggregated to determine the weighted-average dumping margin for the product as a whole, negative dumping margins for particular models could not be used to offset positive margins for other models. In other words, in aggregating the model-specific results to determining the numerator in the "weighted average dumping margin" calculation, the Department used only positive dumping margins.[272]

In annual administrative reviews, where DOC assesses the final antidumping duties to be imposed on entries of the merchandise entered during the prior year, the Department calculates the duty owed by an importer by using the average-to-transaction method, i.e., by comparing the price of each individual export transaction with a monthly weighted-average normal value,[273] and employing what is sometimes referred to as "simple zeroing." Thus, where the export price of the transaction exceeds the normal value, DOC will consider the dumping margin for the export transaction to be zero. The overall weighted average dumping margin for the product is then calculated by combining the results of these multiple comparisons and, again, the numerator for the overall weighted average margin is determined only on the basis of positive dumping margins. DOC ordinarily uses average-to-transaction comparisons with simple zeroing in new shipper and changed circumstances reviews.[274] In sunset reviews, the Department relies on dumping margins obtained through zeroing in determining whether dumping is likely to continue or recur if the antidumping order at issue is revoked.

Domestic Legal Basis for Zeroing

Although the Tariff Act of 1930, at section 735(A), 19 U.S.C. § 1677(35), defines the terms "dumping margin" and "weighted average dumping margin," it does not expressly address the practice of zeroing.[275] Using the *Chevron* standard of judicial review, U.S. courts have held that the statute does not unambiguously require zeroing, but the Commerce Department's interpretation of the statute as allowing the practice is a permissible one.[276] Courts have also refused to implement adverse WTO decisions on zeroing, leaving determinations as to "whether, when, and how" to comply with such rulings to the executive branch.[277]

The U.S. Court of International Trade ruled in July 2009 that the Commerce Department's determination under section 123 of the Uruguay Round Agreements Act to eliminate zeroing in average-to-average comparisons in original antidumping investigations and to offset sales made at less than fair value with fair value sales, an action taken in response to the WTO decision in DS294, was based on a reasonable interpretation of U.S. antidumping law for purposes of *Chevron* and was thus in accordance with law.[278] As discussed earlier, section 123 sets out statutory requirements for U.S. regulatory modifications taken to implement WTO decisions. The court also took into consideration the fact that the Department was undertaking this interpretation in the context of authorities and requirements in section 123, stating that the "deference accorded to Commerce's interpretation [under *Chevron*] is at its highest when that agency acts under the authority of a Congressional mandate to harmonize U.S. practices with international obligations, particularly when it allows the Executive Branch to speak on behalf of the U.S. to the international community on matters of trade and commerce."[279] The court further held that, because the section 123 action was in accordance with law, the Department's use of this new approach in a Section 129 Determination taken to comply with the WTO decision was "not unlawful."[280] Industry plaintiffs have since appealed the decision.

U.S. courts, under Step 2 of *Chevron,* have also refused to find it unreasonable for the Commerce Department to construe section 735(A) of the Tariff Act as simultaneously permitting the use of zeroing in administrative reviews and the abandonment of the practice in average-to-average comparisons in original investigations.[281]

Challenges to the U.S. Use of Zeroing in the WTO

In addition to the four pending disputes and the resolved dispute with Thailand discussed earlier in this chapter, three new challenges against the United States for its use of zeroing are currently active. In the first of these, *United States—Antidumping Measures on Polyethylene Retail Carrier Bags from Thailand*, WT/DS383, Thailand challenged the U.S. use of zeroing in an original antidumping investigation, an issue dealt with in earlier WTO decisions adverse to the United States. On January 22, 2010, the dispute panel issued a report finding that the United States was in violation of its obligations under the WTO Antidumping Agreement.[282] U.S. implementation of the panel report, which has not yet been adopted by the WTO Dispute Settlement Body, is subject to a procedural agreement between the United States and Thailand, notified to the WTO on January 7, 2010. Among other things, the United States pledged not to contest Thailand's claim and the parties agreed that the United States will have six months to implement the panel report once the report is adopted, provided the panel makes the adverse finding specified in the agreement.[283] A panel was established in the second case, *United States—Anti-Dumping Administrative Reviews and Other Measures Related to Imports of Certain Orange Juice from Brazil*, WT/DS382, on September 25, 2009. Korea requested consultations with the United States on November 24, 2009, in a third case, *United States—Use of Zeroing in Anti-Dumping Measures Involving Products from Korea,* WT/DS402.[284]

The conduct of antidumping investigations and the imposition of antidumping duties is subject to obligations in the WTO Agreement on Antidumping and Article VI of the General Agreement on Tariffs and Trade. While neither of these agreements expressly address the use of zeroing in antidumping investigations or in the various reviews and duty assessments carried out in antidumping proceedings, WTO panels and the Appellate Body have found that the use of zeroing in original investigations, except in one type of price comparison, is inconsistent with obligations in Article 2.4.2 of the WTO Antidumping Agreement requiring WTO Members to determine dumping margins by comparing normal and export values of "all comparable export transactions."[285] In addition, with the exception of some early panels, WTO panels and the Appellate Body have concluded that the use of zeroing in subsequent phases of antidumping proceedings violates GATT and Antidumping Agreement prohibitions on imposing antidumping duties that exceed the dumping margin for the goods under investigation. Further, reliance on zeroing-based dumping margins in mandatory five-year sunset reviews of antidumping duty orders has been found to violate Article 11.3 of the WTO Antidumping Agreement on the ground that such reliance taints the fundamental determination made in sunset reviews, namely, whether revocation of the antidumping order is likely to lead to the recurrence or continuation of dumping and injury.

As a result of these cases, the use of zeroing has been found to be broadly prohibited in the calculation of duties in antidumping proceedings. Moreover, particularly important for the U.S. "retrospective" antidumping duty system are findings in related compliance panel proceedings that WTO decisions faulting the use of zeroing in original antidumping investigations continue to apply with respect to subsequent administrative reviews. It has also been found in these proceedings that, where goods have entered the United States before the end of the compliance period established in a WTO dispute but final duties have not been collected, zeroing-based duties may not be applied to such goods once this period has ended. In addition, the Appellate Body recently found that an additional claim may be made in an initial WTO complaint against zeroing, namely, the "continued use" of the practice in subsequent domestic proceedings relating to a particular antidumping duty order.

The United States has expressed concerns with Appellate Body's broad prohibition on the use of zeroing at meetings of the WTO Dispute Settlement Body and in related documents circulated to Members. In addition, the United States submitted proposals in June 2007 to the WTO Negotiating Group of Rules, which has been negotiating revisions to antidumping and subsidy rules in the Doha Round, asking that negotiators evaluate the reasoning of the WTO panels that have examined the issue of zeroing and stating that "the proper resolution of this issue requires clear text providing that margins of dumping may be determined without offsets for non-dumped transactions, consistent with the long-held concept of dumping."[286] The United States also proposed revised language for the Antidumping Agreement to this effect.[287] While the draft negotiating text issued by the Chairman of the Doha Negotiating Group in November 2007 contained proposed language reflecting U.S. concerns,[288] the draft text issued in December 2008 does not contain such language and instead notes that, with regard to zeroing, "[d]elegations remain profoundly divided on this issue," with positions ranging from "insistence on a total prohibition of zeroing irrespective of the comparison methodology used and in respect of all proceedings to a demand that zeroing be specifically authorized in all contexts."[289]

Laws, Regulations, and Methodology for Calculating Dumping Margins ("Zeroing") (DS294)

In June 2003, the European Union (EU) requested consultations with the United States over the use of zeroing by the Commerce Department in determining dumping margins, arguing that the practice as it relates to original antidumping investigations and subsequent administrative, new shipper, changed circumstances, and sunset reviews was inconsistent "as such" with provisions of the WTO Agreement on Antidumping and Article VI of the GATT 1994. That is, complainants argued that the existence of the practice violated these agreements regardless of any specific application.[290] The EU also alleged that the United States had acted inconsistently with its WTO obligations in applying zeroing in 31 specific cases, including 15 original investigations and 16 administrative reviews.[291] The EU further claimed that insofar as dumping margins in original investigations should be calculated without the use of zeroing and some exporters may thus have de miminis dumping margins, these imports should be excluded from the volume of dumped imports that the ITC takes into account in determining whether such imports are causing material injury to domestic industry. The EU argued that WTO obligations require the United States to make this determination based only on the volume of imports remaining after this exclusion. A panel was established in March 2004.

Panel and Appellate Body Reports

In a report issued October 31, 2005, the WTO panel found that zeroing, as applied in the weighted-average-to-weighted average price comparisons made in the 15 original investigations cited in the EU's complaint, was inconsistent with Article 2.4.2 of the Antidumping Agreement. This article provides, in pertinent part, that "[s]ubject to the provisions governing fair comparison in [Article 2] paragraph 4, the existence of margins of dumping during the investigation phase shall normally be established on the basis of a comparison of weighted-average normal value of prices of all comparable export transactions or by a comparison of normal value and export prices on a transaction-to-transaction basis."[292] The panel based its conclusion on Appellate Body rulings in earlier cases that "when a margin of dumping is calculated on the basis of multiple averaging by model type, the margin of dumping for the products in question must reflect the results of *all such comparisons*, including weighted average export prices that are above the normal value for individual models."[293] The Appellate Body had earlier concluded that the term "dumping" in WTO agreements is defined "in relation to a product as a whole" and that, as a result, dumping can thus be found to exist "only for the product under investigation as a whole" and not solely "for a type, model, or category of that product."[294] Thus, in considering the U.S. multiple averaging technique in light of WTO obligations, the Appellate Body concluded that the only was that a dumping margin could be properly established for the product as a whole would be to aggregate "*all* of the 'results' of the multiple comparisons for *all* product types."[295]

The panel also found that zeroing, as it relates to original investigations, was a "well established and well-defined norm" that could be challenged "as such" in a WTO dispute even though it was not in written form, and that, with respect to its use in weighted-average-to-weighted-average price comparisons in original investigations, the norm "as such" was inconsistent with Article 2.4.2.[296]

The panel rejected the EU's claims regarding the application of zeroing in the 16 administrative reviews cited by the EU, as well as on the use of zeroing "as such" in administrative reviews, new shipper reviews, changed circumstances reviews, and sunset reviews. One dissenting panelist would have struck down the use of the practice in proceedings other than original investigations, however. The panel did not address EU claims involving the need for a new injury determination based on excluded imports, viewing this as a dependent claim and finding that any conclusion would not provide the United States with additional guidance as to how to remedy the primary violation.

The panel report was appealed by the United States and the EU. While the United States appealed the panel's finding that zeroing was a challengeable norm, it did not appeal the panel's conclusion that the use of zeroing in weighted-average-to-weighted-average price comparisons in the cited original investigations violated the Antidumping Agreement.[297]

On April 18, 2006, the Appellate Body found, although on different grounds from the panel, that the zeroing methodology could be challenged "as such" as it relates to original investigations and upheld the panel's finding that the practice is inconsistent with Article 2.4.2 of the Antidumping Agreement.[298]

The AB also expanded the range of proceedings in which zeroing was prohibited, finding, contrary to the panel, that the United States could not use zeroing in making weighted-average-totransaction comparisons to assess duties and set cash deposit rates in the 16 administrative reviews challenged by the EU. The AB found that the application of zeroing in these reviews violated Article 9.3 of the Antidumping Agreement and Article VI:2 of the GATT 1994 since the practice resulted in the imposition of antidumping duties that exceeded the exporters' or producers' dumping margins.[299] Article 9.3, which sets out obligations regarding the assessment of antidumping duties, provides that the "amount of the anti-dumping duty" imposed by a WTO Member "shall not exceed the margin of dumping as established under Article 2" of the Agreement. Article VI:2 of the GATT 1994 provides that a WTO Member may impose an antidumping duty on a dumped product "no greater in amount than the margin of dumping in respect of such product." The Appellate Body did not determine whether the use of zeroing in these reviews was "as such" inconsistent with WTO obligations, however, due to insufficient facts in the panel record to complete this analysis.

The AB report, which also addressed other issues, and the modified panel report were adopted on May 9, 2006.[300] While the United States vigorously disputed the Appellate Body decision,[301] it stated at a subsequent DSB meeting that it intended to comply.[302] The disputing parties later agreed on an implementation deadline of April 9, 2007.[303]

U.S. Actions in Response

Shortly before the AB report was issued, the DOC had announced in the *Federal Register* that, in response to the WTO panel report, it would abandon the use of zeroing in weighted-average-toweighted-average comparisons in antidumping investigations and was seeking comments on alternative approaches that might be appropriate in future investigations.[304] The Department noted that the United States had not appealed the panel's finding that the zeroing could not be used in making such comparisons in the specific antidumping investigations challenged by the EU. Agreement.

On December 26, 2006, the Department, following the requirements in section 123 of the Uruguay Round Agreements Act (URAA), published a *Federal Register* notice stating that it was modifying its antidumping practice as announced earlier, noting that the modification would be used in implementing the findings of the WTO panel pursuant to section 129 of the URAA with regard to the specific antidumping investigations challenged by the EU in the dispute and, moreover, that it would apply the modification in all current and future antidumping investigation as of the effective date, which at the time was planned for January 16, 2007.[305] The Department later extended the date to January 23, 2007, and then to February 22, 2007, noting each time that it was acting "[a]fter further consultations with Congress and in order to afford adequate time for review."[306]

The Department also announced on February 22, 2007, that it was initiating section 129 proceedings in which it would implement the WTO ruling with respect to 12 of the 15 original antidumping investigations cited by the EU, three of the cited AD orders having been revoked.[307] On April 9, 2007, the Department of Commerce issued new Section 129 Determinations in 11 of the proceedings using average-to-average comparisons in which offsets were provided, two of which resulted in findings of no dumping.[308] The DOC also postponed its determination in the twelfth investigation, a proceeding involving stainless steel products from Italy, as it was investigating a possible clerical error in the original investigation alleged by the respondent. Recalculations were done without the use of zeroing as provided in the modification originally announced in December 2006.[309] Regarding the administrative reviews at issue in the dispute, the United States stated that since they had been superseded by new administrative reviews, it did not need to take any further action to bring these reviews into compliance with the WTO decision.[310] The USTR instructed DOC to implement the new determinations on April 23, 2007.[311]

While the United States considered itself in compliance,[312] the EU questioned the prospective nature of the new determinations, that is, that they did not cover duties on goods entered before the date the Section 129 Determinations were implemented; claimed that DOC had "massively increased the 'all others' rate (applicable to exporters who do not have an individual duty rate, notably new exporters)"; and stated that the United States was obligated to review the dumping margins in the 16 challenged administrative reviews, claiming that to its knowledge the United States had not taken any action to bring these reviews into compliance with the WTO decision.[313]

On May 4, 2007, the United States and the EU entered into a procedural agreement regarding possible Article 21.5 compliance panel proceedings and the sequencing of a possible retaliation request in the event the United States was found not to have complied in the case.[314] The EU requested consultations with the United States under Article 21.5 in July 2007.[315]

In September 2007, DOC issued a new determination in the outstanding antidumping case involving steel products from Italy, finding that the alleged clerical errors were not raised in the WTO dispute and thus were outside the scope of the Section 129 proceeding.[316]

Compliance Proceedings

The EU requested a compliance panel in September 2007, claiming that the United States had failed to take compliance actions in some cases and that measures that it had taken in others were inconsistent with WTO obligations.[317] In its panel request, the EU cited specific administrative reviews and sunset reviews undertaken by the United States in the 15 original investigations and 16 administrative review that were successfully challenged in the original proceeding. The EU also claimed that United States violated its WTO obligations in those cases where it had recalculated dumping margins in original investigations without the use of zeroing, found that some exporters were not dumping or had *de miminis* margins, and maintained the antidumping order without determining whether the remaining amount of dumped were causing material injury to domestic industry.

The compliance proceeding was complex not only because of the number of U.S. antidumping determinations that the EU claimed were WTO-inconsistent, but also because of the interaction of the retrospective U.S. duty system with what has generally been considered to be the prospective nature of remedies in a WTO dispute. As described by the WTO Appellate Body, the WTO dispute settlement system is one under which "compliance has to be accomplished at the latest from the end of the reasonable period of time [i.e. the compliance period] with prospective effect."[318] At the same time, due to the U.S. retrospective system, there were goods that had entered the United States before the date on which the compliance period ended but for which final duty assessments would not be made until after this date, or for which final assessments were made before this date, but the duties were not collected until after the period expired. While the United States and the EU agreed that the WTO Dispute Settlement Understanding provides only for prospective remedies, the parties disagreed on what this entailed for the United States with regard to these earlier-entered goods.[319]

Questions also arose as to whether dumping determinations made in a phase of the proceeding that occurred after the one at issue in the original WTO dispute were considered measures taken to comply or whether they were properly before the panel for other reasons. Some of the challenged determinations, which had been rendered in original investigations, were the subject of later administrative or sunset reviews. In addition, the challenged administrative reviews had been superseded by determinations made in subsequent administrative reviews. Further, the United States had taken new action in some of the challenged proceedings before the panel and Appellate Body reports were issued.

The United States argued that administrative reviews of challenged dumping determinations made in original investigations were not measures taken to comply with the WTO decision and thus outside the panel's terms of reference.[320] In its view, the compliance panel could only review whether the original determination now complied with the WTO decision and could not examine whether the United State had employed zeroing in the subsequent review. The United States made the same argument with regard to administrative reviews that occurred after those that were challenged in the dispute and protested the inclusion of sunset reviews of challenged determinations as well.[321] As noted above, the United States maintained that since the challenged administrative reviews had been superseded by later reviews, the United States was not required to take any action to ensure that the challenged determinations were in compliance. The EU argued that under this approach, the EU would need to initiate a new dispute settlement proceeding for each subsequent administrative review with which it disagreed, thus allowing the United States to avoid permanent compliance with a WTO decision as it related to a specific investigation or review that was successfully challenged.[322] In addition, the United States had undertaken sunset reviews of some of the challenged original determinations and administrative reviews prior to the adoption of the panel and Appellate Body reports by the Dispute Settlement Body, actions that the EU claimed could not be considered measures taken to comply with the WTO rulings and recommendations in these reports.

Compliance Proceedings: Panel and Appellate Body Reports

In December 2008, the panel issued a mixed report regarding U.S. compliance,[323] which the EU appealed. In a report issued May 20, 2009, the Appellate Body found that the United States remained out of compliance with its WTO obligations in a variety of respects.[324]

Regarding whether actions taken by the United States before the panel and Appellate Body reports were adopted were within the panel's terms of reference, the Appellate Body, reversing the panel, found that measures taken before this date were potentially reviewable as compliance measures. The Appellate Body found that the relevant inquiry was not whether the measures were intentionally taken to comply, but instead whether they each had a "sufficiently close nexus, in terms of *nature, effects,* and *timing*," with the WTO decision and with the declared measures that were in fact taken to comply.[325] The AB found that of the five sunset reviews that met this test determinations in four of these, having relied on dumping margins calculated with the use of zeroing, were inconsistent with WTO obligations; no findings were made on the fifth.[326]

Regarding whether subsequent administrative and sunset reviews of challenged measures were amenable to review, it was determined in the compliance proceeding that administrative reviews involving the calculation of a dumping margin based on zeroing and subsequent sunset reviews in which DOC relies on dumping margins calculated with the use of zeroing, could potentially fall within the scope of the compliance proceeding, This conclusion was based on two grounds: (1) the "close nexus that exists in terms of their nature" between the subsequent reviews and measures at issue in the original dispute and (2) the fact that "the subsequent reviews potentially affect or undermine the steps otherwise taken—or the steps that should have been taken—by the United States to comply with the recommendations and rulings of the DSB, notably in the form of Section 129 determinations."[327] The panel had noted that the use of zeroing in an administrative review of an original determination could potentially negate the results of a Section 129 determination in which the dumping margin was calculated without its use, thus undoing an action taken to comply with the WTO decision.[328]

Further, regarding the scope of U.S. obligations involving imports entering the United States before the end of the compliance period, the Appellate Body agreed with the panel that the calculation of dumping margins in administrative reviews, or "definitive duty determinations," that occurred after the end of the compliance period, but that involved imports entered before this date, could not be made with the use of zeroing.[329] Contrary to the panel, however, the Appellate Body determined that duties could not be *collected* after the end of compliance period consistently with WTO obligations if they are based on dumping margins calculated with the use of zeroing during administrative reviews that occur before the end of the compliance period. The panel had found entries could be liquidated on the basis of a zeroing-based dumping determination without violating WTO obligations even though actions taken by the United States after the compliance deadline would ordinarily be expected to comply with the WTO decision.

The Appellate Body found that any measures that "derives *mechanically*" from the assessment of duties, as is the case with the collection (or liquidation) of antidumping duties, would not be WTO-compliant to the extent they are based on zeroing and are applied after the compliance deadline expires.[330]

Before drawing these conclusions, the AB had generally noted that, with respect to the original determinations and administrative reviews in which the use of zeroing was challenged "as applied," the assessment of a final duty for previously imported goods in an administrative review also affects the cash deposit rate for certain future imports, a situation that has implications for the administrative reviews not directly at issue in the case. Thus, in light of the prospective nature of WTO remedies, "compliance is not confined by the limited duration of the original measures at issue, especially when a subsequent measure replaces or supersedes the measure at issue in the original proceeding."[331]

The panel and AB made various findings regarding the inconsistency of particular determinations challenged by the EU with the obligation to eliminate zeroing. Further, the panel, in an issue not reviewed by the AB, determined that, with regard to four original determinations for which Section 129 determinations were issued, the United States violated the Antidumping Agreement by not revisiting its ITC material injury determinations due to revised import volumes. In some cases, the recalculated dumping margins had led to findings of no dumping or de minimis margins for particular exporters and thus the panel found that, in these four cases, the United States was obligated to reconsider whether dumped imports were causing material injury to domestic industry using import volumes that excluded these non-dumped and de minimis imports.[332]

Recent Developments

The adverse Appellate Body report and the modified compliance panel report were adopted on June 11, 2009. With the compliance panel proceeding completed, the EU has stated that the United States is required to comply "without delay" by recalculating dumping margins without the use of zeroing in the numerous dumping determinations faulted in the case and then collecting duties at the recalculated rates.[333] At the same time, the United States has raised concerns about what it views as the expanded scope of U.S. obligations in the case.[334] According to the U.S.-EU procedural agreement, the EU may now request authorization to suspend concessions owed the United

States and may also request negotiations on compensation. In its January 9, 2010, status report to the WTO Dispute Settlement Body, the United States stated that it "will continue to consult with interested parties in order to address the findings contained in these [panel and Appellate Body] reports."[335]

Measures Relating to Zeroing and Sunset Reviews (DS322)

In November 2004, Japan instituted a broad challenge of the use of zeroing by the United States, claiming in its subsequent panel request that the use of this practice in original antidumping investigations, administrative reviews (referred to in the case as "periodic reviews"), new shipper reviews, sunset reviews, and changed circumstances reviews was in violation of obligations in the WTO Antidumping Agreement. Japan also challenged zeroing as applied in 15 specific antidumping proceedings, including one original investigation, 12 administrative reviews, and two sunset reviews. The cited cases involved imports of steel plate and steel flat products, as well as roller, ball, spherical plain, and antifriction bearings. In addition, Japan challenged subsequent material injury determinations made by the U.S. International Trade Commission based on dumping margins determined through zeroing and made further claims regarding sunset reviews and changed circumstances reviews in which determinations were based on dumping margins obtained in this way.

Panel and Appellate Body Reports

In a report circulated September 20, 2006, the WTO panel concluded that zeroing, when used by DOC in weighted-average-to-weighted-average comparisons in original antidumping investigations and consequently, the use of zeroing in the one original investigation cited by Japan, were inconsistent with Article 2.4.2 of the Antidumping Agreement.[336] As in DS294, discussed above, zeroing was found to be a norm that could be challenged "as such" in a WTO dispute settlement proceeding.

At the same time, the panel rejected Japan's claims that the use of zeroing in transaction-totransaction comparisons and weighted-average-to-transaction comparisons in original investigations, its use administrative reviews and new shipper reviews, its application in the 11 cited administrative reviews was violative of the Antidumping Agreement. The panel also found that Japan had failed to make a prima facie case that the use of zeroing in changed circumstances reviews and sunset reviews violated WTO obligations. The panel also rejected Japan's claims that the ITC had improperly relied on dumping margins calculated in previous proceedings in the two sunset reviews cited by Japan. Both Japan and the United States appealed the decision.

In a ruling issued January 9, 2007, the Appellate Body upheld the panel's findings that zeroing could be challenged "as such," but went further in finding that U.S. measures did in fact constitute "as such" violations of the WTO antidumping obligations.[337] The Appellate Body found that, in maintaining zeroing procedures in transaction-to-transaction comparisons in original investigations, the United States was in violation of Articles 2.4 of the Antidumping Agreement, which requires that a "fair comparison ... be made between the export price and the normal value," and Article 2.4.2 of the Agreement, which as noted earlier, provides that "[s]ubject to the provisions governing fair comparison in paragraph 4, the existence of margins of dumping during the investigation phase shall normally be established on the basis of a comparison of weighted- average normal value of prices of all comparable export transactions or by a comparison of normal value and export prices on a transaction-to-transaction basis."

The Appellate Body further found that by maintaining zeroing procedures in administrative reviews, the United States acted inconsistently with Article 2.4 of the Antidumping Agreement, Article 9.3 of the Agreement, which provides that amount of the antidumping duty actually assessed "shall not exceed the margin of dumping" as determined under Article 2 of the Agreement, and Article VI:2 of the GATT 1994, which provides that a WTO Member may impose an antidumping duty on a dumped product "no greater in amount than the margin of dumping in respect of such product."

The Appellate Body also found that, by using zeroing in new shipper reviews, the United States was out of compliance with Articles 2.4 and 9.5 of the Antidumping Agreement, the latter setting out requirements for such reviews.

In addition, the Appellate Body upheld Japan's "as applied" claims, finding that the United States had acted inconsistently with Articles 2.4 and 9.3 of the Antidumping Agreement and Article VI:2 of the GATT 1994 by applying zeroing in the 11 administrative reviews cited by Japan.

The Appellate Body also determined that, in relying on zeroing-based dumping margins in two cited sunset reviews, the United States had acted inconsistently with Article 11.3 of the Antidumping Agreement. Article 11.3 requires that duties be terminated after five years unless authorities determine in a review "that the expiry of the duty would be likely to lead to continuation or recurrence of dumping and injury." The Appellate Body had found in an earlier dispute that WTO Members are not required to rely on dumping margins in making this determination, but that, if Members choose to do so, they must calculate the margin in conformity with the requirements of Article 2.4 of the Agreement.[338] If not, the "likelihood" determination would not serve as a proper foundation for maintaining the duty under Article 11.3 The Appellate Body found in the instant case that the United States, in making its sunset determinations, had relied on zeroing-based margins calculated in earlier administrative reviews. Since the Appellate Body had also found that the use of zeroing in such reviews is inconsistent "as such" with Articles 2.4 and 9.3 of the Antidumping Agreement, it concluded that reliance on these margins in the sunset reviews thus violated Article 11.3.[339]

The Appellate Body report and the panel report, as modified, were adopted by the DSB at its January 23, 2007, meeting.[340] The United States, while once again disputing the Appellate Body's reasoning, told the DSB on February 20, 2007, that it intended to comply with its WTO obligations in the case and that it needed a reasonable period of time to do so.[341] It later circulated a critical analysis of the Appellate Body decision to WTO Members.[342] While Japan had originally requested the compliance period be arbitrated,[343] the parties later agreed on a compliance period ending December 24, 2007.[344]

Actions by the United States and Japan in Response

In its December 7, 2007 WTO status report on the case, the United States made reference to the modification adopted by the Commerce Department in February 2007 under which zeroing would no longer be used in weighted average-to-weighted average comparisons in original investigations and stated only that is was "continually to consult internally on steps to be taken with respect to the other DSB recommendations and rulings."[345] While the Department of Commerce had initiated a proceeding under section 129 of Uruguay Round Agreements in November 2007 regarding the challenged original investigation, a proceeding involving certain steel plate products, and publicly released final results on December 27, 2007, [346] it took no final action to comply by the December 24 deadline.[347]

In January 2008, Japan requested authorization to retaliate by imposing additional import duties on selected products in an initial annual amount of $181.2 million.[348] While the subsequent U.S. objection sent Japan's request to arbitration,[349] the disputing parties entered into a procedural agreement in March 2008 under which Japan was permitted to request a compliance panel without first seeking consultations and, if it made such a request, its retaliation request would be suspended.[350] Under the procedural agreement, either party may request that the arbitration resume in the event that the compliance proceeding results in a finding that U.S. compliance measures are inadequate or non-existent or "there is no disagreement" between Japan and the United States that "a measure taken to comply does not exist" with respect to certain U.S. actions that were successfully challenged in the original dispute.

The United States maintained in a status report to the Dispute Settlement Body and in a DSB meeting held on January 21, 2008, that it was in compliance in the case because it was no longer making average-to-average price comparisons in original investigations without offsets, it had issued a revised dumping determination using this methodology in the one challenged original investigation, and it did not need to take action with respect to the challenged administrative reviews because they had been superseded by subsequent reviews.[351]

Compliance Panel Proceedings

As provided for in the U.S.-Japan procedural agreement, Japan requested a compliance panel on April 7, 2008, stating that the United States was in violation of its WTO obligations by not having fully complied with respect to the one original investigation at issue; by continuing to use zeroing in transaction-to-transaction comparisons in original investigations, administrative reviews, and new shipper reviews; by applying zeroing in five of the administrative reviews originally challenged by Japan and as well as in three "closely connected" administrative reviews that the United States argued had superseded earlier reviews; and by relying on zeroing in one of the originally challenged sunset reviews and a subsequent sunset review of the same antidumping duty order.[352] The compliance panel was established on April 18, 2008. On June 6, 2008, the United States and Japan asked the arbitration panel that was reviewing Japan's January 2008 retaliation request to suspend its work.[353]

In the interim, DOC, on May 20, 2008, announced the results of the section 129 proceeding involving the challenged original investigation, stating in the *Federal Register* that it had recalculated the affected dumping margins, arriving at slightly reduced rates, which, at the direction of the U.S. Trade Representative, went into effect on April 8, 2008.[354]

The compliance panel issued its report on April 20, 2009, finding that the United States had not complied with its WTO antidumping obligations in the administrative reviews cited by Japan and in maintaining zeroing in transaction-to-transaction comparisons in original investigations and in any price comparison used in administrative and new shipper reviews.[355] While the United States had argued that it did not have compliance obligations with respect to five of the reviews because the covered goods had entered the United States before the end of the compliance period, the panel found that the United States was required to bring the importer-specific assessment rates determined in these reviews into compliance with its WTO obligations by the end of the compliance period.[356] The panel also addressed a situation that had not been ruled upon in DS294—that is, one in which duties are assessed before the end of the compliance period, but liquidation instructions are delayed because of injunctions issued under domestic judicial proceedings challenging the assessment—and found that the fact that the delay was due to litigation was of no consequence to compliance with the WTO obligations in the case.[357]

The panel further determined that the United States had violated GATT Article II prohibitions on imposing tariff surcharges on goods subject to negotiated tariff rates (so-called "bound items") by issuing WTO-inconsistent liquidation instructions in four challenged administrative reviews involving ball bearing products after the compliance period expired.[358] These reviews were among the five with delayed liquidations because of pending litigation. While the panel had agreed with the United States that the Article II claims were derivative of Japan's claims under the Antidumping Agreement, it nonetheless found it appropriate to rule on them because "they raise an important point of contention between the parties regarding the right of the United States to continue liquidating entries after the expiry of the RPT [reasonable period of time] on the basis of liquidation measures issued pursuant to administrative reviews that have already been found to be WTO-inconsistent."[359]

The panel additionally concluded that the United States was out of compliance with its WTO obligations by not withdrawing or modifying the likelihood of dumping determination in the challenged 1999 sunset review in which the United States had relied on zeroing-based dumping margins.[360]

Recent Developments

The United States appealed the adverse compliance panel report in May 2009. In a report issued August 18, 2009, the Appellate Body upheld the compliance panel on all issues appealed, including against U.S. claims regarding the judicial delay of liquidation and violations of GATT Article II.[361] The Appellate Body emphasized that all antidumping duties collected after the end of the compliance period needed to be calculated without the use of zeroing. Among other things, it upheld the panel's dismissal of the U.S.

argument that judicial delay of liquidation permits the collection of zeroing-based antidumping duties after the compliance period expires, stating, *inter alia*, that it was "not persuaded that the initiation by private parties of domestic judicial proceedings is relevant for determining the scope of the United States compliance obligations in this case."[362]

The Appellate Body and compliance panel reports issued in the Article 21.5 proceeding were adopted by the WTO Dispute Settlement Body on August 31, 2009. At the meeting, the United States referred Members to its earlier public statements regarding its intent to comply in all the WTO zeroing disputes and stated that it was "working actively to implement these recommendations and rulings, including those made in other disputes for which the reasonable period of time ... is still ongoing." [363] The United States added, however, that in its view the appeal of the compliance panel report in this case "was not about zeroing but rather concerns what a Member with a retrospective antidumping system must do to come into compliance with the DSB's recommendations and rulings with respect to individual administrative reviews" and that the dispute in addition "raised important procedural issues as to the scope of dispute settlement proceedings." Noting the prospective nature of WTO remedies, the United States cited the systemic implications of applying obligations under a WTO decision to governmental actions involving goods that enter the defending Member's customs territory before the end of the compliance period, an approach that, in its view, could be taken toward all border measures imposed on imports, including ordinary tariffs. It also took issue with Appellate Body's finding that the obligation not to use zeroing applied to duty liquidations that take place after the expiration of the compliance period where the liquidation is delayed due to litigation, as well as the Appellate Body's affirmance that a particular administrative review could be reviewed by a compliance panel even though the proceeding was not in existence at the time that Japan made its panel request.

Under the U.S.-Japan procedural agreement, either the United States or Japan may ask that the arbitration on Japan's January 2008 retaliation request be resumed. The arbitration was suspended in June 2008 following Japan's request for a compliance panel. Japan has not yet taken further action in the case.

Final Anti-Dumping Measures on Stainless Steel from Mexico (DS344)

Mexico challenged (1) the use of model zeroing by the United States in original antidumping investigations, both as such and as applied in an original investigation of Mexican stainless steel sheet and strips in coils and (2) the use of simple zeroing in annual administrative reviews, both as such and as applied in five administrative reviews in the antidumping proceeding involved.[364] A panel report issued December 20, 2007, concluded that model zeroing, as used in original investigations, was inconsistent with Article 2.4.2 of the Antidumping Agreement, both as such and as applied in the cited antidumping investigation.[365] The panel ruled in favor of the United States, however, in finding that the use of simple zeroing, either as such or as applied in the cited administrative reviews, was not inconsistent with the GATT Article VI or the Antidumping Agreement.

In an appeal by Mexico, the Appellate Body issued a report on April 30, 2008, in which it reversed the panel's findings on the use of simple zeroing, finding, as it had in earlier disputes, that the use of this practice in administrative reviews, both as such and as applied in cited antidumping cases, was inconsistent with Article VI:2 of the GATT and Article 9.3 of the Antidumping Agreement.[366] The Appellate Body also criticized the panel for not adhering to earlier Appellate Body rulings on this issue, stating that, although it was "well settled that Appellate Body reports are not binding, except with respect to resolving the particular dispute between the parties," this principle "does not mean that subsequent panels are free to disregard the legal interpretations and the *ratio decidendi* contained in previous Appellate Body reports that have been adopted by the DSB."[367] Examining the use made of panel and Appellate Body reports in subsequent disputes and by WTO Members in enacting laws and issuing regulations, and the role played by the Appellate Body in the WTO dispute settlement system *vis à vis* panels, the Appellate Body concluded that the "Panel's failure to follow previously adopted Appellate Body reports addressing the same issues undermines the development of a coherent and predictable body of jurisprudence clarifying Members' rights and obligations under the covered agreements as contemplated under the DSU."[368]

The Appellate Body report and modified panel report were adopted at the May 20, 2008, meeting of the Dispute Settlement Body. During the meeting, the United States stated its support for the panel's conclusions regarding simple zeroing and questioned the approach taken by the Appellate Body in reversing the panel.[369] It did not, however, discuss compliance in the case. The United States later circulated a document in which it questioned in a more detailed fashion the reasoning and approach of the Appellate Body regarding the use of zeroing in the transaction-specific calculations employed in administrative reviews.[370]

Because the parties could not agree on the length of the compliance period, the issue was arbitrated at Mexico's request. In an October 31, 2008, decision, the Arbitrator set a deadline of April 30, 2009.[371]

The Commerce Department issued a determination under section 129 of the Uruguay Round Agreements Act on March 31, 2009, in which it recalculated the dumping margin in the original investigation without the use of zeroing, and later published a notice in the *Federal Register* that the USTR had instructed the Department to implement this determination effective April 23, 2009.[372] The recalculation resulted in a reduction of the dumping margin from 30.85 percent to 30.69 percent for one individually investigated exporter and the same reduction in the "all others" rate.

With respect to the administrative reviews that were challenged "as applied," the United States has reportedly informed the WTO Dispute Settlement Body at its May 20, 2009, meeting "that 'any prospective effect of those reviews has been eliminated and all entries of merchandise under the five reviews have been liquidated for customs purposes.'"[373] With regard to other rulings and recommendations in the dispute, however, the United States "informed the DSB that it 'has also been conferring with Mexico about the steps that the United States has taken to comply with the recommendations and rulings of the DSB.'"[374] On May 19, 2009, the United States and Mexico entered into a sequencing agreement involving the possible request by Mexico of a compliance panel and, if it is later determined that the United States has not taken a measure to comply or its compliance measures are inconsistent with WTO obligations, a request for authorization to suspend concessions owed the United States.[375]

Recent Developments

On August 19, 2009, Mexico requested consultations with the United States under Article 21.5 of the DSU regarding U.S. compliance in the case.[376] Mexico maintains that the United States has not complied with the WTO decision because it: (1) "has not taken any steps" to eliminate the use of simple zeroing in periodic, i.e., administrative, reviews; (2) continues to maintain and use simple zeroing in the five administrative reviews originally challenged in the case; and (3) continues to "impose, assess and/or collect anti-dumping duties in excess of the proper margin of dumping, and evidences its intention to continue to do so, through ... five subsequent periodic reviews [of the original antidumping duty order on stainless steel and sheet in coils from Mexico] ... , any amendments thereto, any measures closely related thereto, any future subsequent periodic reviews, and the United States Government instructions and notices." The U.S.-Mexico procedural agreement gave the parties 15 days to consult on Mexico's request, after which Mexico could request a compliance panel. To date, Mexico has not made such a request.

Continued Existence and Application of Zeroing Methodology (D S350)

Although the European Union (EU) had successfully challenged the U.S. use of zeroing in DS294, it was concerned that the United States had not yet broadly discontinued use of the practice. In October 2006, the EU challenged the continued use and application of zeroing in 18 specific antidumping cases, citing the continued application of antidumping duties at a level in excess of the margins that would result from correct application of the Antidumping Agreement.[377] Ten of the 18 cases had been at issue in the EU's earlier challenge, DS294. The EU also challenged the use of zeroing in administrative and sunset reviews in 13 cases, a sunset review in one case, and original investigations in four others, a total of 52 agency determinations.

Along with challenging the use of zeroing both "as such" and "as applied" in the cited antidumping determinations, the EU also claimed that a duty based on zeroing, while not falling within either of these two categories, was a "measure" subject to WTO dispute settlement.[378] The EU considered this new argument to be "key" to the proceeding since, in its view, its effect "would be that of bringing the future use of United States zeroing in each case within the scope of the panel findings."[379] The EU later abandoned its "as such" claim after Japan successfully obtained a ruling on this point in DS322.[380]

In its October 1, 2008 report, the WTO panel found that the United States acted inconsistently with its obligations in the Antidumping Agreement by (1) using model zeroing in the four cited original investigations; (2) applying simple zeroing in 29 of the cited administrative reviews cited; and (3) relying on dumping margins obtained through model zeroing in the eight sunset reviews at issue.[381] The panel found, however, that claims involving the continued application of antidumping duties in thel 8 antidumping cases were not within the panel's terms of reference. One panelist, while agreeing with these conclusions, disagreed with the legal reasoning used by the panel in considering the EU's claims on simple zeroing in periodic reviews and, in part, on model zeroing in original investigations. The report was appealed by both the EU and the United States.

In a report issued on February 4, 2009, the Appellate Body ruled that "the continued use of zeroing in successive proceedings in which duties resulting from the 18 anti-dumping duty orders are maintained, constitute 'measures' that can be challenged in WTO dispute settlement."[382] The Appellate Body determined that it had a sufficient factual record to make findings on this basis in four of the 18 cases cited by the EU and found that, with respect to these four cases, the application and continued application of antidumping duties was (1) inconsistent with Article 9.3 of the Antidumping Agreement and Article VI:2 of the GATT 1994 to the extent that the duties were calculated with zeroing in administrative reviews, and (2) inconsistent with Article 11.3, to the extent that reliance was placed on a zeroing-based margin in sunset reviews.[383]

The Appellate Body also upheld the panel's findings that zeroing was improperly applied in 29 of the challenged administrative reviews and, contrary to the panel, was able to find that the United States had acted inconsistently with its WTO obligations in five additional administrative reviews originally cited by the EU.[384] In addition, the Appellate Body upheld the panel's finding that the United States had acted inconsistently with Article 11.3 of the Antidumping Agreement in eight sunset reviews.[385]

The Appellate Body Report and the modified panel report were adopted at the February 19, 2009, meeting of the Dispute Settlement Body. As it had with respect to past appellate reports on zeroing, the United States expressed concerns with the Appellate Body's approach to a variety of issues in the case.[386] At the March 20, 2009, meeting of the Dispute Settlement Body, the United States stated that it intended to comply in the dispute, "would be considering carefully how to do so," and would need a reasonable period of time for this undertaking.[387] In June, the United States and the EU agreed on a compliance period ending December 19, 2009.[388]

Recent Developments

With the compliance deadline of December 19, 2009, before it, the United States stated in its December 10, 2009, WTO status report that the USTR had sent a written request to the Secretary of Commerce to issue a Section 129 determination that would render four final antidumping determinations at issue in the case not inconsistent with the recommendations and rulings of the WTO

Dispute Settlement Body.[389] The United States also stated that it would "continue to consult with interested parties in order to address the other findings" contained in the adopted panel and Appellate Body reports.[390] At the December 21, 2009, meeting of the WTO Dispute Settlement Body, the United States added that it was "sure that Members appreciate the difficulties that are raised for the United States by the Appellate Body findings on zeroing in this disputes and others," reiterating the action that it had taken and the ongoing discussions on unresolved issues.[391] At the same meeting, the EU reportedly "expressed its disappointment that the reasonable period of time for implementation had expired and the US had yet to bring itself into compliance."[392] With other issues in the case remaining unaddressed, the United States and the EU entered into a procedural agreement in the case in January 2010 providing for a possible compliance panel request by the EU.[393]

End Notes

[1] The case histories in this chapter are primarily based on WTO documents, available at http://www.wto.org, or the WTO dispute settlement website indicated below. This chapter does not address cases in which the United States has implemented adverse reports to the satisfaction of the complaining party and the dispute has been fully settled, nor does it discuss the compliance history of other WTO Members that have been found to be in violation of their WTO obligations. For further information on WTO disputes, see Office of the U.S. Trade Representative, "WTO Dispute Settlement," at *http://www.ustr.gov/trade-topics/enforcement* the annual Trade Policy Agenda and Annual Report of the President of the United States on the Trade Agreements Program, at http://www.ustr.gov/sites/default/files/uploads/reports/2009/asset_upload_file86_15410.pdf ; and WTO, Update of WTO Dispute Settlement Cases (updated regularly), at http://www.wto.org/english/tratop_e/dispu_e/ dispu_e.htm.

[2] For further information on WTO dispute settlement procedures, *see* "Dispute settlement," at http://www.wto.org/ english/tratop_e/dispu_e/dispu_e.htm, and CRS Report RS20088, *Dispute Settlement in the World Trade Organization (WTO): An Overview*, by Jeanne J. Grimmett.

[3] See Sylvia A. Rhodes, *The Article 21.5/22 Problem: Clarification Through Bilateral Agreements?*, 3 J. INT'L ECON. L. 553 (2000).

[4] The DSU does not expressly set out a procedure for obtaining the removal of countermeasures, though Members may obtain a ruling on whether continued imposition is warranted either through a compliance panel or a new dispute settlement proceeding. The issue of removing such measures arose in connection with the continued levying of increased tariffs on imports from the European Union (EC) by the United States and Canada in response to the EC's failure to comply with WTO decisions faulting European Union import restrictions on beef produced with growth hormones. The EC initiated WTO dispute settlement proceedings against the United States and Canada in 2004. The Appellate Body, reversing the panel on various points, recommended that the disputing parties request an Article 21.5 compliance panel proceeding in order to resolve their differences as to whether the EC is in compliance in the underlying beef hormone cases (DS26/DS48) and whether the U.S. and

Canadian countermeasures thus have a legal basis. Appellate Body Report, *United States—Continued Suspension of Obligations in the EC-Hormones Dispute*, WT/DS320/AB/R (Oct. 16, 2008); Appellate Body Report, *Canada—Continued Suspension of Obligations in the EC- Hormones Dispute*, WT/DS321/AB/R (Oct. 16, 2008). The EC requested consultations under Article 21.5 in December 2008, but the proceeding involving the United States has since been suspended as part of a bilateral agreement intended to resolve the beef hormone dispute. Press Release, Office of the USTR, USTR Announces Agreement with European Union in Beef Hormones Dispute (updated June 22, 2009), at *http://www.ustr.gov/about-us/press-office/press-releases/* 2009/may/ustr-announces-agreement-european-union-beef-hormones-; European Commission, Memorandum on Beef Hormones dispute signed with the United States (May 14, 2009), at *http://ec.europa.eu/trade/issues* dispute/ memo140509_en.htm.

[5] For background discussions regarding the effect of treaties and international agreements in domestic law, see CRS Report RL32528, *International Law and Agreements: Their Effect Upon U.S. Law*, by Michael John Garcia; Ronald A. Brand, *Direct Effect of International Economic Law in the United States and the European Union*, 17 NW. J. INT'L L. & BUS. 556 (1996-97); and John H. Jackson, *Status of Treaties in Domestic Legal Systems: A Policy Analysis*, 86 AM. J. INT'L L. 310 (1992).

[6] Uruguay Round Agreements Act (URAA), § 123(d)-(f), 19 U.S.C. § 3533(d)-(f).

[7] Uruguay Round Agreements, Statement of Administrative Action, H.Doc. 103-316(I) at 659 (1994) [hereinafter cited as Uruguay Round SAA]. The SAA, which was expressly approved in the URAA, is "regarded as an authoritative expression by the United States concerning the interpretation and application of the Uruguay Round Agreements and ... [the URAA] in any judicial proceeding in which a question arises concerning such interpretation or application." URAA, § 102(d), 19 U.S.C. § 3512(d).

[8] H.Rept. 103-826(I), at 25; see also S.Rept. 103-412, at 13.

[9] H.Rept. 103-826(I), at 25; see also S.Rept. 103-412, at 13.

[10] H.Rept. 103-826(I), at 25; see also S.Rept. 103-412, at 13, and the Uruguay Round SAA, *supra* note 7, at 1032-33. The latter states as follows: "Reports issued by panels or the Appellate Body under the DSU have no binding effect under the law of the United States and do not represent an expression of U.S. foreign or trade policy. They are no different in this respect than those issued by GATT panels since 1947. If a report recommends that the United States change federal law to bring it into conformity with a Uruguay Round agreement, it is for the Congress to decide whether any such change will be made."

[11] A challenge by Brazil to Florida's equalizing excise tax on processed orange and grapefruit products (WT/DS250) was resolved in 2004 without panelists having been appointed after Florida amended its statute. Notification of Mutually Agreed Solution, *United States—Equalizing Excise Tax Imposed by Florida on Processed Orange and Grapefruit Products*, WT/DS250/3 (June 2, 2004); *U.S. Brazil Settle Long-standing Dispute Over Florida Tax to Promote Citrus Products*, 21 Int'l Trade Rep. (BNA) 945 (2004). In the challenge by Antigua and Barbuda to both federal and state laws affecting the cross-border supply of gambling and betting services (DS285), the United States prevailed on the issue of whether the state measures infringed market access obligations under the General Agreement on Trade in Services (GATS). The WTO Appellate Body found that the panel had erred in considering whether the eight laws at issue violated the Agreement because the complainant had not presented sufficient evidence and legal arguments to establish a prima facie case. *United States—Measures Affecting the Cross-Border Supply of Gambling and Betting Services*, WT/DS285. See *infra* text accompanying notes 195-23 7 for further discussion of this case.

[12] For further discussion, see Uruguay Round SAA, *supra* note 7, at 676.

[13] URAA, § 102(b)(2)(A), 19 U.S.C. § 3512(b)(2)(A). The term "State law" is defined to include "any law of a political subdivision of a State, as well as any State law that regulates or taxes the business of insurance." URAA, § 102(b)(3), 19 U.S.C. § 3512(b)(3). The term is

intended to encompass "any provision of a state constitution, regulation, practice or other state measure." Uruguay Round SAA, *supra* note 7, at 674.

[14] S.Rept. 103-412, at 15; see also H.Rept. 103-826(I), at 25, and Uruguay Round SAA, supra note 7, at 670.

[15] URAA, § 102(b)(2)(B), 19 U.S.C. § 3512(b)(2)(B). In addition, the United States will have the burden of proving that the State law or its application is inconsistent with the WTO agreement in question; any State whose interests may be impaired or impeded by the suit will have the unconditional right to intervene as a party, and the United States will be entitled to amend its complaint to include a claim or cross-claim concerning the law of a State that does intervene; and any State law that is declared invalid will not be considered to have been invalid in its application during any period before the court's judgment becomes final and all timely appeals are exhausted. The statute also requires the United States Trade Representative to notify Congress before bringing any such suit. URAA, § 102(b)(2)(C), 19 U.S.C. § 3512(b)(2)(C).

[16] Uruguay Round SAA, *supra* note 7, at 674; H.Rept. 103-826(I), at 26; S.Rept. 103-412, at 15. The SAA states, inter alia, that the Attorney General "will be particularly careful in considering recourse to this authority where the state measure involved is aimed at the protection of human, animal, or plant health or of the environment or the state measure is a state tax of a type that has been held to be consistent with the requirements of the U.S. Constitution. In such a case, the Attorney General would entertain use of this statutory authority only if consultations between the President and the Governor of the State concerned failed to yield an appropriate alternative." Uruguay Round SAA, *supra* note 7, at 674.

[17] H.Rept. 103-826(I), at 26.

[18] Uruguay Round SAA, *supra* note 7, at 676.

[19] The provision first came into play in 1996 when the United States took regulatory action to comply with the adverse WTO decision in *United States—Standards for Reformulated and Conventional Gasoline*, WT/DS2, WT/DS4. See World Trade Organization (WTO) Decision on Gasoline Rule (Reformulated and Conventional Gasoline), 61 Fed. Reg. 33703 (1996). The U.S. Court of Appeals for the District of Columbia Circuit upheld the final issued by EPA to resolve the dispute, finding, inter alia, that the agency was not statutorily precluded from considering factors other than air quality in issuing rules under the antidumping provision of the Clean Air Act and could thus consider the effect of the proposed rule on U.S. treaty obligations. George E. Warren Corp. v. U.S. Environmental Protection Agency, 159 F.3d 616 (D.C.Cir. 1998).

[20] URAA, § 121(3), 19 U.S.C. § 353 1(3).

[21] Two 110th Congress bills would have placed restrictions on the use of section 123 authorities. S. 364 (Rockefeller) would have amended section 123 to provide that any regulatory modification or final rule proposed under the section could only enter into force if approved by joint resolution enacted into public law. The bill would also have rescinded certain § 123 regulatory modifications that had already taken effect. S. 1919 (Baucus) would have established a WTO Dispute Settlement Review Commission to evaluate WTO decisions under statutory criteria and prohibited a domestic regulatory modification under section 123 from taking effect unless and until Congress received the Commission's report on the WTO decision involved. No action was taken on either of these bills. See also text at *infra* note 294.

[22] URAA, § 129(e), *adding* Tariff Act of 1930, § 516A(a)(2)(B)(vii), 19 U.S.C. § 1516a(a)(2)(B)(vii)), *and amending* Tariff Act of 1930, § 516A(g)(8)(A)(i), 19 U.S.C. § 1516a(g)(8)(A)(i).

The Uruguay Round SAA states the following regarding the legal implications of possible parallel judicial proceedings regarding the same agency determinations:

Since implemented determinations under section 129 may be appealed, it is possible that Commerce or the ITC maybe in the position of simultaneously defending determinations in which the agency reached different conclusions. In such situations, the Administration expects that courts and binational panels will be sensitive to the fact that under the applicable standard of review, as set forth in statute and case law, multiple permissible interpretations of the law and the facts may be legally permissible in any particular case, and the issuance of a different determination under section 129 does not signify that the initial determination was unlawful.

Uruguay Round SAA, *supra* note 7, at 1027.

[23] URAA, § 129(a)(1), 19 U.S.C. § 3538(a)(1).

[24] URAA, § 129(a)(2), 19 U.S.C. § 3538(a)(2).

[25] Uruguay Round SAA, *supra* note 7, at 1023.

[26] URAA, § 129(a)(3),(4), 19 U.S.C. § 3538(a)(3),(4).

[27] ITC authority to issue a new determination is granted "notwithstanding any provision of Tariff Act of 1930 ... or title II of the Trade Act of 1974." The Uruguay Round SAA explains that "[m]any of the ITC's proceedings are time- limited by statute, and the ITC cannot revisit its actions in those proceedings in the absence of the authority provided by subsection (a)(4) or a remand." Uruguay Round SAA, *supra* note 7, at 1024.

[28] *Id.*

[29] URAA, § 129(a)(6), 19 U.S.C. § 3538(a)(6).

[30] URAA, § 129(a)(5),(6), 19 U.S.C. § 3538(a)(5),(6).

[31] URAA, § 129(a)(7), 19 U.S.C. § 2254(b)(3).

[32] URAA, § 129(c)(2)(B), 19 U.S.C. § 3538(c)(2)(B).

[33] URAA, § 129(b)(1),(2), 19 U.S.C. § 3538(b)(1),(2). Senate legislative history indicates that USTR is expected to "consult closely with Commerce in order to ensure that it benefits from Commerce's expertise with respect to both the panel or Appellate Body reports and the appropriate implementing action (if any), including the implications of any such action on the administration of the antidumping or countervailing duty law." S.Rept. 103-412, at 27. The Senate Finance Committee has further stated that it "expects to be consulted closely by the Administration throughout this process, and to be informed and provided an explanation should USTR decide to implement an adverse panel or Appellate Body decision notwithstanding a contrary recommendation by Commerce." *Id.* If USTR directs Commerce to implement the new determination, "Commerce may do so even if litigation is pending with respect to the initial agency determination." H.Rept. 103-826(I), at 39.

[34] URAA, § 129(b)(2), 19 U.S.C. § 3538(b)(2).

[35] URAA, § 129(b)(3),(4), 19 U.S.C. § 3538(b)(3),(4).

[36] URAA, § 129(c)(1), 19 U.S.C. § 3538(c)(1). This provision has been held to be unambiguous in its prospective effect. E.g., Corus Staal BV, v. United States, 593 F.Supp.2d 1373, 1382-83 (Ct. Int'l Trade 2008).

[37] U.S. Customs and Border Protection, *Importing into the United States; A Guide for Commercial Importers* 105-106 (2002 ed.), *at* http://www.cbp.gov/nafta/cgov/pdf/iius.pdf.

[38] Uruguay Round SAA, *supra* note 7, at 1026. See also H.Rept. 103-826(I), at 39; S.Rept. 103-412, at 27.

[39] Trade Act of 1974, § 751(a), 19 U.S.C. §1675(a), 19 C.F.R, § 351.212(a), 351.213. The rate determined in the administrative review is also the rate at which estimated duties on imports entered during the succeeding year are assessed and will apply until any subsequent administrative review produces a new rate.

[40] Request for the Establishment of a Panel by Canada, *United States—Section 129(c) (1) of the Uruguay Round Agreements Act,* WT/DS221/4 (July 13, 2001).

[41] Second Written Submission of the United States, *United States—Section 129(c) (1) of the Uruguay Round Agreements Act* (WT/DS221), paras. 17-20 (Mar. 8, 2002), at http://www.ustr.gov/webfm_send/688.

[42] Panel Report, *United States—Section 129(c) (1) of the Uruguay Round Agreements Act,* WT/DS221/R (July 15, 2002).

[43] 28 U.S.C. § 1581(c)(enacted in Customs Courts Act of 1980, P.L. 96-417, § 201).

[44] Tariff Act of 1930, § 516A(b)(1)(B)(i), 19 U.S.C. § 1516a(b)(1)(B)(i).

[45] See United States v. Eurodif S.A., 129 S.Ct. 878, 886-87 (2009); United States v. Mead Corp., 533 U.S. 218, 226-27 (2001). See also Wheatland Tube Co. v. United States, 495 F.3d 1355 (Fed. Cir. 2007); Pesquera Mares Australes Ltda. v. United States, 266 F.3d 1372, 1379-82 (Fed. Cir. 2001); Koyo Seiko Co. v. United States, 36 F.3d 1565, 1570 (Fed. Cir. 1994), Corus Staal BV v. United States, 593 F.Supp.2d 1373, 1381-82 (Ct. Int'l Trade 2008); Windmill Int'l PTE v. United States, 193 F.Supp.2d 1303, 1305-306 (Ct. Int'l Trade 2002); Cultivos Miramonte S.A. v. United States, 980 F.Supp. 1268, 1271-72 (Ct. Int'l Trade 1997).

[46] See, e.g, Corus Staal BV v. U.S. Dep't of Commerce, 259 F.Supp.2d 1253, 1262 (Ct. Int'l Trade 2003) and generally Jane A. Restani & Ira Bloom, *Interpreting International Trade Statutes: Is The Charming Betsy Sinking?* 24 FORDHAM INT'L L. J. 1533 (2001). The *Charming Betsy* canon stems from the following Supreme Court language: "It has also been observed, that an act of congress ought never to be construed to violate the law of nations, if any other possible construction remains, and consequently, can never be construed to violate neutral rights, or to affect neutral commerce, further than is warranted by the law of nations as understood in this country." *Murray v. Schooner Charming Betsy,* 6 U.S. (2 Cranch) 64, 118 (1804).

[47] See, e.g, Corus Staal BV v. Dept. of Commerce, 395 F.3d 1343, 1347 (Fed. Cir. 2005), *cert denied*, 126 S.Ct. 1023 (2006); Timken Co. v. United States, 354 F.3d 1334, 1343-44 (Fed. Cir. 2004); Corus Staal BV v. United States, 593 F.Supp.2d 1373, 1383-84 (Ct. Int'l Trade 2008).

[48] E.g., SNR Roulements v. United States, 341 F.Supp.2d 1334, 1341 (Ct. Int'l Trade 2004); Timken v. United States, 240 F.Supp. 2d 1228, 1238 (Ct. Int'l Trade 2002); Gov't of Uzbekistan v. United States, 2001 WL 1012780, at *3 (Ct. Int'l Trade August 30, 2001).

[49] Koyo Seiko Co. v. United States, 442 F. Supp.2d 1360, 1363 (Ct. Intl Trade 2006), *citing, inter alia*, NSK Ltd. v. United States, 358 F.Supp.2d 1276, 1288 (Ct. Int'l Trade 2005). Note also that in *Cummings Inc. v. United States*, the Court of Appeals for the Federal Circuit held that a classification opinion of the World Customs Organization "is not binding and is entitled, at most, to 'respectful consideration'" by a U.S. court. 454 F.3d 1361, 1366 (Fed. Cir. 2006).

[50] Hyundai Electronics Co. v. United States, 53 F.Supp.2d 1334, 1343 (Ct. Int'l Trade 1999); see also, e.g., Allegheny Ludlum Corp. v. United States, 367 F.3d 1339, 1348 (Fed. Cir. 2004).

[51] Corus Staal BV v. Dept. of Commerce, 395 F.3d 1343, 1348-49 (Fed. Cir. 2005), *cert denied*, 126 S.Ct. 1023 (2006). See also Corus Staal BV v. United States, 502 F.3d 1370, 1375 (Fed. Cir. 2007), and Koyo Seiko Co. v. United States, 442 F.Supp.2d 1360, 1363 (Ct. Int'l Trade 2006). For discussions of federal cases addressing the domestic effect of WTO decisions, see, e.g., Robin Miller, *Effect of World Trade Organization (WTO) Decisions Upon United States*, 17 A.L.R.FED.2D 1 (2007) and Patrick C. Reed, *Relationship of WTO Obligations to U.S. International Trade Law: Internationalist Vision Meets Domestic Reality*, 38 GEO. J. INT'L L. 209 (2006). See also John D. Greenwald, *After Corus Staal—Is There Any Role, and Should There Be—for WTO Jurisprudence in the Review of U.S. Trade Measures by U.S. Courts?* 39 GEO. J. INT'L L. 199 (2007).

[52] Koyo Seiko Co. v. United States, 551 F.3d 1286, 1291 (Fed. Cir. 2008)("The determination whether, when, and how to comply with the WTO's decision on 'zeroing', involves delicate and subtle political judgments that are within the authority of the Executive and not the Judicial Branch."); Corus Staal BV v. Dept. of Commerce, 395 F.3d 1343, 1347 (Fed. Cir. 2005), *cert denied*, 126 S.Ct. 1023 (2006); SKF USA v. United States, 611 F.Supp.2d 1351, 1359-60 (Ct. Intl trade 2009); Corus Staal BV v. United States, 593 F.Supp.2d 1373, 1383-85 (Ct. Int'l Trade 2008). See also Koyo Seiko Co. v. United States, 442 F.Supp. 1360, 1363 (Ct. Int'l Trade 2006). In this case, the court refused to permit the plaintiff to amend its complaint to challenge the Commerce Department's "zeroing" methodology on the ground that the WTO had since adopted an Appellate Body decision faulting the U.S.

practice, stating that such an amendment would be futile "given that it is not controlling precedent and is immaterial to the court's examination of the administrative decisions issued by the Department."

[53] E.g., Corus Staal BV v. Dept. of Commerce, 395 F.3d 1343, 1349 (Fed. Cir. 2005), *cert denied*, 126 S.Ct. 1023 (2006) and SNR Roulements v. United States, 341 F.Supp.2d 1334, 1343-44 (Ct. Int'l Trade 2004).

[54] As of December 1, 2009, "European Union" replaced "European Communities" as the official name of this WTO Member. The terms European Communities and EC still appear in older WTO materials, including panel and Appellate Body reports, bilateral procedural agreements in particular disputes, and communications to the WTO Dispute Settlement Body. Except for references to any such older WTO documents, this chapter uses the name "European Union" or the acronym "EU" in the text of the report regardless of the time period being discussed. For further information, see *European Union or Communities?*, at http://www.wto.org/english/thewto_e/countries_e/european_union_or_communities_ popup.htm.

[55] For further discussion of this provision, see CRS Report RS21107, *Copyright Law's "Small Business Exception": Public Performance Exemptions for Certain Establishments*, by Todd B. Tatelman.

[56] See H.Rept. 108-76 at 33, 92. As does the House report on the enacted appropriation, the House report on the House- passed FY2004 appropriation for the USTR (H.R. 2799) points out that approval of the payment was intended as a "one-time only" funding measure and further states that "[t]here is a long-established practice of using suspension of tariff concessions to resolve trade disputes and the Committee does not intend to appropriate funds to settle these matters." H.Rept. 108-22 1 at 65. In addition, the Committee "cautions U.S. negotiators that there should be no commitments made within trade agreements to use funds from the U.S. Treasury that have neither been requested nor appropriated to resolve trade disputes." *Id.*

[57] Notification of a Mutually Satisfactory Temporary Arrangement, *United States—Section 110(5) of the US Copyright Act*, WT/DS160/23 (June 26, 2003).

[58] Dispute Settlement Body, Minutes of Meeting, Nov. 24 and 26, 2004, at 7, WT/DSB/M/178 (Jan. 17, 2005). The continued existence of the provision is also routinely cited in annual European Union (EU) reports on U.S. foreign trade barriers and periodic EU updates of EU WTO disputes. See European Commission, *United States Barriers to Trade and Investment Report for 2008,* at 20, 77 (July 2009) [hereinafter EC 2009 U.S. Trade Barriers Report], at http://trade.ec.europa.eu/doclib/docs/2009/july/tradoc_144160.pdf, and European Commission, *General Overview of Active WTO Dispute Settlement Cases Involving the EC as Complainant or Defendant and of Active Cases under the Trade Barriers Regulation, 22 January 2010,* at 19-20 [hereinafter EC Dispute Settlement Overview (Jan. 2010)], at http:// http://trade.ec.europa.eu/doclib/docs/2007/may/tradoc_134652.pdf.

[59] E.g., Dispute Settlement Body, Minutes of Meeting, Mar. 20, 2009, at 5, 6, WT/DSB/M/266 (May 19, 2009) [hereinafter DSB Minutes (Mar. 20, 2009)]; see also Status Report by the United States, Addendum, *United States— Section 110(5) of the US Copyright Act*, WT/DS160/24/Add.56 (Aug. 21, 2009).

[60] E.g., Dispute Settlement Body, Minutes of Meeting, Sept. 28, 2006, at 5-6, WT/DSB/M/220 (Nov. 2, 2006)[hereinafter DSB Minutes (Sept. 28, 2006)].

[61] See, e.g., Dispute Settlement Body, Minutes of Meeting, June 20, 2007, at 6, WT/DSB/M/234 (July 23, 2007), as corrected, WT/DSB/M/234/Corr. 1 (Aug. 22, 2007).

[62] Press Release, Office of the U.S. Trade Representative, U.S. and EU discuss ways forward on bilateral trade issues (last updated July 14, 2009), at http://www.ustr.gov/about-us/press-office/press-releases/2009/july/eu-and-us-discussways-forward-bilateral-trade-issues.

[63] For more detailed information on the legal issues involved in this case, see CRS Report RS2 1764, *Restricting Trademark Rights of Cubans: WTO Decision and Congressional Response*, by Margaret Mikyung Lee.

[64] Modification of the Agreement under Article 21.3(b) of the DSU, *United States—Section 211 Omnibus Appropriations Act of 1998*, WT/DS176/15 (Dec. 21, 2004).

[65] Understanding between the European Communities and the United States, *United States—Section 211 Omnibus Appropriations Act of 1998*, WT/DS176/16 (July 1, 2005).

[66] E.g., DSB Minutes (Mar. 20, 2009), *supra* note 59, at 2-5. As with the "Irish music" case discussed earlier, the continued existence of § 211 is routinely cited in annual European Union (EU) reports on U.S. foreign trade barriers and periodic EU updates of EU WTO disputes. See EC 2009 U.S. Trade Barriers Report, *supra* note 58, at 21, 79-80, and EC Dispute Settlement Overview (Jan. 2010), *supra* note 58, at 20.

[67] See, e.g., Status Report by the United Status, Addendum, United States—Section 211 Omnibus Appropriations Act of 1998, WT/DS176/11/Add.81 (Aug. 21, 2009).

Bills to repeal or amend the provision were also introduced in the 110th and earlier Congresses. 110th Congress bills included: H.R. 217 (Serrano) and H.R. 624 (Rangel), which would have repealed § 211, as well as removed the current trade embargo on Cuba; H.R. 2819 (Rangel) and S. 1673 (Baucus), which would have repealed the statute along with removing certain other restrictions on trade with Cuba; S. 1806 (Leahy), which would have repealed the statute and required the Secretary of the Treasury to issue regulations as were necessary to carry out the repeal within 30 days after enactment; and H.R. 1306 (Wexler) and S. 749 (Nelson), which would have amended § 211 to apply to all persons claiming rights in trademarks confiscated by Cuba, whatever their nationality. In addition, the Senate Judiciary Committee held a hearing on Section 211 issues on July 13, 2004. See *An Examination of Section 211 of the Omnibus Appropri*ations Act of 1998, at http://judiciary for witness lists, testimony and Members statements.

[68] Panel Report, *United States—Anti-dumping Measures on Certain Hot-Rolled Steel Products from Japan*, WT/DS184/R (Feb. 28, 2001) [hereinafter Hot-Rolled Steel Panel Report]; Appellate Body Report, *United States— Anti-dumping Measures on Certain Hot-Rolled Steel Products from Japan*, WT/DS1 84/AB/R (July 24, 2001) [hereinafter Hot-Rolled Steel AB Report].

[69] Hot-Rolled Steel AB Report, *supra* note 68, paras. 235-236.

[70] After consultations with Japan, the United States requested that deadline be extended to the dates noted; the DSB approved the extension on December 5, 2002. See Status Report by the United States, Addendum, *United States—Antidumping Measures on Certain Hot-Rolled Steel Products from Japan*, WT/DS1 84/15/Add.3 (Dec. 9, 2002).

The United States and Japan had reportedly been in disagreement regarding implementation of the ruling as it relates to the ITC's application of the statutory captive production provision. See *Japan Threatens Retaliation Against U.S. For Hot-Rolled Steel Antidumping Duties*, 19 Int'l Trade Rep. (BNA) 1965 (2002); *U.S. Response Leaves WTO Ruling on Hot-Rolled Injury Claims Untouched*, INSIDE U.S. TRADE, Nov. 15, 2002, at 3; *U.S. Gets Extra Year to Comply with WTO Hot-rolled Steel Decision*, INSIDE U.S. TRADE, Dec. 6, 2002, at 13. No action has been taken by the ITC in response to the WTO decision.

[71] Antidumping Proceedings: Affiliated Party Sales in the Ordinary Course of Trade, 67 Fed. Reg. 69186 (Nov. 15, 2002) [hereinafter Modification of Antidumping Methodology]. See also Antidumping Proceedings: Affiliated Party Sales in the Ordinary Course of Trade, 67 Fed. Reg. 53339 (Aug. 15, 2002)(request for public comment).

[72] Hot-Rolled Steel Panel Report, *supra* note 68, paras. 7.91-7.120, Hot-Rolled Steel AB Report, *supra* note 68, paras. 131-173.

[73] Modification of Antidumping Methodology, *supra* note 71, 67 Fed. Reg. at 69186. The Department noted that its modification was the same as that proposed in August 2002, "with the exception of comparing prices of 'similar' products where an identical comparison product was not sold to unaffiliated parties...." *Id.* at 69187.

[74] *Id.*

[75] *Id.*

[76] Notice of Determination Under Section 129 of the Uruguay Round Agreements Act: Antidumping Measures on Certain Hot-Rolled Flat-Rolled Carbon-Quality Steel Products from Japan, 67 Fed. Reg. 71936 (Dec. 3, 2002).

[77] Article 6.8 provides, in full text, as follows:

In cases in which any interested party refuses access to, or otherwise does not provide, necessary information within a reasonable period or significantly impedes the investigation, preliminary and final determinations, affirmative or negative, may be made on the basis of facts available. The provisions of Annex II shall be observed in the application of this paragraph.

Annex II, titled "Best Information Available in Terms of Paragraph 8 or Article 6," provides guidelines for the collection and use of information by investigating authorities in antidumping proceedings.

[78] Tariff Act of 1930, § 735(c)(5)(A), 19 U.S.C. § 1673d(c)(5)(A)(emphasis added).

[79] The Tariff Act generally directs the Commerce Department and the International Trade Commission to use "the facts otherwise available" in reaching their subsidy, dumping, and injury determinations if: (1) necessary information is not available on the record or (2) an interested party or any other person withholds requested information, fails to provide such information by the deadline or in the form and manner requested, significantly impedes an antidumping or countervailing duty proceeding, or provides information that cannot be verified. Tariff Act of 1930, § 776(a), 19 U.S.C. § 1677e(a). Before using "facts available," however, the agencies must enable a person submitting information in response to an agency request to remedy or explain any deficiencies in the original response. Tariff Act of 1930, § 782(d), 19 U.S.C. § 1677m(d). The agencies are allowed to use adverse inferences in selecting from fact available where an interested party "has failed to cooperate by not acting to the best of its ability" to comply with an agency information request." Tariff Act of 1930, § 776(b), 19 U.S.C. § 1677e(b). As noted by the U.S. Court of International Trade, the ability of an agency to use "facts available" in an investigation acts as "an inducement for respondents to provide complete and accurate information in a timely manner." Maui Pineapple Company v. United States, 264 F.Supp. 2d 1244, 1257 (Ct. Int'l Trade 2003).

[80] Emphasis added. See Hot-Rolled Steel Panel Report, *supra* note 68, paras. 7.83-7.90, 8.1(b); Hot-Rolled Steel AB Report, *supra* note 68, paras. 111-130.

[81] See Dispute Settlement Body, Minutes of Meeting, Aug. 31, 2004, at 6-7, WT/DSB/M/175 (Sept 24, 2004).

[82] Understanding between Japan and the United States, *United States—Anti-dumping Measures on Certain Hot-Rolled Steel Products from Japan*, WT/DS184/19 (July 28, 2005). The United States has agreed not to block any retaliation request on the ground that the 30-day period for requesting authorization to suspend concessions in Article 22.6 has expired, but has reserved the right to have any retaliation request referred to arbitration.

[83] Comments submitted to the Trade Subcommittee of the House Ways and Means Committee on the possible inclusion of this legislation in a future bill are available at http://waysandmeans.house.gov/hearings.asp?formmode=comment& hearing=440.

[84] E.g, DSB Minutes (Mar. 20, 2009), *supra* note 59, at 5-6, and Japan, Ministry of Economy, Trade and Industry, METI Priorities Based on the 2009 Report on Compliance by Major Trading Partners with Trade Agreements 10-11 (May 29, 2009)[hereinafter 2009 METI Report on Japan Trade Priorities], at http://www.meti.go.jp/english/press/data/pdf/20090525_02a.pdf.

[85] *Id.*; Status Report by the United States, Addendum, *United States—Anti-dumping Measures on Certain Hot-Rolled Steel Products from Japan*, WT/DS184/15/Add.81 (Aug. 21, 2009).

[86] *U.S. Seeks to Reverse WTO Ruling on 'Facts Available' Dumping Rates*, 21 Int'l Trade Rep. (BNA) 1540 (2004); Negotiating Group on Rules, All-Others Rate (Article 9.4 ADA); Communication from the United States, TN/RL/GEN/16 (Sept. 15, 2004), as corrected [hereinafter U.S. Communication]. See also Negotiating Group on Rules, Identification of

Certain Major Issues Under the Anti-Dumping and Subsidies Agreements; Submission by the United States, TN/RL/W/72, at 2-3 (Mar. 19, 2003).
In presenting its proposal to WTO negotiating partners, the United States has explained that it interpreted Article 9.4 of the Antidumping Agreement as providing that only margins based entirely on facts available are to be excluded from calculating the all-others rate ceiling because "the United States believed that this was a reasonable interpretation of the statute and because, in the United States' experience, some level of facts available is often necessary to determine a company's dumping margin." U.S. Communication, *supra*, at 1. In the U.S. view, whether the "facts available" data used with respect to a firm are small or substantial, "the resulting margin represents the best estimate of the level of dumping by that particular company" and it is thus "appropriate to use such a margin when establishing a duty rate for unexamined firms based on the dumping found to exist for firms actually examined." *Id.* It continued: "We therefore interpreted the Agreement as distinguishing those situations from situations in which a firm's data are so flawed or unreliable that it is necessary to base its antidumping duty entirely on facts available." *Id.*

[87] See WTO, Negotiating Group on Rules, New Draft Consolidated Chair Texts of the AD and SCM Agreements, at 20, TN/RL/W/236 (Dec. 19, 2008[hereinafter 2008 Draft Rules Text] and WTO, Negotiating Group on Rules, Draft Consolidated Chair Texts of the AD and SCM Agreements, at 21, TN/RL/W/213 (Nov. 30, 2007)[hereinafter 2007 Draft Rules Text].

[88] P.L. 106-387, 114 Stat. 1549A-72, codified at 19 U.S.C. § 1675c (2000). Regulations are set out at 19 C.F.R. §§ 159.6 1-64. For a more detailed examination of the statute and additional discussion of the WTO proceeding, see CRS Report RL33045, *The Continued Dumping and Subsidy Offset Act ("Byrd Amendment")*, by Jeanne J. Grimmett and Vivian C. Jones. See also U.S. Government Accountability Office, *International Trade: Issues and Effects of Implementing the Continued Dumping and Subsidy Offset Act* (Sept. 2005)(GAO-05-979).

[89] Article 18.1 of the Antidumping Agreement had been successfully used by EC and Japan in their WTO challenges of the U.S. Antidumping Act of 1916, 15 U.S.C. § 72, which provided a private right of action and criminal penalties against dumping. See Appellate Body Report, *United States—Anti-Dumping Act of 1916*, paras. 103-138, WT/DS136/AB/R, WT/DS162/AB/R (Aug. 28, 2000)(*adopted* Sept. 26, 2000).

[90] Panel Report, *United States—Continued Dumping and Subsidy Offset Act*, WT/DS217/R, WT/DS234/R (Sept. 16, 2002).

[91] Appellate Body Report, *United States—Continued Dumping and Subsidy Offset Act*, paras. 224-299, WT/DS217/AB/R, WT/DS234/AB/R (Jan. 16, 2003).

[92] Award of the Arbitrator, *United States—Continued Dumping and Subsidy Offset Act of 2000*; WT/DS217/14, WTDS234/22 (June 13, 2003). The Arbitrator emphasized in his award that it was for the United States to decide on the manner of implementation, which might be through repeal or modification of the law. *Id.* para. 50.

[93] See WTO documents WT/DS217/20 (Brazil); WT/DS217/21 (Chile); WT/DS217/22 (EC); WT/DS217/23 (India); WT/DS217/24 (Japan); WT/DS217/25 (Korea); WT/DS234/25 (Canada); WT/DS234/26 (Mexico).

[94] See Dispute Settlement Body, Minutes of Meeting, Jan. 26, 2004, WT/DSB/M/164 (Mar. 12, 2004).

[95] See WTO documents WT/DS217/17 (Thailand); WT/DS217/18 (Australia); and WT/DS217/19 (Indonesia).

[96] E.g., Decision by the Arbitrator, Recourse to Arbitration by the United States under Article 22.6 of the DSU; *United States—Continued Dumping and Subsidy Offset Act of 2000 (Original Complaint by the European Communities)*, paras. 5.1-5.2, WT/DS217/ARB/EEC (Aug. 31, 2004).

[97] *Id.* para. 3.41.

[98] *Id.* paras. 3.72, 3.80-3.151, 4.7.

[99] Absent action to repeal or modify the statute by December 27, 2004, the compliance deadline agreed to by Australia, Indonesia, and Thailand, the three Members entered into entered into new agreements with the United States in which they reserved the right to take further action against U.S. goods in the future. See WTO documents WT/DS217/44 (Australia), WT/DS217/45 (Thailand), and WT/DS217/46 (Indonesia).

[100] Communication from the European Communities, *United States—Continued Dumping and Subsidy Offset Act*, WT/DS217/47 (May 4, 2005); *Canada Implements Retaliatory Surtax on U.S. Goods Due to Byrd Amendment*, 22 Int'l Trade Rep. (BNA) 796 (2005).

[101] *Mexico Announces $20.9 Million in Byrd Retaliation Against U.S. Exports*, INSIDE U.S. TRADE, Aug. 19, 2005, at 1.

[102] Communication from Japan, *United States—Continued Dumping and Subsidy Offset Act of 2000*, WT/DS217/48 (Aug. 19, 2005); Japan, Ministry of Economy, Trade and Industry, "US Byrd Amendment: Japan Decides to Start Retaliation," Press Release, Aug. 1, 2005, at http://www.meti.go.jp/english/information/data/WTOByrd050801e.html [hereinafter METI Press Release]; *Japan OKs Countervailing Duties on 15 U.S. Products Because of Byrd Amendment*, 22 Int'l Trade Rep. (BNA) 1344 (2005). According to Japan, the level of retaliation would not exceed $52 million, which, it stated, was the amount authorized by the WTO based on the amount of CDSOA disbursements involving Japanese goods in fiscal 2004. METI Press Release, *supra.*

[103] Canadian Lumber Trade Alliance v. United States, 425 F.Supp.2d 1321 (Ct. Int'l Trade 2006), 441 F.Supp.2d 1259 (Ct. Int'l Trade 2006), *aff'd in part, vacated in part, and remanded,* 517 F.3d 1319 (Fed. Cir. 2008), *cert. denied* 129 S.Ct. 344 (2008). Canada and Canadian industry groups had challenged CDSOA distributions based on goods from Canada, arguing that, because of a provision in the NAFTA Implementation Act stating after the NAFTA enters into force for the United States, an amendment that is made to Title VII of the Tariff Act of 1930 may apply to goods from a NAFTA country only to the extent specified in the amendment, the CDSOA, in not expressly referring to Canada, did not apply to imports of Canadian products. The provision is set out at P.L. 103-182, § 408, 19 U.S.C. § 3438. While ruling that Canada did not have standing to sue in the case, the USCIT agreed with industry plaintiffs that the statutory provision applied to the CDSOA, which is contained in Title VII of the 1930 act along with authorities for U.S. antidumping and countervailing duty investigations. Since the CDSOA did not refer either to Canada or Mexico, the court ruled that imports from both countries were exempt.

Canadians had been concerned that antidumping and countervailing duties collected on softwood lumber imports, which had at the time of the suit totaled over $4 billion and whose underlying duty orders had been heavily litigated by Canada, might eventually be distributed to U.S. lumber producers. For further information on the U.S.-Canada softwood lumber dispute, which was settled in 2006, see CRS Report RL33752, *Softwood Lumber Imports from Canada: Issues and Events*, by Ross W. Gorte and Jeanne J. Grimmett.

[104] Notice of Withholding of Certain Distributions on Continued Dumping and Subsidy Offset to Affected Producers, 71 Fed. Reg. 57000 (Sept. 28, 2006).

[105] See Canada, Dept. of Foreign Affairs and International Trade, *Dispute Settlement: Questions and Answers— Expiration of Retaliatory Measures*, at http://www.dfait-maeci.gc.ca/tna-nac/disp/byrdqa-en.asp.

[106] *U.S. Dairy Industry Expects Hit from Short-term Mexican Byrd Retaliation*, INSIDE U.S. TRADE, Oct. 6, 2006; *DSB Minutes* (Sept. 28, 2006), *supra* note 60, at 9.

[107] Deficit Reduction Act of 2005, P.L. 109-171, § 7601. Section 7701 of the act provides that Title VII, which contains the CDSOA-related provisions, "shall take effect as if enacted on October 1, 2005."

[108] Distribution of Continued Dumping and Subsidy Offset to Affected Domestic Producers, 74 Fed. Reg. 25,8 14- 25,969 (May 29, 2009).

[109] The mandate for FY2009 currently appears in the Omnibus Appropriations Act, 2009, P.L. 111-8, Division B, Title I, Title IV. See also the pending appropriations bill for the

Departments of Commerce and Justice, and Science, and Related Agencies for FY20 10, H.R. 2847, 111th Cong., 1st Sess. (2009), Title I, Title IV, as passed the House and as reported in the Senate (S.Rept. 111-34).

Although the USTR submitted a proposal of this type to the pertinent Doha Round negotiating group in 2004, a provision addressing this issue has not been included in the draft negotiating texts. See Communication from the United States, *Three Issues Identified for Discussion by the Negotiating Group on Rules*, at 2, TN/RL/W/153 (Apr. 26, 2004); 2007 Draft Rules Text and 2008 Draft Rules Text, *supra* note 87.

[110] Dispute Settlement Body, Minutes of Meeting, Feb. 17, 2006, at 5-10, WT/DSB/M/205 (Mar. 31, 2006).

[111] *Id.*

[112] See, e.g., Dispute Settlement Body, Minutes of Meeting, May 20, 2009, at 13,WT/DSB/M/268 (July 13, 2009). See also EC Dispute Settlement Overview (Jan. 2010), *supra* note 58, at 17; 2009 METI Report on Japan Trade Priorities, *supra* note 84, at 8-9.

[113] Communication from the European Communities, *United States—Continued Dumping and Subsidy Offset Act of 2000*, WT/DS217/55 (Apr. 28, 2009).

[114] Communication from Japan, *United States—Continued Dumping and Subsidy Offset Act of 2000*, WT/DS217/54 (Sept. 2, 2008).

[115] Communication from Japan, *United States—Continued Dumping and Subsidy Offset Act of 2000*, WT/DS217/56 (Aug. 18, 2009).

[116] Request for Consultations by Brazil, *United States—Subsidies on Upland Cotton*, WT/DS267/1 (Oct. 3, 2002). For further information on this dispute, see CRS Report RL32571, *Brazil's WTO Case Against the U.S. Cotton Program*, by Randy Schnepf, available upon request [hereinafter CRS Report RL32571], and CRS Report RS22187, *Brazil's WTO Case Against the U.S. Cotton Program: A Brief Overview*, by Randy Schnepf, available upon request [hereinafter CRS Report RS22187].

[117] Request for the Establishment of a Panel by Brazil, *United States—Subsidies on Upland Cotton*, WT/DS267/7 (Feb. 7, 2003).

[118] Agreement on Agriculture, at http://www.wto.org/english/docs_e/legal_e/14-ag.pdf.

[119] *Id.* art. 3.1.

[120] Agreement on Subsidies and Countervailing Measures (SCM Agreement) arts. 1, 3, 5, at http://www.wto.org/ english/docs_e/legal_e/legal_e.htm.

[121] *Id.* art. 6.3(c).

[122] Panel Report, *United States—Subsidies on Upland Cotton*, WT/DS267/R (Sept. 8, 2004) [hereinafter U.S. Cotton Panel Report]. For further information on the agricultural programs at issue and the bases for panel and Appellate Body findings in the case, see CRS Report RL32571, *supra* note 116. See also Eliza Patterson, *The WTO Decision on U.S. Cotton Subsidies*, ASIL Insight (Mar. 2005), at *http://www.asil.org/insights/2005/03 /insights050323.html.*

[123] U.S. Cotton Panel Report, *supra* note 122, at paras. 7.866-7.867.

[124] *Id.* paras. 7.796-7.803.

[125] *Id.* paras. 7.860-7.866.

[126] *Id.* paras. 7.415-7.608. See Agreement on Agriculture art. 13(b)(ii).

[127] U.S. Cotton Panel Report, *supra* note 122, para. 8.3(b)-(c). Article 4.7 of the SCM Agreement provides that, in the event a panel finds that a prohibited subsidy exists, the panel "shall recommend that the subsidizing Member withdraw its measure without delay" and "shall specify in its recommendation the time-period within which the measure must be withdrawn."

[128] *Id.* para. 8.3(d).

[129] Article 7.9 further provides that the DSB "shall grant authorization to the complaining Member to take countermeasures, commensurate with the degree and nature of the adverse affects determined to exist," subject to the reverse consensus rule.

[130] Appellate Body Report, *United States—Subsidies on Upland Cotton*, WT/DS267/AB/R (Mar. 3, 2005).

[131] Dispute Settlement Body, *Minutes of Meeting*, Mar. 21, 2005, at 7-13, WT/DSB/M/186 (Apr. 14, 2005).

[132] Dispute Settlement Body, Minutes of Meeting, Apr. 20, 2005, at 7, WT/DSB/M/188 (May 18, 2005)[hereinafter DSB Minutes (Apr. 20, 2005)].

[133] *Id.* at 8.

[134] News Release, USDA, USDA Announces Changes to Export Credit Guarantee Programs to Comply with WTO Findings (June 30, 2005).

[135] Recourse to Article 4.10 of the SCM Agreement and Article 22.2 of the DSU by Brazil, *United States—Subsidies on Upland Cotton*, WT/DS267/21 (July 5, 2005).

[136] Brazil stated that this amount represented "Step 2 payments estimated for marketing year 2004-2005 and total amount of applications received for export credit guarantees under GSM 102, GSM 103, and SGCP during fiscal year 2004." *Id.* at 2, note 1.

[137] News Release, USDA, USDA Proposes Legislative Changes to Cotton and Export Credit Programs to Comply with WTO Findings (July 5, 2005).

[138] *Id.*

[139] Understanding between Brazil and the United States Regarding Procedures under Articles 21 and 22 of the DSU and Article 4 of the SCM Agreement, *United States—Subsidies on Upland Cotton*, WT/DS267/22 (July 8, 2005).

[140] Dispute Settlement Body, Minutes of Meeting, July 15, 2005, WT/DSB/M/193 (July 28, 2005).

[141] See Communication from the Arbitrator, Recourse by the United States to Article 22.6 of the DSU and Article 4.11 of the SCM Agreement, *United States—Subsidies on Upland Cotton*, WT/DS267/25 (Aug. 18, 2005).

[142] Recourse to Article 7.9 of the SCM Agreement and Article 22.2 of the DSU by Brazil, *United States—Subsidies on Upland Cotton*, WT/DS267/26 (Oct. 7, 2005).

[143] Request by the United States for Arbitration under Article 22.6 of the DSU and Article 7.10 of the SCM Agreement, *United States—Subsidies on Upland Cotton*, WT/DS267/27 (Oct. 18, 2005); see Note by the Secretariat, Constitution of the Arbitrator, Recourse by the United States to Article 22.6 of the DSU and Article 7.10 of the SCM Agreement, *United States—Subsidies on Upland Cotton*, WT/DS267/29 (Dec. 7, 2005).

[144] See Communication from the Arbitrator, Recourse by the United States to Article 22.6 of the DSU and Article 7.10 of the SCM Agreement, *United States—Subsidies on Upland Cotton*, WT/DS267/29 (Dec. 7, 2005).

[145] See § 1103 of P.L. 109-171, the Deficit Reduction Act of 2005, signed by the President on February 8, 2006. For further information on U.S. actions taken in response to the WTO decision, see CRS Report RS221 87, *supra* note 116.

[146] Panel Report, *United States—Subsidies on Upland Cotton, Recourse to Article 21.5 of the DSU by Brazil*,WT/DS267/RW (Dec. 18, 2007)[U.S Cotton Article 21.5 Panel Report].

[147] The compliance panel rejected Brazil's argument that the United States had failed to comply with the panel's recommendations, as adopted by the WTO Dispute Settlement Body, to withdraw the export subsidy with respect to payments issued before July 1, 2005. *Id.* paras. 14.19-14.39.

[148] *Id.* paras. 14.139-14.150.

[149] *Id.* paras. 14.151-14.157.

[150] *Id.* para. 14.133.

[151] *Id.* para. 14.131.

[152] Appellate Body Report, *United States—Subsidies on Upland Cotton, Recourse to Article 21.5 of the DSU by Brazil*,WT/DS267/AB/RW (June 2, 2008)[hereinafter U.S. Cotton Article 21.5 AB Report].

[153] *Id.* paras. 279-295.

[154] See U.S. Cotton Article 21.5 Panel Report, *supra* note 146, para. 14.78.

[155] U.S. Cotton Article 21.5 AB Report, *supra* note 152, paras. 321-322. The Appellate Body upheld the panel's comparison of OECD MPRs with GSM-102 fees as an element of the panel's analysis because, in the Appellate Body's view, the comparison was used only as evidence of the magnitude of the difference between the two and thus possibly indicative of the inadequacy of the GSM-102 fees to the program's long-term costs and losses, and was not relied upon to make a definitive determination as to whether the criterion of item (j) of the Illustrative List was met. *Id.* paras. 302- 307.

[156] *Id.*

[157] Food, Conservation, and Energy Act of 2008 (FCE Act), P.L. 110-246, § 3 101(a)(1)(B), (2), *repealing* Agricultural Trade Act of 1978, § 202(a)(2),(3), (b), 7 U.S.C. § 5622(a)(2),(3), (b).

[158] FCE Act, § 3101(b), *amending* Agricultural Trade Act of 1978, § 211(b), 7 U.S.C. § 5641(b).

[159] FCE Act, § 3 101(a)(4), *adding* Agricultural Trade Act of 1978, § 202(k)(2), 7 U.S.C. § 5622(k)(2).

[160] FCE Act, § 3 101(a)(4), *adding* Agricultural Trade Act of 1978, § 202(k)(1), 7 U.S.C. § 5622(k)(1).

[161] H.Rept. 110-627 at 758. See FCE Act, § 3101(b), *amending* Agricultural Trade Act of 1978, § 211(b), 7 U.S.C. § 564 1(b). As stated in the conference report, it was expected that USDA would be able to make available "approximately $4 billion annually in export credit guarantees on $40 million in budget authority." H.Rept. 110-627 at 728. Regarding the export credit guarantee authorization, see generally CRS Report RL33553, *Agricultural Export and Food Aid Programs*, by Charles E. Hanrahan, at 8.

[162] FCE Act, §§ 1104, 1201-1204. See generally CRS Report RL34594, *Farm Commodity Programs in the 2008 Farm Bill*, by Jim Monke.

[163] See *United States—Subsidies on Upland Cotton, Arbitration under Article 22.6 of the DSU and Article 7.10 of the SCM Agreement*, Oral Statement of the United States, Mar. 2, 2009, paras. 5, 60, at http://www.ustr.gov/webfm_send/ *585*; *United States—Subsidies on Upland Cotton, Arbitration under Article 22.6 of the DSU and Article 7.10 of the SCM Agreement*, Oral Statement of the United States, Mar. 3, 2009, para. 6, at *http:// www.ustr.gov/webfm_send/587.*

[164] SCM Agreement art. 4.11 and n. 10.

[165] SCM Agreement art. 7.10.

[166] Decision by the Arbitrator, *United States—Subsidies on Upland Cotton, Recourse to Arbitration by the United States under Article 22.6 of the DSU and Article 4.11 of the* SCM Agreement, WT/DS267/ARB/1 (Aug. 31, 2009) [hereinafter U.S. Cotton Arbitrator's Decision I]; Decision by the Arbitrator, *United States—Subsidies on Upland Cotton, Recourse to Arbitration by the United States under Article 22.6 of the DSU and Article 7.10 of the* SCM Agreement, WT/DS267/ARB/2 (Aug. 31, 2009) [hereinafter U.S. Cotton Arbitrator's Decision II].

[167] U.S. Cotton Arbitrator's Decision I, *supra* note 166, paras. 3.5-3.64.

[168] *Id.* para. 4.203.

[169] *Id.* para. 4.278. See *id.* paras. 4.203-4.278 for a full discussion of this portion of the decision.

[170] *Id.* para. 4.279.

[171] *Id.* paras. 5.198, 5.200; see *id.* paras. 5.61-5.201 for full discussion of this issue. Along with determining whether or not retaliating solely in trade in goods would be "practicable or effective," the Arbitrator also needed to determine whether Brazil met the second requirement for cross-retaliation, that is, whether it had adequately shown that the "circumstances are serious enough" to warrant suspension of concessions under another agreement. Brazil maintained that this was the case because of the continued maintenance and expansion of U.S. subsidy programs, their long term distortion of world markets, and the disproportionately costly effects on the Brazilian economy and the welfare of the Brazilian population if countermeasures were confined to trade in goods. *Id.* para. 5.216. The Arbitrator found that Brazil's determination was "reasonable in light of the

circumstances of the case." *Id.* paras. 5.217-5.218. While the Arbitrator was not persuaded that the "very granting" of the subsidies by the United States was sufficient to create the required "serious enough" circumstances, the Arbitrator agreed with Brazil that "the specific design and structure of the subsidies at issue, as they have been maintained over a significant period of time, is such as to have created an artificial and persisting competitive advantage for US producers over all other operators, and that this has a significant trade-distorting impact, not just on the US domestic market, but on the world market in these products." *Id.* para. 5.219. Adding to this the amplified trade-distorting impact of the increased payments under GSM-102 program during the current credit crisis, a situation also cited by Brazil, the Arbitrator found that these factors in combination supported the required determination. *Id.* para. 5.220. In addition, the Arbitrator agreed that the disproportionate adverse impact of suspending concessions or other obligations on a Member's economy was also a relevant consideration. The Arbitrator found that the fact that countermeasures involving trade in goods would no longer be "practicable or effective" for Brazil if a specified monetary threshold is reached would in this case "also directly contribute to the circumstances being 'serious enough' to justify recourse to suspension under another agreement." *Id.* para. 5.221.

[172] *Id.* para. 5.201.

[173] *Id.* para. 5.181.

[174] *Id.* paras. 5.201, 5.230-5.236.

[175] U.S. Cotton Arbitrator's Decision II, *supra* note 166, para. 3.19, *quoting* Appellate Body Report, *United States- Continued Suspension of Obligations in the EC – Hormones Dispute*, para. 308, WT/DS320/AB/R (Oct. 16, 2008).

[176] *Id.* paras. 3.25-3.28.

[177] *Id.* para. 3.28

[178] *Id.* para. 3.29.

[179] *Id.* paras. 3.30.

[180] *Id.* paras. 3.31-3.32.

[181] U.S. Cotton Arbitrator's Decision II, *supra* note 166, paras. 4.193-4.195.

[182] *Id.* paras. 5.230-5.233.

[183] Communication from Brazil, *United States – Subsidies on Upland Cotton* ,WT/DS267/40 (Sept. 30, 2009).

[184] *Brazil to Seek WTO Okay for Cotton Sanctions, Issues List of Possible U.S. Imports Targeted,* 26 Int'l Trade Rep. (BNA) 1552 (Nov. 12, 2009).

[185] WTO News Item, DSB authorizes Brazil countermeasures in "cotton" case, established "COOL" and poultry panels (Nov. 19, 2009), at *http://www.wto.org/english /news_e/news09_e/dsb_19nov09_e.htmPhttp://www.wto.org/english/* news _e/news09 _e/dsb _19nov09 _e.htm.

[186] Statements by the United States at the DSB Meeting, Item 7, Nov. 19, 2009, at http://geneva.usmission.gov/2009/ 11/19/11 19dsb.

[187] Solicitation of Input from Stakeholders on Revised Fees for the Export Credit Guarantee (GSM-102) Program, 74 Fed. Reg. 48014 (Sept. 21, 2009).

[188] *Id.* at 48015.

[189] USDA, Foreign Agricultural Service, GSM-102 Guarantee Fee Rate Schedule, updated on Nov. 17, 2009, at http://www.fas.usda.gov/excredits/gsm102fees.html.

[190] News Release, USDA, Foreign Agricultural Service, Notice to GSM-102 Program Participants, at *http://www.fas.usda.gov/scriptsw/PressRelease/pressrel_ dout.asp?PrNum= 0280-09;* USDA, Foreign Agricultural Service, Country Risk Ratings (for the GSM-102 Program), updated on Dec. 7, 2009, at http://www.fas.usda.gov/ excredits/countryrisk.html.

[191] *Id.*

[192] USDA, Foreign Agricultural Service, FY 2010 GSM-102 Announcements, As of 12/08/09, at http://www.fas.usda.gov/excredits/ecgp.asp.

[193] E.g., Letter from Export Credit Working Group (ECWG) to USTR Ronald Kirk, Sept. 22, 2009, and attached ECWG Press Release, Sept. 2, 2009, at *http://www.nopa.org/content /newsroom/2009/* ECWG%20to%20Amb%20Kirk_Mtg%20Request%20Letter_Press%20Release_9-22-09.pdf. See also *Kirk: U.S. Will Work Hard for Negotiated Solution to Brazil Cotton Dispute*, INSIDE U.S. TRADE, Dec. 4, 2009, at 1 [hereinafter Kirk]; *USTR Under Pressure to Bring Cotton Compliance Panel After Ruling*, INSIDE U.S. TRADE, Sept. 4, 2009, at 1; *U.S. Prepared to Discuss with Brazil Settlement of Dispute Over Cotton Subsidies*, Daily Rep. for Executives (BNA), Sept. 2, 2009, at A-22.

[194] See *Kirk: U.S. Will Work Hard for Negotiated Solution to Brazil Cotton Dispute*, INSIDE U.S. TRADE, Dec. 4, 2009, at 1.

[195] *Brazil Sets February Time Frame to Decide Key Elements of Cotton Retaliation*, INSIDE U.S. TRADE, Dec. 18. 2009, at 6; *Brazil Delays Final List of U.S. Goods To Be Sanctioned in WTO Cotton Dispute*, 26 Int'l Trade Rep. (BNA) 1777 (Dec. 24, 2009)[hereinafter *Brazil Delays Final List*].

[196] *Brazil Delays Final List*, *supra* note 196.

[197] WTO News Item, DSB establishes panel to examine China's export restrictions of raw materials (Dec. 21, 2009), at *http://www.wto.org/english/news_e/news09_e/dsb_ 21dec09_e.htm* [hereinafter WTO News Item (Dec. 21, 2009)]; *Brazil Says Entitled to Impose $829 Million in Annual Sanctions on U.S. in Cotton Case*, 26 Int'l Trade Rep. (BNA) 1776 (Dec. 24, 2009).

[198] Regarding the difficulties that may be encountered in the removal of sanctions where disagreement over compliance remains, see *supra* note 4.

[199] Note U.S. Cotton Arbitrator's Decision I, *supra* note 166, para. 5.235; U.S. Cotton Arbitrator's Decision II, *supra* note 166, para. 5.23 7.

[200] See *Brazil, U.S. Remain in Stalemate Over Cotton Case Settlement*, INSIDE U.S. TRADE, Dec. 18, 2009, at 7; *Settling with Brazil on Cotton*, WASH.TRADE DAILY, Dec. 15, 2009.

[201] Request for Consultations by Antigua and Barbuda, *United States—Measures Affecting the Cross-Border Supply of Gambling and Betting Services*, WT/DS285/1 (Mar. 27, 2003).

[202] Panel Report, *United States—Measures Affecting the Cross-Border Supply of Gambling and Betting Services*, WT/DS285/R (Nov. 10, 2004) [hereinafter U.S. Gambling Panel Report].

[203] The Wire Act, P.L. 87-216, § 2, 18 U.S.C. § 1084, prohibits the transmission of wagering information. The Travel Act, P.L. 87-228, § 1(a), 18 U.S.C. § 1952, prohibits interstate and foreign travel or transportation in aid of certain unlawful activities, including business enterprises involving gambling in violation of U.S. or state law. The Interstate Gambling Business Act, P.L. 91-452, § 803(a), 18 U.S.C. § 1955, prohibits illegal gambling businesses, as defined in the statute.

[204] See U.S. Gambling Panel Report, *supra* note 202, para. 6.578.

[205] Appellate Body Report, *United States—Measures Affecting the Cross-Border Supply of Gambling and Betting Services*, WT/DS285/AB/R (Apr. 7, 2005) [hereinafter U.S. Gambling AB Report].

[206] The AB stated that "limitations amounting to a zero quota are quantitative limitations and fall within the scope of Article XVI:2(a)" and that prohibitions on service supply "amount to a 'zero quota' on service operations or output with respect to such services ... [and a]s such fall within the scope of Article XVI:2(c)." *Id.* paras. 238, 251.

[207] Because it had found that the U.S. statutes were "necessary" for purposes of XVI(a), the AB did not address whether the statutes fulfilled the "necessity" test of Article XIV(c), the GATS exception for measures necessary to enforce GATS-consistent laws and regulations. *Id.* paras. 337, 373(D)(iv)(b).

[208] *Id.* paras. 338-372, 373(v),(vi).

[209] Interstate Horseracing Act of 1978 (IHA), P.L. 95-5 15, 15 U.S.C §§ 3001-3006. See U.S. Gambling AB Report, *supra* note 205, para. 361.

[210] Section 4 of the IHA, 15 U.S.C. § 3003, prohibits a person from accepting an "interstate off-track wager" except as provided in the act. Section 5(a) of the IHA, 15 U.S.C. § 3004(a), states that "[a]n interstate off-track wager may be accepted by an off-track betting system only if consent is obtained from—(1) the host racing association ...; (2) the host racing commission; (3) the off-track racing commission."

[211] IHA, § 3(3), 15 U.S.C § 3002(3).

[212] Gambling AB Report, *supra* note 205, para. 361 (footnotes omitted)(emphasis in original).

[213] *Id.* para. 364 (emphasis in original).

[214] Dispute Settlement Body, Minutes of Meeting, May 19, 2005, at 9, WT/DSB/M/189 (June 17, 2005).

[215] Request from Antigua and Barbuda for Arbitration under Article 21.3(c) of the DSU, *United States—Measures Affecting the Cross-Border Supply of Gambling and Betting Services*, WT/DS285/1 1 (June 9, 2005).

[216] Submission of the United States, *United States—Measures Affecting the Cross-Border Supply of Gambling and Betting Services* (WT/DS285): Arbitration under Article 21.3(c) of the DSU, at 4 (July 12, 2005), at http://www.ustr.gov/webfm_send/768.

[217] The United States argued as follows regarding the complexity of the foreseen legislative action:

... It requires consideration of the relationship between the IHA and three different federal criminal statutes—the Wire Act, the Travel Act, and the Illegal Gambling Business statute The Appellate Body has made no finding as to whether the activity that is prohibited by these statutes is permitted under the IHA. Instead the Appellate Body has emphasized the need to "demonstrate[] that—in the light of the existence of the Interstate Horseracing Act—the Wire Act, the Travel Act, and the Illegal Gambling Business Act are applied consistently with the requirements of the [Article XIV] chapeau." Accordingly a reasonable legislative option would have the effect of clarifying that relevant U.S. federal laws entail no discrimination between foreign and domestic service suppliers in the application of measures prohibiting remote supply of gambling and betting services.

... There will be ample room for reasonable and principled disagreements among legislators as to precisely how to achieve such a clarification in the context of Internet gambling....

... A legislative clarification will be further complicated by the fact that , starting in the 105th Congress (1997-98), and continuing in each subsequent Congress through the 108th Congress (2003-04), U.S. federal lawmakers have considered a wide range of proposals to address Internet gambling. Members of Congress are actively considering introduction of Internet gambling bills in the current 109th Congress (2005-2006), and will undoubtedly find it necessary to consider the need for compliance with the DSB's recommendations and rulings in the context of this continuing debate, and the variety of broader proposals already supported by different groups of legislators. The issue of how to achieve compliance with the DSB's recommendations and rulings is thus further complicated by its potential to affect, and be affected by, elements of an already complex legislative debate that has gone unresolved over the past four Congresses.

Id. at 5-7.

[218] Award of the Arbitrator, Arbitration under Article 21.3 of the Understanding on Rules and Procedures Governing the Settlement of Dispute, *United States—Measures Affecting the Cross-Border Supply of Gambling and Betting Services*, WT/DS285/13 (Aug. 19, 2005).

[219] Status Report by the United States, Addendum, United States—Measures Affecting the Cross-Border Supply of Gambling and Betting Services, WT/DS285/15/Add. 1 (Apr. 11, 2006). *Internet Gambling Prohibition Act of 2006: Hearing Before the Subcomm. on Crime, Terrorism, and Homeland Security of the H. Comm. on the Judiciary*, 109th Cong. 14 (2006)(statement of Bruce G. Ohr, Chief, Organized Crime and Racketeering Section, Criminal Division, U.S. Department of Justice), at http://frwebgate.access.gpo.gov/cgi-bin/getdoc.cgi?dbname=109_house_hearings& docid=f:26913.pdf.

[220] Agreement between Antigua and Barbuda and the United States Regarding Procedures under Articles 21 and 22 of the DSU, *United States—Measures Affecting the Cross-Border Supply of Gambling and Betting Services*, WT/DS285/16 (May 26, 2006). Note also Dispute Settlement Body, *Minutes of Meeting*, Apr. 21, 2006, at 8-10, WT/DSB/M/210 (May 30, 2006).

[221] Request for the Establishment of a Panel, Recourse to Article 21.5 of the DSU by Antigua and Barbuda, *United States—Measures Affecting the Cross-Border Supply of Gambling and Betting Services*, WT/DS285/1 8 (July 7, 2006). Antigua also made separate arguments regarding the inconsistency of the then-pending bills with U.S. GATS obligations, faulting in particular their exclusions for transactions made in accordance with the Interstate Horseracing Act (IHA), intrastate transactions, and remote gambling conducted by Native American tribes in accordance with existing federal laws applicable to Native American gaming.

In October 2006, the President signed into law the SAFE Port Act, which contains an Internet gambling title that generally following the House-reported language of H.R. 4411. Unlawful Internet Gambling Enforcement Act (UIGEA), P.L. 109-347, Title VIII. The statute prohibits gambling businesses from accepting checks, credit cards, electronic transfers and similar forms of payment in connection with illegal Internet gambling, while exempting intrastate and intratribal Internet gambling operations that include age and location verification requirements imposed as a matter of law. The legislation also leaves unresolved questions as to the extent to which the Interstate Horseracing Act restrains the reach of other federal statutes. For further information, see CRS Report RS22749, *Unlawful Internet Gambling Enforcement Act (UIGEA) and Its Implementing Regulations*, by Charles Doyle and Brian T. Yeh [hereinafter CRS Report RS22749]; CRS Report RS2 1984, *Internet Gambling: An Abridged Overview of Federal Criminal Law*, by Charles Doyle.

[222] Panel Report, Recourse to Article 21.5 of the DSU by Antigua and Barbuda, *United States—Measures Affecting the Cross-Border Supply of Gambling and Betting Services*, WT/DS285/RW (Mar. 30, 2007)[hereinafter U.S. Gambling Article 21.5 Report]. Among other things, the panel concluded that enactment of the UIGEA, see *supra* note 221, did not resolve any of the issues involved in the dispute, citing the statute's express exclusion of activities allowed under the Interstate Horseracing Act and its "sense of Congress" statement that UIGEA "is not intended to resolve any existing disagreements over how to interpret the relationship between the IHA and other Federal statutes." U.S. Gambling Article 21.5 Report, *supra*, paras. 6.130-6.135.

[223] *Id.* para. 6.90

[224] Press Release, Office of the U.S. Trade Representative, Statement of Deputy United States Trade Representative John K. Veroneau Regarding U.S. Actions under GATS Article XXI (May 4, 2007)[hereinafter USTR Press Release, May 4, 2007], at *http://www.ustr.gov/about-us/press-office/press-releases/archives/2007/may/statement-deputy-unitedstates-trade-represen;* Press Release, U.S. Diplomatic Mission to the United Nations in Geneva , Statements by the United States at the WTO Dispute Settlement Body Meeting, Geneva, May 22, 2007, at http://www.us-mission.ch/ Press2007/0522DSB.html.

[225] USTR Press Release, May 4, 2007, *supra* note 225.

[226] See Request for Public Comment on the Negotiations for Compensatory Adjustments to U.S. Schedule of Services Commitments Under WTO General Agreement on Trade in Services (GATS) in Response to Notice of the United States of Intent to Modify Its Schedule Under Article XXI of the GATS, 72 Fed. Reg. 38846 (July 16, 2007) [hereinafter USTR Request for Public Comment]; WTO Council on Trade in Services, Procedures for the Implementation of Article XXI of the General Agreement on Trade in Services (GATS)(Modification of Schedules), para. 3, S/L/80 (Oct. 29, 1999)[hereinafter GATS Article XXI Procedures].

[227] USTR Request for Public Comment, *supra* note 226.

[228] *U.S. Extends Gambling Negotiations on Compensation with Claimants*, INSIDE U.S. TRADE, Oct. 26, 2007, at 9 [hereinafter *U.S. Extends Negotiations*]. See GATS Article XXI Procedures, *supra* note 226, para. 4.

[229] Office of the U.S. Trade Representative, Statement by USTR Spokeswoman Gretchen Hamel on Gambling (Dec. 17, 2007)[hereinafter USTR Statement on Gambling Case (Dec. 17. 2007)]; Office of the U.S. Trade Representative, Statement on Internet Gambling (Dec. 21, 2007); European Union, News Release No. 128/17, EU and US Agree on Compensation in WTO for Loss of Trade Opportunities in US Gambling Sector (Dec. 17, 2007), at http://www.eurunion.org/News/press/2007/20070128.htm.

[230] USTR Statement on Gambling Case (Dec. 17, 2007), *supra* note 229.

[231] *U.S. Extends Negotiations, supra* note 228; *U.S. Japan Reach WTO Settlement on Compensation for Gambling Claim*, Daily Report for Executives (BNA), Sept. 28, 2007, at A-29; *U.S. Compensation Package for WTO Members Unlikely to Satisfy Antigua*, INSIDE U.S. TRADE, at Aug. 24, 2007, at 1.

[232] *Antigua, Costa Rica Request Arbitration on Compensation in U.S. Gambling Dispute*, 25 Int'l Trade Rep. (BNA) 166 (Jan. 31, 2008).

[233] *Id.*; *Costa Rica Drops Gambling Arbitration Claim in WTO Against U.S. After Compensation Deal*, 25 Int'l Trade Rep. (BNA) 355 (Mar. 6, 2008)[hereinafter *Costa Rica Drops Claim*].

[234] *Costa Rica Drops Claim, supra* note 233.

[235] See GATS Article XXI Procedures, *supra* note 226, paras. 7-19.

[236] Recourse by Antigua and Barbuda to Article 22.2 of the DSU, *United States—Measures Affecting the Cross-Border Supply of Gambling and Betting Services*, WT/DS285/22 (June 22, 2007). Along with obligations under the Agreement on Trade Related Intellectual Property Rights, Antigua has also proposed possible suspension of GATS concessions involving telecommunications services. Antigua argues in its request that imposing tariff surcharges on U.S. products (the most commonly used form of retaliation) or placing added restrictions on U.S. services would have a "disproportionate adverse impact" on Antigua because any such fees or restrictions would make the goods and services "materially more expensive" to Antiguan citizens and would have little or no impact on the United States. Antigua also argues that retaliating solely under the GATS would prevent it from recovering the full amount of trade damage caused by the U.S. measures.

[237] Request by the United States for Arbitration under Article 22.6 of the DSU, *United States—Measures Affecting the Cross-Border Supply of Gambling and Betting Services*, WT/DS285/23 (July 24, 2007). The United States challenged both the economic data used by Antigua and its measurement of losses against the hypothetical legalization of all remote gambling in the United States instead of the legalization of remote gambling on horseracing. The United States argued that by its calculations Antigua's trade injury should amount to $500,000 per year and, in any event, no more than $3.3 million per year. Written Submission of the United States, *United States-Measures Affecting the Cross- Border Supply of Gambling and Betting Services—Arbitration Pursuant to Article 22.6 of the DSU*, WT/DS285 (Sept. 19, 2007), at http://www.ustr.gov/webfm_send/769.

[238] Decision by the Arbitrator, Recourse to Arbitration by the United States for Arbitration under Article 22.6 of the DSU, *United States—Measures Affecting the Cross-Border Supply of Gambling and Betting Services*, WT/DS285/ARB (Dec. 21, 2007).

[239] Antiguan Government Statement on Unauthorized Representations by *Zookz.com* Regarding its Entertainment Download Web Site, at *http://www.antiguawto.com/pr_zookz _antiguan_gov_jul09.pdf.*

[240] Office of the U.S. Trade Representative, 2009 TRADE POLICY AGENDA AND 2008 ANNUAL REPORT 83 (Mar. 2009), at http://www.ustr.gov/about-us/press-office/reports-and-publications/2009/2009-trade-policy-agenda-and-2008-annualreport.

[241] European Commission, Report to the Trade Barriers Regulation Committee (Commission Staff Working Paper), Examination Procedure Concerning an Obstacle to Trade, Within the Meaning of Council Regulation (EC) No 3286/94, Consisting of Measures Adopted by the

United States of America Affecting Trade in Remote gambling Services at http://trade.ec.europa.eu/doclib/docs/2009/june/tradoc_143405.pdf.

[242] European Commission, Fact Sheet: Trade Barriers Regulation report on US Internet gambling laws (June 10, 2009), at http://trade.ec.europa.eu/doclib/docs/2009/june/tradoc_143429.pdf.

[243] Press Release, Office of the U.S. Trade Representative, U.S. and EU discuss ways forward on bilateral trade issues (last updated July 14, 2009).

[244] 73 Fed. Reg. 69382 (Nov. 18, 2008), codified at 31 C.F.R. Part 132; Prohibition on Funding of Unlawful Internet Gambling, 74 Fed. Reg. 62687 (Dec. 1, 2009)(extension of compliance date).

[245] For further information on the UIGEA and proposed legislation, see CRS Report RS22749, *supra* note 221.

[246] Panel Report, *United States—Measures Related to Shrimp from Thailand*, WT/DS343/R (Feb. 29, 2008); Panel Report, *United States—Customs Bond Directive for Merchandise Subject to Anti-Dumping/Countervailing Duties,* WT/DS345/R (Feb. 29, 2008); Appellate Body Report, *United States—Measures Related to Shrimp from Thailand, United States—Customs Bond Directive for Merchandise Subject to Anti-Dumping/Countervailing Duties,* WT/DS343/AB/R, WT/DS345/AB/R (July 16, 2008).

[247] Implementation of the Findings of the WTO Panel in United States—Antidumping Measure on Shrimp From Thailand: Notice of Determination Under Section 129 of the Uruguay Round Agreements Act and Partial Revocation of the Antidumping Duty Order on Frozen Warmwater Shrimp from Thailand, 74 Fed. Reg. 5638 (Jan. 30, 2009).

[248] Enhanced Bonding Requirement for Certain Shrimp Importers, 74 Fed. Reg. 14809 (Apr. 1, 2009) [hereinafter April 2009 EBR Notice]. U.S. Customs and Border Protection had proposed this change in January 2009. Enhanced Bonding Requirement for Certain Shrimp Importers, 74 Fed. Reg. 1224 (Jan. 12, 2009).

[249] April 2009 EBR Notice, *supra* note 248, 74 Fed. Reg. at 14811-12.

[250] Dispute Settlement Body, Minutes of Meeting, Apr. 20, 2009, at 15, WT/DSB/M/267 (June 26, 2009) [hereinafter DSB Minutes (Apr. 20, 2009)]. The United States also stated that, in response to another ruling and recommendation in the dispute involving India, it had notified documents relating to the EBR to the WTO Committee on Antidumping Practices and the Committee on Subsidies and Countervailing Measures. *Id.* at 16.

[251] *Id.* at 15, 16.

[252] National Fisheries Institute, Inc. v. U.S. Bureau of Customs and Border Protection, 637 F.Supp.2d 1270 (Ct. Int'l Trade).

[253] Tariff Act of 1930, § 731, 19 U.S.C. § 1673. The U.S. International Trade Commission may also find that the establishment of a industry in the United States is materially retarded by reason of the dumped products, but this situation has rarely been alleged in an antidumping investigation.

[254] Tariff Act of 1930, § 771(35)(A), 19 U.S.C. § 1677(35)(A).

[255] See Tariff Act of 1930, § 733(b)(3)m, 19 U.S.C. § 1673b(b)(3).

[256] See, e.g, http://ia.ita.doc.gov/download/section123/final-123-modification-notice-20061220.pdf

[257] 19 C.F.R. § 351.212(a).

[258] 19 C.F.R. § 351.204(b)(1).

[259] 19 C.F.R. § 341.204(c)(1).

[260] Tariff Act of 1930, § 735(c)(1)(B)(i)(II), 19 U.S.C. § 1673d(c)(1)(B)(i)(II). Liquidation of entries may also be delayed because of litigation challenging a dumping or injury determination.

[261] 19 C.F.R. § 351.213.

[262] 19 C.F.R. § 351.212(a).

[263] Tariff Act of 1930, § 751(a)(2)(B), 19 U.S.C. § 1675(a)(2)(B); regulations at 19 C.F.R. § 351.214.

[264] Tariff Act of 1930, § 751(b), 19 U.S.C. § 1675(b); regulations at 19 C.F.R. § 351.216.

[265] Tariff Act of 1930, § 751(b), 19 U.S.C. § 1675(c); regulations at 19 C.F.R. § 351.218.

[266] Tariff A ct of 1930, § 777A(d), 19 U.S.C. § 1677f-1(d).

[267] Targeted dumping comparison methodology, authorized under Tariff Act of 1930, § 777A(d)(1)(B), 19 U.S.C. § 1677f-1(d)(1)(B), has been rarely used but may be employed where the other comparison methodologies "cannot account for a pattern of prices that differ significantly among purchasers, regions, or time periods." Uruguay Round SAA, *supra* note 7, at 843. Targeting dumping would occur when an exporter sold a product at a dumped price in certain areas or to certain customers, while masking these sales with non-dumped exports elsewhere.;

In October 2007, DOC requested comment on the use of targeted dumping in original antidumping investigations, the one type of price comparison that has not been affected by the adverse zeroing decisions discussed in this chapter. DOC specifically requested "comments and suggestions on what guidelines, threshold, and tests it should use in determining whether targeting dumping is occurring." Targeted Dumping in Antidumping Investigations; Request for Comment, 72 Fed. Reg. 60651 (Oct. 25, 2007). On May 9, 2008, DOC announced in the *Federal Register* that it proposed to adopt, for future antidumping investigations, the new targeted dumping methodology that it had recently announced and applied in a proceeding involving certain steel nails from the United Arab Emirates and the People's Republic of China, and requested comment on this action. The new methodology involves a two-stage test addressing the "pattern" and "significant difference" requirements set out in the statute. Proposed Methodology for Identifying and Analyzing Targeted Dumping in Antidumping Investigations; Request for Comment, 73 Fed. Reg. 26371 (May 9, 2008).

On December 10, 2008, DOC issued an interim final rule withdrawing 19 C.F.R. § 351.414 (f) and (g), the regulatory provisions addressing targeted dumping, noting that these provisions had been promulgated before DOC had performed a targeted dumping analysis and stating that their withdrawal "will provide the agency with the opportunity to analyze extensively the concept of targeted dumping and develop a meaningful practice in this area as it gains experience in evaluating such allegations." It further stated that withdrawal of the rule was "not significant" and "will allow the Department to exercise the discretion intended by the statute and, thereby, develop a practice that will allow interested parties to pursue all statutory avenues of relief in this area." DOC also stated that it was not replacing the provisions at this time and is instead "returning to a case-by-case adjudication, until additional experience allows the Department to gain a greater understanding of the issue. Withdrawal of the Regulatory Provisions Governing Targeted Dumping in Antidumping Investigations; Request for Comment, 73 Fed. Reg. 74930 (Dec. 10, 2008).

[268] 19 C.F.R. § 351.414(c)(1).

[269] 19 C.F.R. § 351.414(d)(1). The products in a sub-group, or "averaging group," are identical or virtually identical in all physical characteristics and sold at the same level of trade. 19 C.F.R. § 351.414(d)(2).

[270] 19 C.F.R. § 351.414(d)(1).

[271] Tariff Act of 1930, § 7771(35)(B), 19 U.S.C. § 1677(35)(B). See also Dept. of Commerce, *Import Administration Antidumping Manual*, ch. 6, at 9 (1997 ed.)[hereinafter DOC AD Manual], at http://ia.ita.doc.gov/admanual/index.html.

[272] See Antidumping Proceedings: Calculation of the Weighted-Average Dumping Margin During an Antidumping Investigation; Final Modification, 71 Fed. Reg. 77722 (Dec. 27, 2006) [hereinafter Notice of Antidumping Modification]. For another description of "model zeroing," see Panel Report, *United States—Laws, Regulations and Methodology for Calculating Dumping Margins ("Zeroing")*, para. 7.31, WT/DS294/R (Oct. 31, 2005).

[273] 19 C.F.R. § 351.414(c)(2).

[274] See Panel Report, *United States—Measures Relating to Zeroing and Sunset Reviews*, paras. 7.3, 7.30, 7.35, WT/DS322/R (Sept. 20, 2006); Panel Report, *United States—Continued*

Existence and Application of Zeroing Methodology, paras. 7.159-7.161, WT/DS350/R (Oct. 1, 2008). See generally DOC AD Manual, *supra* note 271, ch. 18, at 24.

275 The term "dumping margin" is defined as "the amount by which the normal value exceeds the export price or constructed export price of the subject merchandise." Tariff Act of 1930, § 777(35)(A), 19 U.S.C. § 1677(35)(A).

276 SKF USA Inc. v. United States, 491 F. Supp. 1354, 1364-66 (Ct. Int'l Trade 2007), *aff'd*, 537 F.3d 1373 (Fed. Cir. 2008); Corus Staal BV v. Department of Commerce, 395 F.3d 1343, 1347 (Fed. Cir. 2005), *cert denied*, 126 S.Ct. 1023 (2006); Timken Co. v. United States, 354 F.3d 1334, 1341-42 (Fed. Cir.), *cert denied sub nom.* Koyo Seiko Co. v. United States, 543 U.S. 976 (2004).

277 Koyo Seiko Co. v. United States, 551 F.3d 1286, 1290-91 (Fed. Cir. 2008).

278 U.S. Steel Corp. v. United States, 637 F.Supp.2d 1199, 1209-16 (Ct. Int'l Trade 2009), *appeal docketed*, No. 2009- 1572 (Fed. Cir. Sept. 16, 2009).

279 *Id.* at 1212.

280 *Id.* at 1216.

281 Union Steel v. United States, 645 F. Supp.2d 1298 (Ct. Int'l Trade 2009); see also Corus Staal BV v. United States, 502 F.3d 1370 (Fed. Cir. 2007).

282 Panel Report, *United States—Antidumping Measures on Polyethylene Retail Carrier Bags from Thailand*, WT/DS383/R (Jan. 22, 2010)[hereinafter Thai Carrier Bags Panel Report].

283 Agreement on Procedures between Thailand and the United States, *United States—Antidumping Measures on Polyethylene Retail Carrier Bags from Thailand*, WT/DS383/4 (Jan. 12, 2010).

284 Along with the eight cases discussed or otherwise mentioned in the text, eight other WTO disputes have involved challenges to the U.S. use of zeroing, though not all of these have resulted in panels. These include: *United States— Anti-dumping Measure on Shrimp from Ecuador,* WT/DS335 (adverse panel report; dispute appears to have been resolved with the August 2007 revocation of the AD order in question); *United States—Anti-dumping Determinations Regarding Stainless Steel from Mexico,* WT/DS325 (consultations only; see WT/DS355, discussed in text, for further action); *United States—Provisional Anti-Dumping Measures on Shrimp from Thailand,* WT/DS324 (consultations only; see WT/DS343, *supra,* for further action); *United States—Anti-dumping Measures on Cement from Mexico,* WT/DS28 1 (panel established but work suspended; dispute settled with 2006 bilateral Trade in Cement Agreement); *United States—Final Dumping Determination on Softwood Lumber from Canada,* WT/DS264 (adverse panel and AB reports in original dispute; adverse AB report in compliance panel proceeding; dispute settled with 2006 bilateral Softwood Lumber Agreement); *United States—Provisional Anti-Dumping Measures on Import of Certain Softwood Lumber from Canada,* WT/DS247 (consultations only; dispute settled with 2006 bilateral Softwood Lumber Agreement,); *United States—Sunset Review of Anti-Dumping Duties on Corrosion-Resistant Carbon Steel Flat Products from Japan,* WT/DS255 (Appellate Body reversed panel finding that United States did not violate WTO Antidumping Agreement in relying on zeroing-based dumping margin in challenged sunset review, but found that it had insufficient factual basis to complete analysis of Japan's claim); *United States—Anti-dumping Duties on Silicon Metal from Brazil,* WT/DS239 (consultations only).

285 Article 2.4.2 states, in pertinent part, as follows: "Subject to the provisions governing fair comparison in paragraph 4, the existence of margins of dumping during the investigation phase shall normally be established on the basis of a comparison of a weighted average normal value with a weighted average of prices of all comparable export transactions or by a comparison of normal value and export prices on a transaction-to-transaction basis."

The first WTO decision in which the U.S. practice of zeroing was ruled to be inconsistent with this provision of the WTO Antidumping Agreement was *United States – Final Dumping Determination on Softwood Lumber from Canada (Softwood Lumber)*, WT/DS264. The case involved the application of zeroing in an average-to-average price comparison in an original antidumping investigation. As summarized in the January 2010 panel report in *Thai Carrier Bags*, the WTO Appellate Body found in *Softwood Lumber* "that the terms 'margins of dumping' and 'all comparable export transactions' in Article 2.4.2 must be interpreted in an 'integrated manner', such that where 'an investigating authority has chosen to undertake multiple comparisons, the investigating authority necessarily has to take into account the results of all those comparisons in order to establish margins of dumping for the product as a whole under Article 2.4.2'." Thai Carrier Bags Panel Report, *supra* note 282, para. 7.20.

[286] Communication from the United States, *Offsets for Non-Dumped Comparisons*, TN/RL/W/208 (June 5, 2007).

[287] Proposal from the United States, *Proposal on Offsets for Non-Dumped Comparisons*, TN/RL/GEN/147 (June 27, 2007).

[288] 2007 Draft Rules Text, *supra* note 87, at 6, 20.

[289] 2008 Draft Rules Text, *supra* note 87, at 6. See also *16 Members Propose Complete Ban of All 'Zeroing' in WTO Rules Talks*, 25 Int'l Trade Rep. (BNA) 149 (Jan. 31, 2008); *China, Other WTO Members Add Support to Proposal on Elimination of Zeroing*, 25 Int'l Trade Rep. (BNA) 185 (Feb. 7, 2008).

[290] Request for the Establishment of a Panel by the European Communities, *United States—Laws, Regulations and Methodology for Calculating Dumping Margins ("Zeroing")*, WT/DS294/7 (Feb. 6, 2004) and WT/DS294/7/Rev. 1 (Feb. 19, 2004). The EC's use of zeroing in establishing the existence of dumping margins in antidumping investigations, as applied in a case involving goods from India, had been successfully challenged by India in 2001. See panel and Appellate Body reports in *European Communities—Anti-Dumping Duties on Imports of Cotton-type Bed Linen from India*, WT/DS141.

[291] Request for Consultations by the European Communities, *United States—Laws, Regulations and Methodology for Calculating Dumping Margins ("Zeroing")*, WT/DS294/1 (June 19, 2003) and WT/DS294/1/Add. 1 (Sept. 15, 2003). : The WTO Appellate Body has described "as such" claims as follows: "By definition, an 'as such' claim challenges laws, regulations, or other instruments of a Member that have general and prospective application, asserting that a Member's conduct—not only in a particular instance that has occurred, but in future situation as well—will necessarily be inconsistent with that Member's WTO obligations. In essence, complaining parties brining 'as such' challenges seek to prevent Members *ex ante* from engaging in certain conduct. The implications of such challenges are obviously more far-reaching than 'as applied' claims." Appellate Body Report, *United States—Sunset Review of Anti-Dumping Measures on Oil Country Tubular Goods from Argentina*, para. 172, WT/DS268/AB/R (Nov. 29, 2004).

[292] Panel Report, *United States—Laws, Regulations and Methodology for Calculating Dumping Margins ("Zeroing")*, WT/DS294/R (Oct. 31, 2005) [hereinafter U.S. Zeroing Panel Report (EC I)].

[293] *Id.* paras. 7.27-7.32 (emphasis added).

[294] Appellate Body Report, *United States—Final Dumping Determination on Softwood Lumber from Canada*, WT/DS264/AB/R, para. 93 (Aug. 11, 2004).

[295] *Id.* para. 98 (emphasis added).

[296] U.S. Zeroing Panel Report (EC I), *supra* note 292, paras. 7.91-7.106. The panel rejected the EC's claims that various provisions of the Tariff Act of 1930, which define terms "dumping margin" and "weighted average dumping margin," establish the basic authority for imposing antidumping duties, and authorize the price comparison methodologies discussed above, were inconsistent with WTO obligations, finding that these provisions did not address the issue of zeroing. *Id.* paras. 7.50-7.69. The cited provisions were Tariff Act of 1930, §§ 771(35)(A),(B), 731, 777A(d), 19 U.S.C. §§ 1677(35)(A),(B), 1673, 1677f-1(d).

[297] Notification of an Other Appeal by the United States, *United States—Laws, Regulations and Methodology for Calculating Dumping Margins ("Zeroing")*, WT/DS294/13 (Feb. 1, 2006).

[298] Appellate Body Report, *United States—Laws, Regulations and Methodology for Calculating Dumping Margins ("Zeroing")*, WT/DS294/AB/R (Apr. 18, 2006).

[299] *Id.* para. 133.

[300] Dispute Settlement Body, *Minutes of Meeting*, May 9, 2006, at 7-13, WT/DSB/M/21 1 (June 12, 2006).

[301] Along with criticizing the Appellate Body report at DSB meetings, the United States took the uncommon step of circulating detailed critiques of the decision to WTO Members. See Communication from the United States, *United States—Laws, Regulations and Methodology for Calculating Dumping Margins ("Zeroing")*, WT/DS294/16 (May 17, 2006); Communication from the United States, *United States—Laws, Regulations and Methodology for Calculating Dumping Margins ("Zeroing")*, WT/DS294/18 (June 19, 2006).

[302] Dispute Settlement Body, *Minutes of Meeting*, May 30, 2006, at [1], WT/DSB/M/213 (June 21, 2006).

[303] Agreement under Article 21.3(b) of the DSU, *United States—Laws, Regulations and Methodology for Calculating Dumping Margins ("Zeroing")*, WT/DS294/19 (Aug. 1, 2006).

[304] Antidumping Proceedings: Calculation of the Weighted Average Dumping Margin During an Antidumping Duty Investigation, 71 Fed. Reg. 11189 (Mar. 6, 2006).

[305] Notice of Antidumping Modification, *supra* note 272.

[306] Antidumping Proceedings: Calculation of the Weighted-Average Dumping Margin During an Antidumping Duty Investigation; Change in Effective Date of Final Modification, 72 Fed. Reg. 1704 (Jan. 16, 2007); Antidumping Proceedings: Calculation of the Weighted-Average Dumping Margin During an Antidumping Duty Investigation; Change in Effective Date of Final Modification, 72 Fed. Reg. 3783 (Jan. 26, 2007).

Representative Rangel, Chairman of the House Ways and Means Committee, and Senator Baucus, Chairman of the Senate Finance Committee, had written to the Secretary of Commerce and the USTR on January 19, 2007, requesting that DOC postpone its decision whether to modify the practice to March 31, 2007, to give Committee members additional time to consider the issue. The letter stated that the 60-day consultation period, which in this case ended in mid-January, was insufficient given the limited actual time for consultation, the complexity of the matter, and the controversial nature of the ruling. Text of letter available at http://finance.senate.gov/press/Bpress/2007press/ prb012207.pdf. The House Ways and Means Committee went on to solicit comments on the DOC action. See Advisory from the Committee on Ways and Means, FC-7 (Jan. 31, 2007), at http://waysandmeans.house.gov.

In mid-December 2006, 11 Senators signed a letter to the same Administration recipients in which they took issue with the Appellate Body decision in DS294, favorably referred to several earlier GATT and WTO panels that had ruled differently, and expressed their disagreement with any modification of the U.S. practice. Text of December 2006 letter and of USTR memo to Congress under section 123 regarding the modification available at *In side U.S. Trade,* Dec. 15, 2006, at 19-21.

In addition, H.R. 496 (Rangel), introduced January 14, 2009, provides that the 2007 regulatory modification will expire March 1, 2009, and the prior departmental practice will thenceforth apply, unless and until the department issues a revised methodology pursuant to procedures laid out in the bill. Note also S. 364 (Rockefeller), 1 10th Cong., 1st Sess. (2007), discussed at *supra* note 21.

[307] See Department of Commerce *Federal Register* notice and fact sheet at http://ia.ita.doc.gov/ia-highlights-andnews.html. The Department stated in its *Federal Register* notice that since a Section 129 Determination is implemented prospectively, the date on which the USTR directs the Commerce Department to implement the determination "will necessarily be after the effective date of the revocation" of the AD orders in the three

referenced cases and that "[a]s a result, the Department is not conducting section 129 proceedings with respect to the three investigations."

308 Department of Commerce, Issues and Decision Memorandum for the Final Results of the Section 129 Determination (Apr. 9, 2007), at *http://ia.ita.doc.gov/download/zeroing /zeroing-sec-129-final-decision-memo20070410.pdf.*

309 *Id.*

310 Status Report by the United States, Addendum, *United States—Laws, Regulations and Methodology for Calculating Dumping Margins ("Zeroing")*, at 2, WT/DS294/20/Add.2 (Apr. 13, 2007) [hereinafter April 2007 Zeroing Status Report].

311 See Implementation of the Findings of the WTO Panel in US—Zeroing (EC): Notice of Determinations Under Section 129 of the Uruguay Round Agreements Act and Revocations and Partial Revocations of Certain Antidumping Duty Orders, 72 Fed. Reg. 25261 (May 4, 2007).

312 April 2007 Zeroing Status Report, *supra* note 310.

313 European Commission, EU response to US action on WTO zeroing judgement (Apr. 12, 2007), at http://ec.europa.eu/trade/issues

314 Understanding between the United States and the European Communities Regarding Procedures under Articles 21 and 22 of the DSU, *United States—Laws, Regulations and Methodology for Calculating Dumping Margins ("Zeroing")*, WT/DS294/21 (May 9, 2007).

315 Request for Consultations, Recourse to Article 21.5 of the DSU by the European Communities, *United States— Laws, Regulations and Methodology for Calculating Dumping Margins ("Zeroing")*, WT/DS294/22 (July 12, 2007).

316 The final antidumping margins were 2.11 percent for the individually investigated producer and 2.11 for all other exporters and producers, the same as the preliminary margins, each a reduction from an original margin of 11.23 percent. Implementation of the Findings of the WTO Panel in US-Zeroing (EC); Notice of Determination Under Section 129 of the Uruguay Round Agreements Act: Antidumping Duty Order on Stainless Steel Sheet and Strip from in Coils from Italy, 72 Fed. Reg. 54640 (Sept. 29, 2007); Department of Commerce, Issues and Decision Memorandum for the Final Results of the Section 129 Determination (Aug. 20, 2007), at http://ia.ita.doc.gov/download/section129/ Italy-SSSS-in-Coils-129-Final-Decision-Memo-08-20-07.pdf.

317 Request for the Establishment of a Panel, Recourse to Article 21.5 of the DSU by the European Communities, *United States—Laws, Regulations and Methodology for Calculating Dumping Margins ("Zeroing")*, WT/DS294/25 (Sept. 14, 2007).

318 Report of the Appellate Body, *United States—Laws, Regulations and Methodology for Calculating Dumping Margins ("Zeroing"); Recourse to Article 21.5 of the DSU by the European Communities,* para. 305, WT/DS294/AB/RW (May 14, 2009)[hereinafter U.S. Zeroing Article 21.5 AB Report (EC I)].

319 Report of the Panel, *United States—Laws, Regulations and Methodology for Calculating Dumping Margins ("Zeroing"); Recourse to Article 21.5 of the DSU by the European Communities*, paras. 8.165-8.169, WT/DS294/RW (Dec. 17, 2008)[hereinafter U.S. Zeroing Article 21.5 Panel Report (EC I].

320 *Id.* para. 8.33.

321 *Id.* paras. 8.33-8.34, 8.36.

322 *Id.* paras. 8.40, 8.42.

323 U.S. Zeroing Article 21.5 Panel Report (EC I), *supra* note 319.

324 U.S. Zeroing Article 21.5 AB Report (EC I), *supra* note 318.

325 *Id*, para. 226 (emphasis in original).

326 *Id.* paras. 233-35, 392-97.

327 U.S. Zeroing Article 21.5 Panel Report (EC I), *supra* note 319, paras. 8.165-8.169.

328 *Id.* para. 8.108

329 U.S. Zeroing Article 21.5 AB Report (EC I), *supra* note 318, para. 311.

[330] *Id.* (emphasis in original).

[331] *Id.* para. 304.

[332] U.S. Zeroing Article 21.5 Panel Report (EC I), *supra* note 319, para. 8.118.

[333] WTO News Item, WTO adopts compliance rulings in the US "zeroing" case brought by the EC (June 11, 2009), at http://www.wto.org/english/news_e/news09_e/dsb_11jun09_e.htm.

[334] *Id.*

[335] Status Report by the United States, *United States—Laws, Regulations and Methodology for Calculating Dumping Margins ("Zeroing"),* WT/DS294/34/Add. 5 (Jan. 8, 2010).

[336] Panel Report, *United States—Measures Relating to Zeroing and Sunset Reviews,* WT/DS322/R (Sept. 20, 2006).

[337] Appellate Body Report, *United States—Measures Relating to Zeroing and Sunset Reviews,* WT/DS322/AB/R (Jan. 9, 2007) [hereinafter U.S. Zeroing AB Report (Japan)].

[338] *Id.* para. 183, *citing Appellate Body Report, United States—Sunset Review of Corrosion-Resistant Carbon Steel Products from Japan*, para. 127, WT/DS244/AB/R (Dec. 15, 2003).

[339] U.S. Zeroing AB Report (Japan), *supra* note 337, paras. 184-185.

[340] Dispute Settlement Body, Minutes of Meeting, Jan. 23, 2007, at 15-22 ,WT/DSB/M/225 (Mar. 8, 2007) [hereinafter DSB Minutes (Jan. 23, 2007)].

[341] Dispute Settlement Body, Minutes of Meeting, Feb. 20, 2007, at 7, WT/DSB/M/226 (Mar. 26, 2007); see also DSB Minutes (Jan. 23, 2007), *supra* note 340 at 15-17, and *Administration, Congress Explore Zeroing Compliance Options*, INSIDE U.S. TRADE, Feb. 9, 2007, at 1.

[342] Communication from the United States, *United States—Measures Relating to Zeroing and Sunset Reviews*, WT/DS322/16 (Feb. 26, 2007). On June 1, 2007, the United States submitted a proposal to the WTO Negotiating Committee on Rules asking that negotiators evaluate the reasoning of the WTO panels that have examined the issue of zeroing and stating its view that "the proper resolution of this issue requires clear text providing that margins of dumping may be determined without offsets for non-dumped transactions, consistent with the long-held concept of dumping." Communication from the United States, *Offsets for Non-Dumped Comparisons*, TN/RL/W/208 (June 5, 2007).

[343] Request by Japan for Arbitration under Article 2 1.3(c) of the DSU, *United States—Measures Relating to Zeroing and Sunset Reviews*, WT/DS322/17 (Mar. 30, 2007).

[344] Agreement under Article 21.3(b) of the DSU, *United States—Measures Relating to Zeroing and Sunset Reviews*, WT/DS322/20 (May 8, 2007).

[345] Status Report by the United States, *United States—Measures Relating to Zeroing and Sunset Reviews*, WT/DS322/Add. 1 (Dec. 7, 2007).

[346] Japan Certain Cut-to-Length Carbon-Quality Steel Plate Products, Final Results Under Section 129: Uruguay Round Agreements Act, Dec. 27, 2007, at *http://ia.ita.doc.gov/ia-news-2007.html;* Issues and Decision Memorandum for the Final Results (undated), at http://ia.ita.doc.gov/download/section129/Japan-CTL-Plate-129-Final-20071227.pdf. The subsequent *Federal Register* notice announcing these results states that the Department issued them on December 21, 2007. See Notice of Implementation of Determination Under Section 129 of the Uruguay Round Agreements Act Regarding the Antidumping Duty Order on Certain Cut-to-Length Carbon –Quality Steel Plate Products from Japan, 73 Fed. Reg. 29109 (May 20, 2008)[hereinafter Notice of Japan Steel Section 129 Determination].

[347] See generally *U.S. Fails to Comply with WTO Challenge on Zeroing by Deadline*, INSIDE U.S. TRADE, Jan. 4, 2008, at 1.

[348] Recourse to Article 22.2 of the DSU by Japan, *United States—Measures Relating to Zeroing and Sunset Reviews*, WT/DS322/24 (Jan. 11, 2008); Recourse to Article 22.2 of the DSU by Japan, *United States—Measures Relating to Zeroing and Sunset Reviews*, WT/DS322/23 (Jan. 11, 2008).

[349] Request by the United States for Arbitration under Article 22.6 of the DSU, *United States—Measures Relating to Zeroing and Sunset Reviews*, WT/DS322/25 (Jan. 21, 2008).

[350] Understanding between the United States and Japan Regarding Procedures under Articles 21 and 22 of the DSU, Recourse to Article 22.2 of the DSU by Japan, *United States—Measures Relating to Zeroing and Sunset Reviews*, WT/DS322/26 (Mar. 12, 2008).

[351] Status Report by the United States, Addendum, *United States—Measures Relating to Zeroing and Sunset Reviews*, WT/DS322/22/Add.2 (Jan. 11, 2008); Dispute Settlement Body, Minutes of Meeting, Jan. 21, 2008, at 6,WT/SB/M/245 (Mar. 14, 2008).

[352] Request for the Establishment of a Panel, Recourse to Article 21.5 of the DSU by Japan, *United States—Measures Relating to Zeroing and Sunset Reviews*, WT/DS322/27 (Apr. 8, 2008).

[353] Communication from the Arbitrator, Recourse by the United States to Article 22.6 of the DSU, *United States— Measures Relating to Zeroing and Sunset Reviews*, WT/DS322/30 (June 10, 2008).

[354] Notice of Japan Steel Section 129 Determination, *supra* note 346.

[355] Panel Report, *United States—Measures Relating to Zeroing and Sunset Reviews; Recourse to Article 21.5 of the DSU by Japan,* WT/DS322/RW (Apr. 24, 2009) [hereinafter U.S. Zeroing Article 21.5 Panel Report (Japan)].

[356] *Id.* para. 7.149.

[357] *Id.* para. 7.153.

[358] *Id.* paras. 7.198-7.208. GATT Article II permits the imposition of antidumping duties on bound items but the duties must be applied consistently with GATT VI. See GATT 1994 art. II:2(b).

[359] U.S. Zeroing Article 21.5 Panel Report (Japan), *supra* note 355, paras. 7.202, 7.203.

[360] *Id.* paras. 7.223-7.229.

[361] Appellate Body Report, *United States—Measures Relating to Zeroing and Sunset Reviews; Recourse to Article 21.5 of the DSU by Japan,* WT/DS322/AB/RW (Aug. 18, 2009).

[362] *Id.* paras. 170-187, 188.

[363] U.S. Diplomatic Mission to the United Nations in Geneva, Statements by the United States at the August 31, 2009 WTO—DSB, at para. 5, at *http://geneva.usmission.gov/news/2009/08/31/ds/.*

[364] Request for the Establishment of a Panel by Mexico, *United States—Final Anti-dumping Measures on Stainless Steel from Mexico,*WT/DS344/3 (Oct. 16, 2006).

[365] Panel Report, *United States—Final Anti-dumping Measures on Stainless Steel from Mexico,*WT/DS344/R (Dec. 20, 2007).

[366] Appellate Body Report, *United States—Final Anti-dumping Measures on Stainless Steel from Mexico,*WT/DS344/AB/R (Apr. 30, 2008).

[367] *Id.* para. 158.

[368] *Id.* paras. 160-61.

[369] Dispute Settlement Body, Minutes of Meeting, May 20, 2008, at 9-11, WT/DSB/M/250 (July 1, 2008).

[370] Communication from the United States, *United States—Final Anti-dumping Measures on Stainless Steel from Mexico,*WT/DS344/11 (June 11, 2008).

[371] Award of the Arbitrator, *United States—Final Anti-dumping Measures on Stainless Steel from Mexico, Arbitration under Article 21.3(c) of the Understanding on Rules and Procedures Governing the Settlement of Disputes*, WT/DS344/15 (Oct. 31, 2008).

[372] Implementation of the Findings of the WTO Dispute Settlement Panel and Appellate Body in United States—Final Anti-Dumping Measures on Stainless Steel from Mexico: Notice of Determination under Section 129 of the Uruguay Round Agreements Act, 74 Fed. Reg. 19527 (Apr. 29, 2009).

[373] Request for Consultations, *United States—Final Anti-dumping Measures on Stainless Steel from Mexico,* Recourse to Article 21.5 of the DSU by Mexico, at 3, WT/DS344/1 8 (Aug. 24, 2009)[hereinafter Mexico Article 21.5 Consultation Request]. Recalculation of dumping margins in the challenged administrative reviews was not part of the Section 129 proceeding for the original antidumping investigation at issue in the case. See Department

of Commerce, Issues and Decision Memorandum for the Final Results of Proceedings Under Section 129 of the Uruguay Round Agreements Act: Antidumping Measures on Stainless Steel from Mexico, [Mar. 31, 2009], at http://ia.ita.doc.gov/ download/ section129/mexico-ssss-coil-129-final-memo-04-03-09.pdf

[374] Mexico Article 21.5 Consultation Request, *supra* note 373, at 3.

[375] Understanding between Mexico and the United States Regarding Procedures under Articles 21 and 22 of the DSU, *United States—Final Anti-dumping Measures on Stainless Steel from Mexico*, WT/DS344/17 (May 20, 2009).

[376] Mexico Article 21.5 Consultation Request, *supra* note 373.

[377] Request for the Establishment of a Panel by the European Communities, *United States—Continued Existence and Application of Zeroing Methodology*, WT/DS350/6 (May 11, 2007).

[378] This issue implicates Article 6.2 of the WTO Dispute Settlement Understanding, which states that a Member's written request for the establishment of a panel must, *inter alia,* "identify the *specific measures* at issue" in the dispute (emphasis added).

[379] EC 2009 U.S. Trade Barriers Report, *supra* note 58, at 60.

[380] *Id.*

[381] Panel Report, *United States—Continued Existence and Application of Zeroing Methodology*, WT/DS350/R (Oct. 1, 2008).

[382] Appellate Body Report, *United States—Continued Existence and Application of Zeroing Methodology*, para. 185, WT/DS350/17 (June 4, 2009)[hereinafter U.S. Zeroing AB Report (EC II)]. The "continued use" argument has since been made by Brazil its consultations and panel requests in *United States—Anti-dumping Administrative Reviews and Other Measures Related to Imports of Certain Orange Juice from Brazil.* Request for Consultations by Brazil, WT/DS3 82/1/Add. 1 (May 27, 2009), at 2; Request for the Establishment of a Panel by Brazil, WT/DS382/4 (Aug. 21, 2009), at 3.

[383] U.S. Zeroing AB Report (EC II), *supra* note 382, paras. 186-99.

[384] *Id.* paras. 242-357. One Appellate Body member, in a concurrence to the AB's findings that zeroing was not permitted in administrative reviews, called for an end to litigation on the issue. Despite "arguments of substance made on both sides," the member stated that Appellate Body had "spoken definitively" on the issue of zeroing, the AB decisions had been adopted, and that it was now "more important for the system of dispute resolution to have a definitive outcome than to pick over the entrails of battles past." *Id.* para. 312.

[385] *Id.* paras. 369-83.

[386] Dispute Settlement Body, Minutes of Meeting, Feb. 19, 2009, at 18-21, WT/DSB/M/265 (Apr. 29, 2009).

[387] DSB Minutes (Mar. 20, 2009), *supra* note 59, at 14.

[388] Agreement under Article 2 1.23(b) of the DSU, *United States—Continued Existence and Application of Zeroing Methodology*, WT/DS350/17 (Feb. 4, 2009).

[389] Status Report by the United States, *United States—Continued Existence and Application of Zeroing Methodology*, WT/DS350/18 (Dec. 11, 2009).

[390] *Id.*

[391] U.S. Diplomatic Mission to the United Nations in Geneva, Satements [sic] by the United States at the December 21, 2009, DSB Meeting, at para. H, at *http://geneva.usmission.gov/ 2009/12/21/1221dsb/.*

[392] WTO News Item (Dec. 21, 2009), *supra* note 197.

[393] Understanding between the European Union and the United States Regarding Procedures under Articles 21 and 22 of the DSU, *United States—Continued Existence and Application of Zeroing Methodology*, WT/DS350/19 (Jan. 6, 2010).

In: Disputed WTO Cases Involving the United... ISBN: 978-1-61761-433-0
Editors: Jacqueline P. Daniels

Chapter 2

BRAZIL'S WTO CASE AGAINST THE U.S. COTTON PROGRAM*

Randy Schnepf

SUMMARY

On April 5, 2010, Brazil's Foreign Trade Council (CAMEX) approved a resolution that would postpone until April 22 the implementation of WTO-approved countermeasures by Brazil against U.S. imports in relation to a long-running dispute over U.S. cotton subsidies. Earlier, on March 10, 2010, Brazil had released a list of 102 goods of U.S. origin valued at $561 million that would be subject to import tariffs of up to 100% within 30 days unless a last-minute agreement was reached. Five days later, on March 15, Brazil released a preliminary list of U.S. patents and intellectual property rights it could restrict, barring a joint settlement. In light of the temporary suspension of countermeasures, negotiations between the United States and Brazil on a proposed settlement continue. If preliminary objectives (discussed in the report) are achieved, it may result in the permanent suspension of any countermeasures related to this case.

This trade dispute had its origins in 2002, when Brazil—a major cotton export competitor— expressed its growing concerns about U.S. cotton

* This is an edited, reformatted and augmented edition of a United States Congressional Research Service publication, Report RL32571, dated April 6, 2010.

subsidies by initiating a World Trade Organization (WTO) dispute settlement case (DS267) against specific provisions of the U.S. cotton program. On September 8, 2004, a WTO dispute settlement panel ruled against the United States on several key issues. It found both (1) prohibited U.S. export subsidies (related to Step 2 program payments and export credit guarantees under the GSM- 102 program) and (2) actionable U.S. domestic support measures (i.e., marketing loan benefits and counter-cyclical program payments) that resulted in adverse effects against Brazil's commercial interests.

The United States appealed the ruling, but on March 3, 2005, a WTO Appellate Body upheld the panel's ruling and provided specific deadlines for removal or modification of the offending U.S. subsidies. Shortly after the March 2005 ruling, the United States made several changes to its cotton programs in an attempt to bring them into compliance with the WTO recommendations. However, Brazil argued that the U.S. response was inadequate, and requested the establishment of a WTO compliance panel in August 2006 to review whether the United States had fully complied with the previous rulings. The compliance panel ruled against the United States in December 2007, and the ruling was upheld on appeal in June 2008.

On August 31, 2009, a WTO arbitration panel (reviewing Brazil's retaliation proposal of nearly $3 billion) released its decision, generally finding in favor of Brazil's retaliation requests but at levels substantially reduced from those requested by Brazil. However, in a key decision, the panel ruled that Brazil would be entitled to cross-retaliation if the overall retaliation amount exceeded a formula-based variable annual threshold. Cross-retaliation involves countermeasures in sectors outside of the trade in goods, most notably in the area of U.S. copyrights and patents.

On December 21, 2009, Brazil announced that it was authorized by the WTO to impose trade retaliation against up to $829.3 million in U.S. goods in 2010 (based on 2008 data). The countermeasure included a fixed annual amount of $147.3 million, reflecting the adverse effects from U.S. price-contingent subsidies, and a balance related to the volume of U.S. export credit guarantees, which may vary annually. The WTO also established a threshold value (related to the value of Brazil's consumer goods imports from the United States) for determining the extent of permissible cross-retaliatory countermeasures. The threshold varies annually based on changes in Brazil's total imports from the United States, but is currently estimated at $561 million, yielding a remaining value of $268.3 million ($829.3 million - $561 million) in eligible cross-retaliatory countermeasures.

OVERVIEW

This chapter provides a description and status report on Brazil's challenge to certain aspects of the U.S. cotton program under the rules of the World Trade Organization's (WTO's) dispute settlement process in case DS267.[1] The "Brazil cotton case" had its WTO origins in 2002 and has since evolved into a sprawling legal enterprise that is still ongoing as of early 2010. The report begins by summarizing the most recent developments in the case. It then provides a detailed history of the case in chronological phases.

Current Status

The latest "retaliation" phase in the case's chronology began on November 19, 2009, when the WTO's Dispute Settlement Body (DSB) granted authorization to Brazil to impose countermeasures against the United States. In addition to traditional tariff measures, the retaliatory countermeasures authorized by the WTO included cross-retaliation in the form of the suspension of U.S. intellectual property rights under the WTO 's Agreement on Trade-Related Aspects of Intellectual Property Rights (TRIPS), and the withholding of services concessions under the General Agreement on Trade in Services (GATS).

On December 21, 2009, Brazil announced that it was authorized by the WTO to impose trade retaliation against up to $829.3 million in U.S. goods in 2010 (based on 2008 data). The countermeasure included a fixed annual amount of $147.3 million, reflecting the adverse effects from U.S. price-contingent subsidies (i.e., marketing loan benefits and counter-cyclical payments), and a balance related to the volume of U.S. export credit guarantees (found to operate as a prohibited export subsidy), which may vary annually. The WTO also established a threshold value (related to the value of Brazil's consumer goods imports from the United States) for determining the extent of permissible cross-retaliatory countermeasures. The threshold varies annually based on changes in Brazil's total imports from the United States, but is currently estimated at $561 million, yielding a remaining value of $268.3 million ($829.3 million - $561 million) in eligible cross-retaliatory countermeasures.

On March 10, 2010, Brazil released a final list of goods of U.S. origin valued at $561 million that would be subject to import tariffs within 30 days unless a last-minute agreement was reached.[2] The following week (March 15), Brazil released a preliminary list of U.S. patents and intellectual property rights it could restrict, barring a joint settlement.[3] The new measures—which were open to public comment for a period of 20 days and subject to public hearings—included the temporary suspension of U.S. patents on pharmaceuticals, chemicals, and biotechnology, and the restriction of copyrights in the music and audiovisual industry.[4]

The United States and Brazil continued to seek a last-minute negotiated settlement to avoid the retaliatory measures. Brazil indicated that it could accept a U.S. pledge to send a reform bill to Congress to alter the offending cotton program provisions, if Brazil were compensated for damages until the bill's approval. Some Brazilian leaders proposed compensation through U.S. investments into cotton research, as well as more U.S. imports of Brazilian beef, orange juice, and ethanol.[5]

On April 1, 2010, Deputy U.S. Trade Representative (USTR) Miriam Sapiro and USDA Undersecretary for Farm and Foreign Agricultural Services Jim Miller met with Ambassador Antonio Patriota, Secretary General of Brazil's Ministry of External Relations, to discuss possible resolution of the dispute.[6] On April 5, 2010, the United States floated a proposal to Brazil on a negotiated settlement.[7] After reviewing the proposal, Brazil's Foreign Trade Council (CAMEX) approved a resolution that would postpone until April 22 the implementation of WTO-approved countermeasures by Brazil against U.S. imports. Key features of the U.S. proposal and the ongoing negotiations include the following:

- The United States would establish a fund in the amount of $147.3 million per year to provide technical assistance and capacity-building for Brazil's cotton sector. Under terms of a memorandum of understanding (MOU), the fund would continue until the passage of the next U.S. farm bill or a mutually agreed solution to the dispute, whichever was sooner. The fund would be subject to transparency and auditing requirements.
- The United States has agreed to make some near-term modifications to the operation of the GSM-102 Export Credit Guarantee Program, and to engage with the government of Brazil in technical discussions regarding further operation of the program. On April 6, 2010, USDA announced that it was amending the GSM- 102 program such that any remaining allocations for FY20 10 would be subject to a new guarantee fee rate schedule starting on April 9, 2010.[8]

- The United States has also agreed to publish a proposed rule by April 16, 2010, to recognize the state of Santa Catarina as free of foot-and-mouth disease, rinderpest, classical swine fever, African swine fever, and swine vesicular disease, based on World Organization for Animal Health guidelines, and to complete a risk evaluation that is currently underway and identify appropriate risk mitigation measures to determine whether fresh beef can be imported from Brazil while preventing the introduction of foot-and-mouth disease into the United States.

In light of the temporary suspension of countermeasures, negotiations between the United States and Brazil on a proposed settlement continue with a view to agreeing on a process for complete negotiated settlement by June 2010. Brazil says that it is still pursuing the full U.S. compliance with the WTO dispute settlement ruling. However, this new "path" towards a negotiated settlement is intended to facilitate reaching a permanent solution to this case.

Report Phases

Along the way, this case has touched on many aspects of WTO legal procedure, including an initial WTO panel and appeal phase, a compliance dispute phase, and the ongoing retaliation phase. Because of the case's longevity and complicated legal twists and turns, this chapter seeks to keep the timeline clear and to footnote official reference documents. The report is broken into six separate components, each representing a different (and somewhat independent) phase of the case. These phases are followed by a summary of the potential role of Congress with respect to the WTO case rulings and their implications for U.S. cotton programs.

1. **Phase I:** Pre-case background on the U.S. cotton sector and its global context.
2. **Phase II:** Brazil's WTO dispute settlement case against U.S. cotton programs.
   a. Brazil's specific charges and the WTO panel's findings.
   b. WTO panel and Appellate Body (AB) recommendations.
   c. Implementation timeline for panel and AB recommendations.

3. **Phase III:** WTO compliance panel and AB review of U.S. compliance with dispute settlement panel's and AB's recommendations.
4. **Phase IV:** WTO arbitration of Brazil's request for retaliatory countermeasures.
5. **Phase V:** Retaliation.
6. **Phase VI:** Discussion of the potential policy implications of this WTO case for the U.S. cotton sector.
7. **Role of Congress.**

The report ends with a timetable of the WTO dispute settlement process (Table 5), to facilitate the reader's understanding of and access to the multifaceted legal procedures involved in the case's slow progression. However, the main thrust of this chapter is to provide an economic and policy perspective on case developments. For more on the legal aspects of WTO dispute settlement cases in general, and the cotton case in particular, see CRS Report RL32014, *WTO Dispute Settlement: Status of U.S. Compliance in Pending Cases*, by Jeanne J. Grimmett.

Phase I. Background on the U.S. Cotton Sector

The cotton industry is a major component of the U.S. agricultural sector. From 1991 to 2008 U.S. cash receipts from cotton production averaged $4.9 billion per year, while export sales averaged nearly $2.9 billion. Cotton is grown across the southern tier of states stretching from Virginia down through the Carolinas and into Georgia, then westward through a belt of contiguous states to California. Texas is the largest cotton-producing state, accounting for an average of 26% of U.S. production since 1990. In 2002, when Brazil first originated its WTO dispute settlement case against U.S. cotton programs, 17 states reported cotton production valued at over $20 million.

The United States is the third-largest producer of cotton in the world, behind China and India, and the world's largest cotton exporter. In the 1990s, U.S. exports accounted for 25% of world trade in cotton. However, since 2000 the United States has accounted for an increasing share of world trade (averaging 3 7%). U.S. exports as a share of domestic production have averaged nearly 70% since 2001, up from a 40% average during the early 1 990s, due in large part to a decline in domestic mill use. (See Figure 1.) U.S.

prominence in global markets coupled with large U.S. subsidy levels have directed international attention to U.S. cotton program outlays in recent years.

Domestic Program Support

Cotton is one of the principal U.S. program crops, along with wheat, rice, feed grains, soybeans, and peanuts. Traditionally, qualifying U.S. cotton producers were eligible for direct payments, counter-cyclical program (CCP) payments, marketing loan benefits, Step 2 payments, and other program benefits.[9] Since 2000, U.S. farm subsidies for cotton production have averaged $3.5 billion per year, while the harvest-time value of production has averaged $4.3 billion (Table 1).

Marketing loan program benefits and CCP payments are price-contingent in the sense that payments are determined by market prices falling below their respective price triggers (i.e., the loan rate and the adjusted target price). For upland cotton, the loan rate is set at $0.52 per pound and the target price is set at $0.71 per pound for calendar years 2010 through 2012 by the 2008 farm bill (P.L. 110-246). The target price is adjusted by subtracting the direct payment for upland cotton of $0.0667 per pound for calculating any CCP payment.

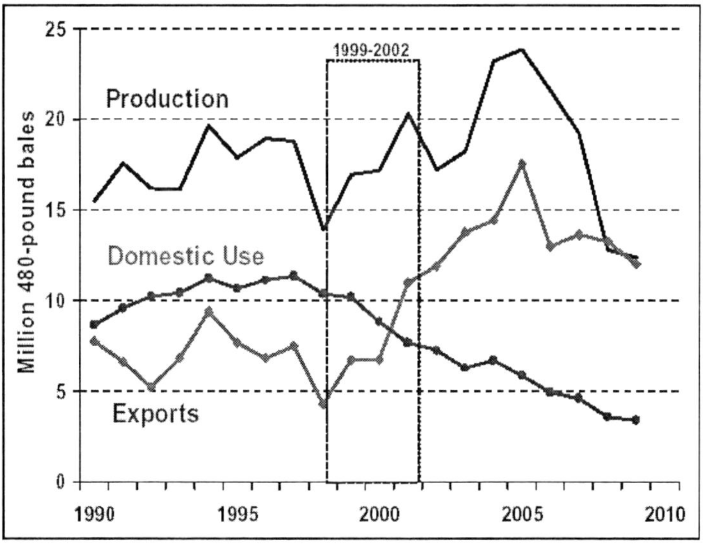

Source: USDA, PSD database, February 11, 2010.

Figure 1. U.S. Cotton Production, Use, and Exports

Table 1. U.S. Upland Cotton Program Outlays and Harvest-Time Value of Production, FY1991 -FY2010 ($ millions)

Fiscal year[a]	Outlays			Value of production[b]
	Cash[c]	Non-Cash[d]	Total	
1991	382	13	395	5,076
1992	1,443	373	1,816	4,912
1993	2,239	572	2,810	4,274
1994	1,539	292	1,831	4,523
1995	99	3	101	6,795
1996	685	0	685	6,573
1997	561	0	561	6,410
1998	1,132	25	1,157	5,972
1999	1,882	230	2,112	4,122
2000	3,809	862	4,671	3,812
2001	1,868	381	2,249	4,257
2002	3,307	1,818	5,125	2,904
2003	2,889	689	3,578	3,676
2004	1,372	169	1,541	5,415
2005	4,245	1,458	5,703	4,643
2006	3,982	939	4,921	5,470
2007	2,592	973	3,565	4,819
2008[e]	1,604	398	2,002	5,468
2009[e]	3,191	na	3,191	3,014
201 0[e]	2,472	na	2,472	3,424
Sum: 1991-2010	41,292	9,194	50,486	95,559
Average: 1991-1999	1,107	167	1,274	5,406
Average: 2000-2010	2,852	854	3,547	4,264

Source: USDA, Farm Service Agency (FSA), Budget Division, History of Budgetary Expenditures of the Commodity Credit Corporation, Books 3 (April 9, 2001) and 4 (July 15, 2003); and FSA Budget Table No. 35, Aug. 25, 2009, available at http://www.fsa.usda.gov/FSA/webapp?area=about&subject=landing&topic=bap-bu-cc.

Note: na = not available. Data are for program outlays within the reported fiscal year. Payments may be specific to cotton from several different crop or marketing year.

a. The fiscal year starts Oct. 1 and ends Sept. 30 of the following year. Fiscal year identification is with the second year. For example, FY1993 starts Oct. 1, 1992, and runs through Sept. 30, 1993.

b. Production is valued at harvest-time prices. Each production value is for the crop harvested during the crop year preceding the designated fiscal year.

c. Includes deficiency payments, production flexibility contract payments, loan deficiency payments, user market payments (Step 2), marketing loss payments, outlays from general loan operations, and other miscellaneous payments.
d. Includes loan repayment write-offs (otherwise referred to as producer marketing loan gains) and certificate sales proceeds/losses, both of which are treated as non-cash transactions.
e. USDA estimate, Table 35, "CCC Net Outlays by Commodity and Function," August 25, 2008, available at http://www.fsa.usda.gov/FSA/webapp?area=about&subject=landing&topic=bap-bu-cc; and USDA FY20 10 Mid-Session Review, Commodity Estimates Book, August 25, 2009.

If the price triggers are set too far above market prices, they act as an incentive to encourage greater production (and exports) than what the market would otherwise demand. This results in lower prices than would exist in the absence of these programs. It is this "price effect" that was found by the WTO to cause adverse effects and serious prejudice in the international cotton market, as described below. Indeed, a comparison of relative support prices versus market prices for major U.S. program crops reveals that cotton producers receive payments under these programs far more routinely than do other crops.[10] This would suggest that cotton support prices are set too high relative to general cotton market conditions, as well as to other crop prices.

Export Credit Guarantee Programs

In 2002, at the time that Brazil first initiated the WTO case, the United States operated three principal export credit guarantee programs to facilitate the export of U.S. agricultural products (including but not limited to cotton). These were the GSM-102 program (which extended credit for periods ranging from 90 days to 3 years), the GSM- 103 program (which extended credit for periods of more than 3 years, but not more than 10 years) and the Supplier Credit Guarantee Program (SCGP). The GSM-103 and SCGP programs were part of Brazil's original case; however, they both were eliminated by congressional action in 2008, as described below.

The GSM- 102 export credit guarantee program (hereafter referred to as the GSM- 102 program) is authorized under the Agricultural Trade Act of 1978 (7 USC Sec. 5622), as amended. The program, backed by USDA's Commodity Credit Corporation (CCC), guarantees the repayment of credit made available to finance export sales of agricultural commodities on credit terms between 90 days and 3 years. Typically, 98% of principal and a portion of interest are covered by a guarantee. To obtain a guarantee, an exporter has to pay a fee (or "premium") calculated on the basis of guaranteed value, according to a schedule of rates applicable to different credit terms and repayment intervals. At the time that Brazil initiated DS267, the fee was capped by law at 1% of the guaranteed value.

PHASE II. BRAZIL'S WTO DISPUTE SETTLEMENT CASE AGAINST THE U.S. COTTON PROGRAM

In 2002, Brazil—a major cotton export competitor—expressed its growing concerns about U.S. cotton subsidies by initiating a WTO dispute settlement case (DS267) against certain features of the U.S. cotton program. Once initiated, a dispute settlement case follows a sequence of events designed to produce resolution of the dispute within a 12-15 month time frame. However, the WTO dispute settlement (DS) process that reviewed Brazil's charges against the U.S. cotton program has extended well beyond the hypothetical 15-month time frame. In this particular case, the initial WTO panel review took 17 months from the establishment of the panel in March 2003 to its final ruling in September 2004.

Furthermore, substantial additional time has since been added to the dispute settlement process— first, for an Appellate Body review of the initial ruling on appeal, then for a WTO compliance panel to review a dispute over U.S. compliance with the initial panel's ruling, and finally for an arbitrator to review a disagreement between Brazil and the United States over Brazil's proposed retaliation amounts. See Table 5 for a timeline of the dispute settlement case and related events.

With respect to the initial dispute settlement case, it was broadly written and touched on almost every aspect of U.S. commodity programs, although the focus was on the six principal claims described below along with the WTO dispute settlement panel finding (of September 8, 2004) and Appellate Body (AB) ruling (of March 3, 2005).[11]

Brazil's Six Principal Claims against U.S. Cotton Programs

Claim 1: Peace Clause Violation

Brazil claimed that the United States was no longer exempt from WTO dispute proceedings under the so-called "peace clause" (Article 13) of the WTO's Agreement on Agriculture (AA) because U.S. domestic and export subsidies to its cotton sector were in excess of its 1992 benchmark level.[12] Prior to its expiry in January of 2004, Article 13 exempted domestic support measures that complied with the AA's requirements from being challenged as illegal subsidies through dispute settlement proceedings, as long as the level of support for a commodity remained at or below the benchmark 1992 marketing year (MY) levels.[13] Brazil argued that U.S. cotton subsidies were about $2 billion in MY1 992 compared with over $4 billion in MY200 1. Therefore, Brazil argued that the United States was no longer in compliance with the requisite conditions and could no longer seek protection under the WTO's peace clause rule.

In response, U.S. trade officials argued that WTO members agreed to the peace clause recognizing that agricultural subsidies could not be eliminated immediately and needed, under certain conditions, to be exempted from the Subsidies and Countervailing Measures (SCM) Agreement and GATT 1994 subsidies disciplines. As a result, U.S. officials argued that the words "exempt from actions" as used in Article 13 of the AA were of overarching importance and precluded not only the "taking of legal steps to ... obtain a remedy," as Brazil has argued, but also the "taking of legal steps to establish a claim."[14] Furthermore, U.S. trade officials argued that the immunity granted by the peace clause was still important, since even if a country was no longer in compliance with the peace clause, it was incumbent on the complaining party to prove there had been injury. (See "Claim 5: U.S. Subsidies Have Caused "Serious Prejudice",'" below.)

Table 2. Comparison of U.S. Domestic Cotton Support in Accordance with Article 13(b)(ii)

$ million	MY1992	MY1999	MY2000	MY2001	MY2002
Total	$ 2,012.7	$ 3,404.4	$ 2,429.3	$ 4,144.2	$ 3,140.3

Source: *United States—Subsidies on Upland Cotton*, "Report of the Panel," WTO, WT/DS267/R, Sept. 8, 2004; p. 157.

Finding 1

The panel found (and was upheld by the AB in finding) that Brazil had successfully discharged its burden to show that U.S. domestic cotton support measures during MY1999-MY2002 (which averaged $3.28 billion) were in excess of WTO commitments (of $2.0 billion) during MY1992. (See **Table 2.**) As a result, U.S. domestic cotton support measures lost the protection afforded by the "Peace Clause," which had shielded them from substantive challenges in the past. This occurred in part because, under Finding 2, Production Flexibility Contract and Direct Payment outlays were included with other commodity program outlays and evaluated against "peace clause" limits.

Claim 2: U.S. Direct Payments Do Not Qualify for Exemption from Reduction Commitments as Decoupled Income Support

Brazil claimed that two types of U.S. payments—production flexibility contract (PFC) payments made under the 1996 farm bill and direct payments (DP) made under the 2002 farm bill—failed to fully meet the conditions for decoupled income support in Annex 2 of the Agreement on Agriculture and should therefore be counted against the U.S. "Peace Clause" domestic support benchmark limit.

The United States considers both PFC and DP programs to be consistent with WTO language for exempt domestic support that has "no, or at most minimal, trade-distorting effects or effects on production."[15] As a result, the United States notifies both the PFC and DP outlays as "green box" where they are not subject to any limits. Furthermore, the United States argued strongly against including such "minimally distorting, non-commodity specific" payments in evaluating whether the United States has met or exceeded its "peace clause" limits.

Finding 2

The panel found (and was upheld by the AB in finding) that U.S. payments made under the PFC and DP programs, because of the prohibition on planting fruits, vegetables, and wild rice on covered program acreage,[16] do not qualify for the WTO's green box category of domestic spending. (The green box contains only non-distorting program payments and is not subject to any limit). Instead, they should be counted as domestic subsidies directly affecting cotton production (i.e., distorting) and be included with other commodity program outlays to evaluate whether the United States has met or exceeded its "peace clause" limits.

Claim 3: The Step 2 Program Functions as an Export Subsidy

Brazil argued that Step 2 payments made under the U.S. cotton program functioned as export subsidies and were inconsistent with U.S. WTO obligations regarding export subsidies as specified under the SCM Agreement.

Step 2 payments were part of special cotton marketing provisions authorized under U.S. farm program legislation to keep U.S. upland cotton competitive on the world market.[17] Step 2 payments were made to exporters and domestic mill users to compensate them for their purchase of higher priced U.S. upland cotton. Under the 2002 farm act, the Step 2 payment rate for the 2002-2005 marketing years was calculated as the difference between the price of U.S. upland cotton, delivered c.i.f. (cost, insurance, freight) in Northern Europe, and the average of the five lowest prices of upland cotton delivered c.i.f. Northern Europe from any source.[18]

The United States argued that Step 2 payments were part of its domestic support program since they were targeted to domestic cotton users as well as exporters. As a result, Step 2 payments were notified to the WTO as "amber" box (trade-distorting) domestic support payments and not as export subsidies. Consequently, U.S. trade officials contended that Step 2 payments were not subject to any limitations placed on export subsidies.

Finding 3

In its finding, the panel considered Step 2 program payments to eligible exporters separately from payments to domestic users.

- Payments to exporters were found to be "contingent upon export performance" and therefore qualified as prohibited export subsidies in violation of WTO commitments.
- Payments to domestic users were found to be "contingent on the use of domestic over imported goods" and therefore qualified as prohibited import substitution subsidies.

The DS panel finding was upheld by the AB.

Claim 4. U.S. Export Credit Guarantees Function as Export Subsidies

Brazil argued that the U.S. GSM-102 program operated as a prohibited export subsidy under item (j) of Annex I of the Agreement on Subsidies and Countervailing Measures (SCM) because the premium rates (i.e., fees) charged to GSM-102 program beneficiaries were inadequate to cover the long-term operating costs of the program, thus imparting an implicit subsidy benefit.

Item (j) of Annex I identifies a prohibited export subsidy as:

> [t]he provision by governments (or special institutions controlled by governments) of export credit guarantee or insurance programs, of insurance or guarantee programs against increases in the cost of exported products or of exchange risk programs, at premium rates which are inadequate to cover the long term operating costs and losses of the programs.[19]

Brazil claimed that the favorable terms (i.e., the interest rate and time period that countries have to pay back the financing) provided under U.S. export credit guarantee programs—GSM-102, GSM-103, and the Supplier Credit Guarantee Program (SCGP)[20]—were effectively export subsidies inconsistent with the WTO's AA and SCM Agreements. Further, the subsidy effects of export credit guarantees applied not only to cotton, but to other eligible commodities.[21]

U.S. trade officials argued that the U.S. export credit guarantee programs were consistent with WTO obligations. Furthermore, the United States asserted that Article 10.2 of the AA reflected the deferral of disciplines on export credit guarantee programs contemplated by WTO members to the next WTO multilateral negotiating round—the Doha Round.

Finding 4

The panel found (and was upheld by the AB in finding) that U.S. export credit guarantees effectively functioned as export subsidies because the financial benefits returned by these programs failed to cover their long-run operating cost as specified by item (j) of the SCM. Furthermore, the panel found that this applied, not just to cotton, but to all commodities that benefit from U.S. commodity support programs and receive export credit guarantees. As a result, export credit guarantees for any recipient commodity were subject to previously scheduled export subsidy commitments for that commodity. This referred to those U.S. export subsidies under the Export Enhancement Program (EEP) and the Dairy Export Incentive Program (DEIP).[22] Under these criteria, export credit guarantees benefits extended to cotton and other "unscheduled" commodities (that are supported under U.S. agricultural programs) were found to be in violation of previous WTO commitments.[23] With respect to "scheduled" commodities, export credit guarantees extended to U.S. rice exports were found to be in violation of previous EEP volume commitments. The panel found (and was upheld by the AB) that "unscheduled" commodities not supported under U.S. agricultural programs, as well as scheduled agricultural products that remain within WTO commitments are exempt from actions under this dispute settlement case.

Claim 5: U.S. Subsidies Have Caused "Serious Prejudice"

Brazil argued that domestic farm subsidies provided to U.S. cotton growers contributed to significant overproduction and resulted in a surge in U.S. cotton exports, particularly during the 1999-2002 marketing years, when unusually large outlays were made under provisions of the U.S. cotton program (see Table 1 and Figure 1). Brazil claimed that the resultant rise in U.S. exports led to three market conditions, each of which contributed to serious injury to Brazilian cotton exporters: (1) an increase in the U.S. share of the world upland cotton market; (2) a displacement of Brazilian upland cotton sales in third-country markets; and (3) a steep decline in world cotton prices (see Figure 2 and Figure 3).[24]

In particular, Brazil claimed that injury to its economy due to low cotton prices, measured as the sum of individual negative impacts on income, foreign trade revenue, fiscal revenues, related services (transportation and ginning), and employment, exceeded $600 million in 2001 alone. Brazil asserted that injury under each of these three circumstances are in violation of the SCM Agreement.[25] In addition, Brazil argued that these same programs would be harmful (i.e., threatened serious prejudice) in future years.

U.S. trade officials argued that the subsidies provided to U.S. cotton growers have been within the allowable WTO limits and are consistent with U.S. WTO obligations. Furthermore, they argued that the decline in U.S. domestic use (due to declining U.S. competitiveness in textile and apparel production), rather than government support program outlays, contributed to larger U.S. raw cotton exports. In addition, they contended that international market forces—including weakness in world demand for cotton due to competing, low-priced synthetic fibers, and weak world economic growth—have played a larger role in determining the generally weak price level during the period in question, rather than U.S. export levels. For example, see Figure 4 for a visibly strong correlation between China cotton imports and the international cotton "A-index."

In evaluating this particular claim, the DS panel separated U.S. cotton support programs into two groups: those that are directly contingent on market price levels (i.e., loan deficiency payments, marketing loss assistance payments, counter-cyclical payments, and Step 2 payments), and those that are not (i.e., PFC and Direct Payments, and the federal crop insurance program).

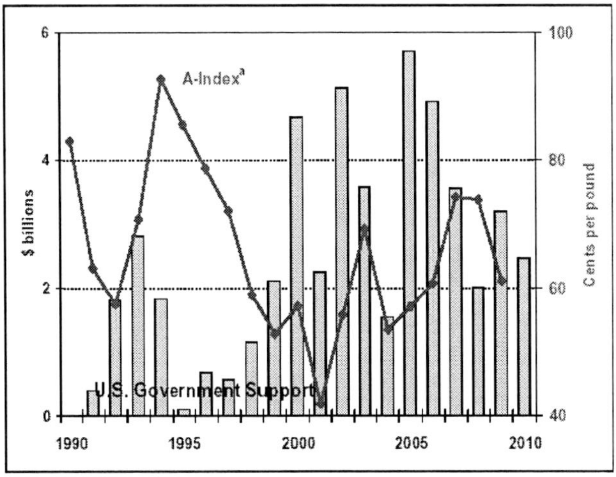

Source: USDA, FSA budget data (cash and non-cash support).

Note: Data for 2009 and 2010 are forecasts.

a. The A-index is an average of the five lowest priced types of 1-3/32 inch staple length cotton offered on the European market from 1990 through 2008, and in Far East markets in 2009.

Figure 2. USDA Cotton Support, 1992 to 2010

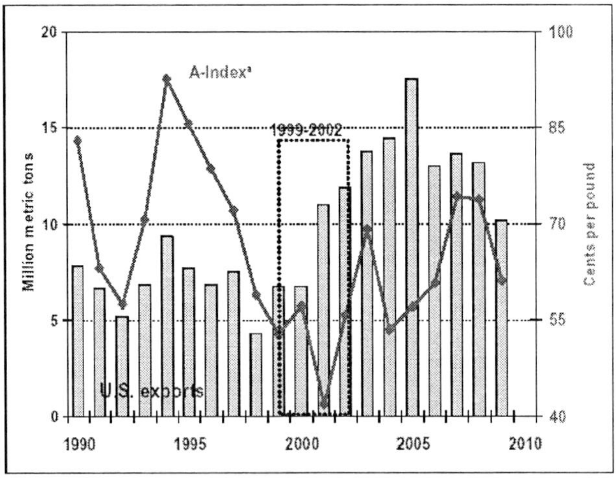

Source: USDA, PSD online data base, August 12, 2009.

a. The A-index is an average of the five lowest priced types of 1-3/32 inch staple length cotton offered on the European market from 1990 through 2008, and in Far East markets in 2009.

Figure 3. U.S. Cotton Exports and International Cotton Price Index

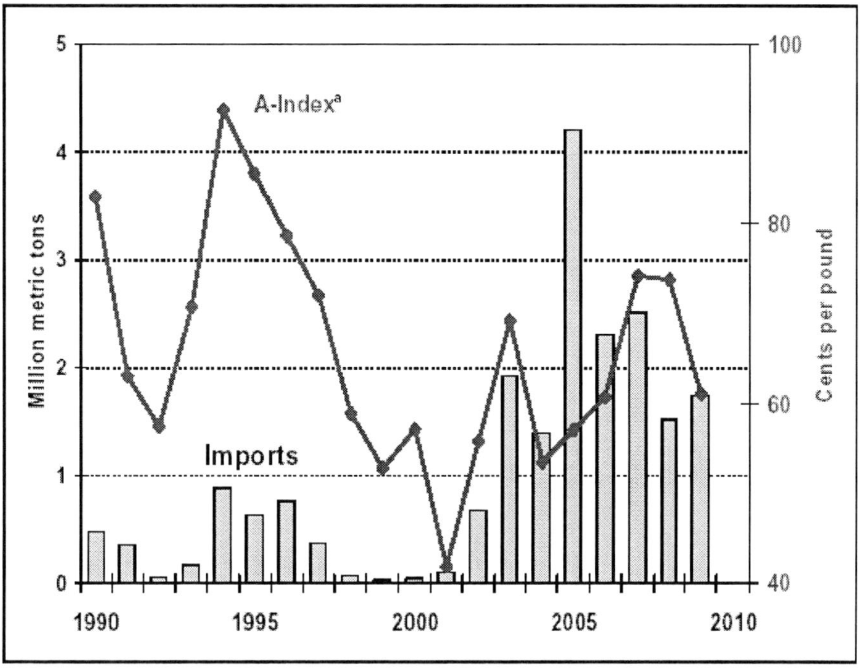

Source: USDA, PSD online data base, August 12, 2009.

a. The A-index is an average of the five lowest priced types of 1-3/32 inch staple length cotton offered on the European market from 1990 through 2008, and in Far East markets in 2009.

Figure 4. China Cotton Imports and International Cotton Price Index

Finding 5

The panel found (and was upheld by the AB in finding) that U.S. domestic support measures that are directly contingent on market price levels caused serious prejudice in terms of market price suppression for the period 1999 to 2002. However, U.S. domestic support measures that are not contingent on market price levels were not included in this finding as the panel could not find enough of a connection between the direct payments program and cotton planting decisions to declare the direct payments program a serious factor in price suppression.[26]

The panel also did not find in favor of Brazil's alleged serious prejudice in terms of an effect on international market share. Article 6.3 of the SCM lists several factors indicating serious prejudice; the panel only had to find one of the factors in violation to rule in Brazil's favor on the claim of serious prejudice during the 1999 to 2002 period.

With respect to Brazil's claim of a threat of serious prejudice going forward (2003 to 2007, the remaining life of the 2002 farm act), the panel stated in its final report that those "prohibited" subsidies that caused serious prejudice during the 1 999-to-2002 period—namely, user marketing (Step 2) payments to exporters and domestic users; and export credit guarantees in respect of certain products under the GSM-102, GSM-103, and SCGP programs—must be withdrawn "without delay" pursuant to Article 4.7 of the SCM Agreement.[27] According to the panel, required withdrawal of the prohibited subsidies, within the time frame set by the panel, would curtail the future threat posed by U.S. cotton support programs. As a result, the panel stated that "it is not necessary or appropriate to address Brazil's claims of threat of serious prejudice."[28]

Claim 6: FSC-ETI Act of 2000 Acts as an Export Subsidy to Upland Cotton

Brazil claimed that the Foreign Sales Corporation Repeal and Extraterritorial Income Act of 2000 (ETI Act of 2000), by eliminating tax liabilities for U.S. upland cotton exporters who sell to foreign markets, constitutes an export subsidy and is inconsistent with U.S. export subsidy commitments for cotton.

The United States asserted throughout the proceedings that Brazil failed to make any specific case with respect to the ETI Act of 2000 and U.S. upland cotton exports.

Finding 6

The panel concurred with the United States (and was upheld by the AB) in stating that Brazil failed to present any new arguments or evidence concerning effects upon upland cotton, but instead simply repeated the arguments that the European Union made in its WTO dispute settlement case with the United States (DS 108).[29] As a result, the panel declined to further examine Brazil's claims on this particular issue.

Panel and Appellate Body Recommendations

The initial panel's final ruling was released publicly on September 8, 2004. The following month (October 18, 2004) the United States notified the WTO of its intent to appeal the panel's ruling. A WTO Appellate Body (AB) reviewed the legality of the case and issued its final report on March 3, 2005, upholding most of the initial panel's rulings. The policy recommendations that emerged from the panel and AB rulings are described below.

Prohibited Subsidies

The AB recommended that the United States withdraw those support programs identified as prohibited subsidies within six months of the date of adoption of the panel report by the Dispute Settlement Body (DSB) or by July 1, 2005 (whichever was earlier).[30] Since the DSB adopted the AB and panel reports on March 21, 2005, the relevant deadline for withdrawal was July 1, 2005. The list of prohibited subsidies subject to withdrawal "without delay" included the following.

Prohibited Export Subsidies

- Export credit guarantees under GSM-102, GSM-103, and SCGP that assist exports of upland cotton and other unscheduled agricultural products that are supported under government agricultural support programs.
- Export credit guarantees under GSM-102, GSM-103, and SCGP that assist exports of one scheduled agricultural product (rice), but in excess of the scheduled volume.
- Step 2 program payments to exporters of upland cotton.

Prohibited Import Substitution Subsidy

- Step 2 payments to domestic users of upland cotton.

In contrast, unscheduled agricultural products not supported under government agricultural support programs and scheduled agricultural product exports that remain within their schedules were judged not to circumvent U.S. export commitments and therefore were not subject to trade remedy actions in this case.

Actionable Subsidies

The panel recommended that the United States take appropriate steps by September 21, 2005, to remove the adverse effects or to withdraw those U.S. subsidy measures singled out as pricecontingent—marketing loan provisions, Step 2 payments, and CCP payments. These subsidies were identified as "actionable" subsidies that contributed adverse effects to the interests of Brazil during the marketing years 1999-2002.

It is noteworthy that the actionable subsidies remedy dealt with adverse effects that occurred during a historical time period and not future prejudice or injury. In support of this concept, the panel stated (in its original ruling on the "threat of serious prejudice" by actionable subsidies) that U.S. compliance with recommendations on prohibited subsidies—the Step 2 provisions and export credit guarantees—could so significantly transform the basket of measures in question that it was not necessary or appropriate to address Brazil's claims of threat of serious prejudice.[31] This appeared to leave open the possibility that removal of the prohibited subsidies might resolve the dispute under the actionable subsidies recommendation.

Implementation of Panel/Appellate Body Recommendations[32]

Following is a discussion of how the implementation phase was to unfold in accordance with WTO rules and how the actual implementation has unfolded.

In accordance with WTO rules, the evolution of the implementation phase depends on how both parties choose to respond to the different sequences of events as they unfold. In addition to the potential time tracks described below, the implementation phase also provides opportunities for the disputing parties to mutually resolve the dispute. If the United States failed to comply, Brazil could (upon visible evidence of noncompliance) request negotiations with the United States to determine mutually acceptable compensation (e.g., tariff reductions in areas of particular interest). Furthermore, if Brazil did not want to press ahead full force with imposing sanctions, there would be considerable opportunity to delay compliance steps.

The time track for compliance with panel and AB recommendations could diverge depending on whether the United States chose to respond separately to the rulings on prohibited subsidies and actionable subsidies. This is because prohibited subsidies are given expedited treatment under SCM, Article 4.12, which states that, "except for time-periods specifically prescribed in [SCM,

Article 4], time-periods applicable under the DSU for the conduct of such disputes shall be half the time prescribed therein."

Prohibited Subsidies Potential Time Track

As a result of their expedited treatment, the AB recommended that the United States remove the prohibited export subsidies by July 1, 2005. Within 15 days after the AB and panel reports were adopted by the DSB (done on March 21, 2005),[33] the United States was expected to present an implementation plan to the DSB, although precedence suggests that such a plan could be as minimal as stating intentions to work with Congress to bring U.S. policies into compliance. This was indeed the case when, on April 20, the U.S. representative to the WTO announced that the United States intended to implement the recommendations and rulings of the DSB in a manner that respected U.S. WTO obligations.[34] The representative noted, however, that determining acceptable options would take a reasonable period of time and requested that Brazil be willing to consult on the potential timetable.

If, 10 days after the designated period (July 1, 2005) expires, no satisfactory compensation is agreed to, the complaining side (Brazil) may ask the DSB for permission to impose limited trade sanctions against the United States.[35] The trade sanctions are limited to a value equivalent to no more than the level of nullification or impairment of benefits. The DSB must grant this authorization within 15 days of expiry of the "reasonable" time period unless a consensus exists against the request.[36]

If the United States objects to the amount proposed by Brazil, the level of suspension would be arbitrated (by the original panel if available). Arbitration shall be completed within 30 days after the date of expiry of the designated period (July 1, 2005).[37] No trade sanctions are to be imposed during the arbitration period.

Once armed with the authority to impose trade sanctions, Brazil could still choose to wait. A precedent for this occurred under the WTO dispute settlement case (DS108) involving the U.S. Foreign Sales Corporation Statute. Under DS108, the European Communities (EC) requested and received authorization to impose retaliatory measures against the United States on May 7, 2003.[38] However, the EC refrained from immediate action, stating that it would review U.S. actions for a period of time before proceeding. The EC eventually began imposing additional duties on U.S. products in March 2004.

Actionable Subsidies Potential Time Track

In contrast to the July 1, 2005, deadline, the removal of actionable subsidies was subject to a six- month period starting on the date of adoption of the AB and panel reports (March 21, 2005).[39] As a result, the panel recommended that, upon adoption of its final report, the United States take appropriate steps to remove the adverse effects or to withdraw those subsidies identified as contributing to serious prejudice to the interests of Brazil—marketing loan provisions, Step 2 payments, and CCP payments—by September 21, 2005. Thus, in every other respect, the timetable for actionable subsidies would follow the same sequence of events listed above for prohibited subsidies, but subject to the full time allotment for each event as described in the preceding footnotes rather than the "halved" time periods.

U.S. Compliance Actions

A spokesperson for the Office of the U.S. Trade Representative (USTR) expressed disappointment in the AB ruling, but also said that USTR would study the AB report carefully and work closely with Congress and U.S. farmers on its next steps.[40] However, U.S. officials said that they preferred to resolve the cotton case through trade negotiations in the WTO Doha Round rather than a separate settlement.[41] The National Cotton Council (NCC) of America—the principal national organization representing the interests of U.S. producers, ginners, warehousers, merchants, cottonseed processors/dealers, cooperatives and textile manufacturers—also expressed disappointment in the AB ruling, but stated that it would work with USTR and USDA to coordinate a response to the decision.[42]

On July 1, 2005, USDA instituted a temporary fix for its export credit guarantee programs, whereby the Commodity Credit Corporation (CCC) would use a risk-based fee structure for the GSM-102 and SCGP programs. The new structure responded to a key finding by the WTO that the fees charged by the programs should be risk-based. The 1% cap on user fees for GSM- 102, the primary export credit program, was cited by the DS panel as contributing to the subsidy component of the GSM program. Higher fees would ensure that the financial benefits returned by these programs would fully cover their long-run operating costs, and eliminate the subsidy component. USDA could not remove the cap administratively as it is required by statute (7 U.S.C. 5641). In addition, the CCC stopped accepting applications for payment guarantees under GSM- 103.

On August 1, 2006, the Step 2 cotton program, which was authorized by the 2002 farm act (P.L. 107-171, Section 1207), was eliminated by a provision (Section 1103) in the Deficit Reduction Act of 2005 (P.L. 109-171).

On June 18, 2008, the date of enactment of the 2008 farm bill (P.L. 110-246), a provision (Sec. 3101(a)) in the Trade title (Title III) eliminated the GSM-103 and SCGP programs, and removed the 1% cap on fees that can be charged under the GSM- 102 program. In addition, the same 2008 farm bill provision explicitly requires the Secretary of Agriculture, in carrying out the GSM-102 program, to "work with the industry to ensure, to the maximum extent practicable, that risk-based fees associated with the guarantees cover, but do not exceed, the operating costs and losses over the long-term."

However, the 2008 farm bill defined the "long-term" as a period of 10 or more years. While the WTO panel did not explicitly define its view of the "long-term," it clearly is less than 10 years and more likely is on the order of a period of two years—that is, a net loss in one year must be offset by a net gain in the following year.

At this point the Administration likely felt that sufficient program changes had been enacted to fully comply with the both the prohibited and actionable subsidies portions of the WTO ruling.

PHASE III. WTO COMPLIANCE PANEL REVIEW AND RULING

This section describes Brazil's charges of noncompliance, the proposed retaliation, the beginning of WTO arbitration over the size and nature of the proposed retaliation, and a ruling by a WTO compliance panel reviewing whether the U.S. had fully complied with earlier recommendations.

Arbitration Requested, Then Suspended, Over Brazil's Proposed Retaliation Amounts

As the reform deadlines under the two different subsidy types expired, Brazil first requested (July 4, 2005) authorization from the WTO to impose $3 billion in countermeasures against the prohibited U.S. subsidies. According to WTO rules, trade sanctions are limited to a value not to exceed the level of lost benefits. The $3 billion value corresponded to (1) Step 2 payments made in the then-most-recently-concluded marketing year (2004/2005) and (2) the total of exporter applications received under the three export credit guarantee programs, for all unscheduled commodities and for rice, for the then-most-recent fiscal year (2004).[43] This amount was later pared back to $1.1 55 billion in annual retaliation to counter the prohibited subsidies based on Brazil's methodology applied to FY2006 data.[44] The United States objected to the amount of Brazil's proposed sanctions and requested WTO arbitration.[45] However, on August 18, 2005, the United States and Brazil reached a procedural agreement temporarily suspending arbitration proceedings concerning the prohibited subsidies.[46]

Then, as the September 21, 2005, deadline to address the actionable subsidy ruling expired, Brazil charged that the United States had neither taken nor announced any specific initiative for the price-contingent programs deemed to cause adverse effects to Brazil's trade interest. Brazil then requested authorization from the WTO to impose countermeasures valued at $1 .037 billion as retaliation against the actionable programs. According to WTO rules, trade retaliation should take place within the sector where the violation occurred. In this case, retaliation would be restricted to punitive tariffs on U.S. goods entering Brazil. However, Brazil argued that limiting retaliation to the goods sector alone would have a more deleterious effect on the Brazilian economy (via higher input costs) and Brazilian consumers (via higher inflation) than on U.S. exporters due to the asymmetries between the two economies.[47] Instead, Brazil proposed to suspend tariff concessions as well as obligations under the WTO Agreement on Trade-Related Intellectual Property Rights (TRIPS) and the General Agreement on Trade in Services (GATS) in the amount of $1.307 billion until the United States withdrew the four domestic subsidies (counter-cyclical payments, market loss assistance payments, market loan program benefits, and Step 2 payments) or removed their adverse effects. This type of "cross-retaliation" has been permitted twice previously in WTO dispute settlement cases, so it is not without precedent. However, its impact is potentially very far-ranging and could include the protection of copyrights, trademarks, industrial designs, patents, and undisclosed information, as well as withdrawal of concessions in services related to communication, construction, distribution, finance, tourism, and transport.[48]

Once again, the United States objected to both the amount and nature of Brazil's proposed request and asked for WTO arbitration over the level of the proposed sanctions (October 18, 2005).[49] Again, the United States and Brazil reached a procedural agreement (December 7, 2005), thereby temporarily suspending further retaliation proceedings on the actionable subsidies.[50]

The suspensions were likely intended to permit policy reform to occur in a less confrontational forum under either the then-ongoing congressional debate on an extension or revision of U.S. farm legislation (as current farm law was set to expire in 2007) or the ongoing Doha negotiations.

Brazil Requests WTO Compliance Panel

Initially Brazil showed a willingness to permit the U.S. legislative process—motivated by the 2007 expiration of U.S. farm programs and the prospects of a successful Doha Round of trade negotiations[51]—to bring U.S. farm programs into compliance with the WTO ruling, even if this process extended well beyond the deadlines established under the WTO dispute settlement ruling. However, Brazil argued that U.S. program changes were insufficient and, on August 21, 2006, requested the establishment of a WTO compliance panel to review whether the United States had fully complied with panel and AB rulings.

Brazil identified below-market premium rates (i.e., user fees) charged to GSM-102 program beneficiaries as the primary reason that the revised GSM-102 program operated at a net loss and was still out of compliance with WTO rules. The WTO Compliance Panel (upheld on appeal) concurred with Brazil, after an examination of new evidence on GSM- 102 operations for the 2006-2008 period showing that it continued to operate at a net loss. See Table 3 for the most recent estimates of credit subsidies under CCC export credit guarantee programs.

The GSM- 102 premium rates were identified as below-market rates, in part, because they failed to fully account for the risk of non-payment or default for individual countries. There is no widely accepted international standard for determining country risk and assigning "market" premium rates. In its determination, the Compliance Panel used a list of "minimum premium rates" as reported in the Organization for Economic Cooperation and Development (OECD) *Arrangement on Officially Supported Export Credits.*[52] A comparison with premium rates charged under the GSM- 102 program found the GSM-102 rates to be significantly below the OECD measures, suggesting that they were under-valued.

Table 3. Estimated Credit Subsidies on CCC Export Credit Guarantees

Fiscal Year	Budget Loss ($ millions)
2001	$1,410
2002	—
2003	$ 13
2004	$ 230
2005	$ 205
2006	$ 366
2007	$ 232
2008	$ 225
2009	$ 39
Average	**$ 302**

Source: President's FY2011 Budget, *Analytic Perspectives*, "Special Topics," Table 22-3, "Re-estimates of credit subsidies on loans disbursed between 1992-2009," p. 366, available at http://www.whitehouse.gov/omb/budget/fy2011 /assets/topics .pdf.

In addition, Brazil charged that U.S. farm programs continued to provide significant (and injurious) support to U.S. cotton producers (Table 1 and Table 4).

WTO Compliance Panel Rules against the United States

Following Brazil's request, the WTO's Dispute Settlement Body (DSB) agreed to establish a compliance panel to review U.S. farm program changes at the September 28, 2006, DSB meeting.

On July 27, 2007, the compliance panel released a confidential interim ruling to the two countries that the United States had not fully complied with the March 2005 WTO ruling against certain U.S. cotton support programs. On October 15, 2007, the compliance panel's final report was released confidentially to the U.S. and Brazilian governments and, two months later on December 18, 2007, it was released publicly. The panel's final ruling confirmed the earlier interim ruling against the United States.

In February 2008, the United States appealed the compliance panel's ruling. On June 2, 2008, a WTO Appellate Body (AB) publicly released its final report upholding the compliance panel's ruling that the United States had not fully complied with the March 2005 WTO ruling. The AB report was adopted by the WTO's Dispute Settlement Body on June 25, 2008.

PHASE IV. WTO ARBITRATION OF BRAZIL'S PROPOSED COUNTERMEASURES

Brazil Requests Resumption of Arbitration

On August 25, 2008, Brazil requested a resumption of the arbitration proceedings to review its proposed retaliatory countermeasures. On October 1, 2008, Brazil and the United States agreed on the arbitration panelists, who then were to produce a ruling within 60 days. However, the arbitration review continued past the normally allotted 60 days and into 2009. During that period, both parties made written submissions to the WTO arbitrator stating their positions with respect to retaliation in this case.[53]

Brazil Alters Its Countermeasure Request

At a March 3, 2009, Dispute Settlement Body meeting, Brazil revised its total retaliation request to $2.5 billion, down from an earlier $3 billion request. Brazil's proposed sanctions total comprised both prohibited and actionable subsidy countermeasure components.

Under the prohibited subsidies arbitration case, Brazil was seeking two countermeasures:

1. a one-time countermeasure in relation to the Step 2 program of $350 million based on U.S. government payments made under the Step 2 program in marketing year 2005 (this corresponds roughly to the period that elapsed between the expiration of the prohibited subsidy compliance period on July 1, 2005, and the effective repeal of the Step 2 program by the U.S. Congress on August 1, 2006); and
2. annual countermeasures proportionate to the entire annual amount of GSM 102 export credit guarantees issued to all countries for export transactions involving unscheduled products—rice, pork, and poultry—valued at $1.1 55 billion during FY2006 (initially Brazil

valued this countermeasure at $1 .294 million) and composed of three parts:

a. an interest rate subsidy component amounting to $234.7 million;
b. the additional export sales obtained by the United States as a result of these discounts, including sales to creditworthy foreign obligors, referred to as marginal additionality and valued at $62.3 million; and
c. the additional export sales to noncreditworthy foreign obligors, referred to as full additionality and valued at $855 million.

Under the actionable subsidies arbitration case, Brazil again asked for:

3. annual countermeasures valued at $1.037 billion until the United States withdrew the relevant subsidies or removed their adverse effects (based on marketing year 2005 data, Brazil calculated the amount of adverse effects on the rest of the world at $3.335 billion, although it only requested countermeasures of $1.037 billion).

Under the combined prohibited and actionable subsidy cases, Brazil asked for:

4. the right to engage in cross-retaliation (i.e., countermeasures in sectors outside of the trade in goods, most notably in the area of U.S. copyrights and patents, as well as services), stating that retaliation in goods would not be practicable or effective due to limited trade in goods between Brazil and the United States.

The United States argued that it had removed the prohibited subsidy component of its export credit program via provision 3101(a) of the 2008 farm bill (P.L. 110-246). Furthermore, the United States argued that it had operated its remaining GSM- 102 export credit program at "no net cost" to the government since 2005.[54] The United States asked the arbitrators to dismiss all claims related to prohibited subsidies since they currently operated at "no net cost" to the government. Furthermore, the United States argued that Brazil's prohibited-subsidy countermeasure request continued to include a program that no longer exists (i.e., Step 2). Finally, with respect to Brazil's actionable-subsidy countermeasure request, the United States pointed out that Brazil included a calculation for the entire global adverse effect, not just those adverse effects relevant to Brazil. According to U.S. calculations, the total effects of U.S. counter-cyclical payments and marketing loan payments on Brazil during the 2005-2007 period averaged $30.4 million per year.[55]

Arbitration Panel Ruling

On August 31, 2009, the arbitrator ruled on Brazil's arbitration requests in two separate reports.[56] The first report (WT/DS267/ARB/1) ruled on Brazil's retaliation requests regarding the prohibited subsidies—the Step 2 cotton program and the GSM 102 program (under certain conditions)—based on Article 4.11 of the SCM Agreement. The second report (WT/DS267/ARB/2) ruled on Brazil's retaliation requests regarding the actionable subsidies—market loss assistance payments, marketing loan benefits, counter-cyclical payments (CCP), and Step 2 payments—based on Article 7.9 of the SCM Agreement. The arbitrator's decisions are final and are not subject to appeal.

With respect to the four main countermeasure requests, the arbitrator issued four key findings, discussed below.

First Finding

Brazil was not entitled to its request of a one-time $350 million retaliation award to compensate for previous Step 2 injury. In rejecting Brazil's request on this point the arbitrator stated that countermeasures are an exceptional temporary remedy, available only where compliance has not been achieved, and aimed at inducing such compliance, and that in fact the United States had fully (albeit belatedly) complied with the panel's recommendation to eliminate the Step 2 program.

Second Finding

With respect to Brazil's request for $1.1 55 billion in countermeasures related to the "prohibited" subsidies, the arbitrator found that Brazil was only entitled to retaliate for the effects of these subsidies on Brazilian products and not for their full effect on the rest of the world (ROW). The arbitrator used Brazil's share of world exports of those products receiving GSM 102 credit guarantees (estimated to be 11.7% in 2006) to apportion Brazil's share of the subsidy effect from the entire global market effect. With this revision to Brazil's formula, the arbitrator estimated the countermeasure at $147.4 million in FY2006—comprising an interest rate effect of $25.27 million, marginal additionality of $41.3 million, and full additionality of $80.8 million.

Furthermore, the arbitrator ruled that the retaliatory amount accorded Brazil would vary each year (via formula) based on the total of exporter applications received by the U.S. government under the GSM 102 program for the most recently concluded fiscal year. The formula would consider an interest rate subsidy component and the trade displacement additionality (both full and marginal) of the subsidy component of GSM 102.

Third Finding

The arbitrator found that the amount of countermeasures specific to Brazil and commensurate with the degree and nature of adverse effects resulting from the actionable subsidies was fixed at an annual amount of $147.3 million. This figure was obtained, first, by a recalculation of the total adverse effects on the ROW resulting from the actionable subsidies, to an amount of $2.905 billion in the 2005 marketing year. The adverse effect was calculated as a price effect whereby it was determined that the world price of cotton would have been 9.38 cents per pound higher in the absence of U.S. marketing loan benefits and CCP payments, and that the lower world price resulted in both lost income effects in the ROW of $2.384 billion and reduced production effects of $521.5 billion, for a total of $2.905 billion. However, the WTO arbitrator determined that Brazil should be entitled to retaliation on only a specific portion of the $2.905 billion. The share apportioned to Brazil was based on Brazil's share of cotton production in the ROW in marketing year 2005, which equaled 5.1% or $147.3 million. Furthermore, the panel fixed Brazil's maximum annual retaliation with respect to the "actionable" U.S. subsidies at this same $147.3 million (in other words, this amount will not vary from year to year).

Thus, the overall annual permissible retaliation amount for 2006 was $294.7 billion. Furthermore, this amount varies annually, since it consists of both a fixed retaliatory amount in response to "actionable" U.S. subsidies, and a variable retaliatory amount in response to "prohibited" U.S. subsidies.

Fourth Finding

Finally, Brazil had requested the right to engage in cross-retaliation, that is, retaliatory countermeasures in sectors outside of the trade in goods, most notably in the area of intellectual property (IP) rights such as copyrights and patents. A key determinant in ruling on this request was Brazil's contention that there is insufficient trade in consumer goods with the United States to permit compensatory retaliatory action, and that a substantial portion of those imports were of critical importance to Brazil's economy such that punitive sanctions on them would harm Brazil's economy. However, the panel felt that a certain percentage of Brazil's imports of consumer goods originating from the United States should be eligible for countermeasures without causing harm to Brazil's economy because there was available to Brazil a sufficient amount of alternate sources of imports or of sufficiently close substitutes in consumption so as to avoid economic harm. As a result, the panel ruled that Brazil would be entitled to cross-retaliation, if (and only if) the overall retaliation amount (combining both the variable and fixed components) to which it would otherwise be entitled exceeds a variable annual threshold (described below). If the threshold is surpassed, then Brazil would be entitled to suspend certain obligations under the TRIPS Agreement and/or the GATS in the amount in excess of the threshold.

Threshold for Permitting Cross-Retaliation Countermeasures

For purposes of determining eligibility to apply cross-retaliation, the panel established an initial threshold amount of $409.7 million that could be subject to countermeasures without harming Brazil's economy based on the volume and composition of Brazil's imports of consumer goods in the year 2007. The amount of $409.7 million represents the sum of the value of those consumer goods imported by Brazil where the U.S. share is less than 20%, excluding books and automotive parts which are considered essential to Brazil's economy.

The threshold amount may vary from year to year according to the following formula:

$$T_{t+1} = T_t * (1 + g_{t+1}) \qquad \text{where } T_{2007} = \$409.7 \text{ million}$$

where

T_{t+1} = threshold value in year t+1

T_t = threshold value in year t

g_{t+1} = percentage change in the value of Brazil's total imports from the United States between years t and t+1.

Brazil's Reaction

Following the arbitration panel's ruling, Brazil claimed that application of the panel's countermeasure determination formulas to preliminary 2009 data would allow for $800 million in total retaliation, including both the fixed $147.3 million of actionable subsidy countermeasures and $650 million of prohibited subsidy countermeasures.[57] The $650 million figure resulted from expanded use of GSM 102 credit guarantees by the United States during the recent fiscal year— rising from $1.36 billion in FY2006 to $5.5 million in FY2009.[58] According to Brazil, using 2009 data to calculate the threshold for cross-retaliation would produce an amount of $460 million. If confirmed, these data would suggest that Brazil would be authorized to engage in cross-retaliation equal to $340 million (i.e., the difference between $800 million and $460 million) by suspending commitments it made under the WTO concerning the protection of intellectual property and services.

U.S. Reaction

USTR spokeswoman Carol Guthrie issued the following statement:[59]

> While we remain disappointed with the outcome of this dispute, we are pleased that the Arbitrators awarded Brazil far below the amount of countermeasures it asked for. In its first requests for countermeasures in the Cotton dispute, Brazil asked for more than $4 billion in annual countermeasures. During the arbitration proceedings, Brazil argued for more than $2 billion annually. Further, we are grateful that the Arbitrators denied Brazil's request for unlimited ability to suspend concessions on intellectual property or services. And we are pleased that the Arbitrators denied Brazil's request for an additional one-time $350 million in countermeasures in connection with the repealed Step 2 payment program for cotton.
>
> At this time, we do not know when or if Brazil will move to obtain final authorization to suspend concessions or when or if Brazil would act on any such authorization.
>
> The Administration will be actively consulting within the U.S. Government and with stakeholders on how to move forward.

U.S. industry groups, led by the National Cotton Council (NCC), argued that substantial changes had been made to the GSM 102 programs since the initial WTO dispute settlement panel issued its ruling in 2005 and that, as a consequence of those changes, the GSM 102 program now operates in a fully WTO-compliant manner.[60] Similarly, the NCC argued that changes under the 2008 farm bill (P.L. 110-246) to the marketing loan and CCP programs had made them more WTO-compliant. Finally, the NCC complained that the WTO arbitration ruling was based almost entirely on 2005 data, when U.S. cotton support programs were at their peak and the U.S. share of the world cotton market was near 40%, compared with about 12% today.[61]

As a result of these changed circumstances, the NCC and other U.S. farm groups publicly stated that USTR should seek the establishment of a new

WTO compliance panel in order to prove that U.S. cotton subsidy programs and export credit programs no longer violate WTO rules. However, in accordance with WTO rules, even if the United States were to initiate such a new compliance panel, Brazil would be able to proceed with its WTO-authorized retaliation.

PHASE V. RETALIATION

The arbitrator's decisions are final and are not subject to appeal, and Brazil has complete freedom to decide which products will be subject to retaliatory hikes in import tariffs and which IP and services rights may be targeted by supplementary countermeasures.[62] However, before Brazil could proceed with any retaliation, it first had to request the WTO Dispute Settlement Body to authorize its retaliation request in an amount, and with respect to types of trade, consistent with these decisions. Following the circulation of the arbitrator's decisions on August 31, 2009, Brazil accordingly submitted requests to the DSB to authorize the suspension of concessions or other obligations (WT/DS267/41 and WT/DS267/42).[63] Such approval is decided under reverse consensus, such that WTO members would have to decide by consensus (including Brazil voting against itself) to not allow Brazil to proceed. On November 29, 2009, the DSB agreed to grant Brazil authorization to impose countermeasures consistent with the arbitrator's decisions contained in documents WT/DS267/ARB/1 and WT/DS267/ARB/2 and Corr.1.

WTO dispute settlement rules do not require that Brazil pursue its retaliation request or, if it does so, that it request authorization to retaliate by a given date. Other possible options that were reported include negotiation of a settlement of the case before Brazil takes further action in the WTO to impose retaliatory measures or, as suggested by some, a request by the United States for a ruling by a new compliance panel that the objectionable elements of the prohibited subsidy have been eliminated.

On December 21, 2009, Brazil announced that it was authorized by the WTO to impose trade retaliation against up to $829.3 million in U.S. goods in 2010 (based on 2008 U.S. trade data).[64] The countermeasure included a fixed annual amount of $147.3 million, reflecting the adverse effects from U.S. price-contingent subsidies (i.e., marketing loan benefits and counter-cyclical payments), and a balance related to the volume of U.S. export credit guarantees (found to operate as a prohibited export subsidy), which may vary annually. The WTO also established a threshold value (related to the value of Brazil's consumer goods imports from the United States) for determining the extent of permissible cross-retaliatory countermeasures. The threshold varies annually based on changes in Brazil's total imports from the United States, but is currently estimated at $561 million, yielding a remaining value of $268.3 million ($829.3 million - $561 million) in eligible cross-retaliatory countermeasures.

On March 10, 2010, Brazil released a final list of goods of U.S. origin valued at $561 million that would be subject to import tariffs within 30 days unless a last-minute agreement was reached. [65] The following week (March 15), Brazil released a preliminary list of U.S. patents and intellectual property rights it could restrict, barring a joint settlement.[66] The new measures—which were open to public comment for a period of 20 days and subject to public hearings—included the temporary suspension of U.S. patents on pharmaceuticals, chemicals, and biotechnology, and the restriction of copyrights in the music and audiovisual industry.[67]

The United States and Brazil continued to seek a last-minute negotiated settlement to avoid the retaliatory measures. Brazil has said that it would only apply sanctions if the United States refuses to eliminate its cotton subsidies. The United States reiterated its intention to comply with the DSB's recommendations and rulings and therefore did not believe that it would be necessary for Brazil to exercise that authorization. The United States added that suspending concessions or obligations could present economic and other challenges for both Brazil and the United States.

Brazil indicated that it could accept a U.S. pledge to send a reform bill to Congress to alter the offending cotton program provisions, if Brazil were compensated for damages until the bill's approval. Some Brazilian leaders proposed compensation through U.S. investments into cotton research, as well as more U.S. imports of Brazilian beef, orange juice, and ethanol.[68] In contrast, some have speculated that the United States could suspend the more than $2.5 billion in trade privileges that it offers Brazil under its Generalized System of Preferences (GSP).

Several U.S. trade associations—including the Brazil-U.S. Business Council, the National Association of Manufacturers, the U.S. Chamber of Commerce, the Council of the Americas, and the American Chamber of Commerce in Brazil, and others—voiced strong concerns that the U.S. government take every measure possible to avoid Brazil's imposition of trade retaliation. [69]

Steven Bipes, executive director of the Brazil-U.S. Business Council, argued that settlement of the dispute would likely have to occur in two stages:[70]

- the first stage would involve administrative action by the U.S. government on any number of several pending trade issues with Brazil as a gesture of good faith;
- the second stage would have to occur in the context of the 2012 farm bill, where Congress could make further substantive changes to U.S. cotton subsidies or to the GSM 102 export credit guarantee program.

On April 1, 2010, Deputy U.S. Trade Representative (USTR) Miriam Sapiro and USDA Undersecretary for Farm and Foreign Agricultural Services Jim Miller met with Ambassador Antonio Patriota, Secretary General of Brazil's Ministry of External Relations, to discuss possible resolution of the dispute.[71] On April 5, 2010, the United States floated a proposal to Brazil on a negotiated settlement.[72] After reviewing the proposal, Brazil's Foreign Trade Council (CAMEX) approved a resolution that would postpone until April 22 the implementation of WTO-approved countermeasures by Brazil against U.S. imports. Key features of the U.S. proposal and the ongoing negotiations include the following:

- The United States would establish a fund in the amount of $147.3 million per year to provide technical assistance and capacity-building for Brazil's cotton sector. Under terms of a memorandum of understanding (MOU), the fund would continue until the passage of the next U.S. farm bill or a mutually agreed solution to the dispute, whichever was sooner. The fund would be subject to transparency and auditing requirements.
- The United States has agreed to make some near-term modifications to the operation of the GSM-102 Export Credit Guarantee Program, and to engage with the government of Brazil in technical discussions regarding further operation of the program. On April 6, 2010, USDA announced that it was amending the GSM- 102 program such that any remaining allocations for FY20 10 would be subject to a new guarantee fee rate schedule starting on April 9, 2010.[73]
- The United States has also agreed to publish a proposed rule by April 16, 2010, to recognize the state of Santa Catarina as free of foot-and-mouth disease, rinderpest, classical swine fever, African swine fever,

and swine vesicular disease, based on World Organization for Animal Health Guidelines, and to complete a risk evaluation that is currently underway and identify appropriate risk mitigation measures to determine whether fresh beef can be imported from Brazil while preventing the introduction of foot-and-mouth disease in the United States.

In light of the temporary suspension of countermeasures, negotiations between the United States and Brazil on a proposed settlement continue with a view to agreeing on a process for complete negotiated settlement by June 2010. Brazil says that it is still pursuing the full U.S. compliance with the WTO dispute settlement ruling. However, this new "path" towards a negotiated settlement is intended to facilitate reaching a permanent solution to this case.

PHASE VI. POTENTIAL POLICY IMPLICATIONS OF WTO PANEL RULING

The arbitration ruling in favor of Brazil's requested cross-retaliation countermeasure could raise the stakes in this particular dispute by expanding retaliation into TRIPS and the General Agreement on Trade in Services. The U.S. response to the WTO cotton ruling is being watched closely by developing countries, particularly by a consortium of four African cotton-producing countries that has submitted its own proposal to the WTO calling for a global agreement to end all production-related support for cotton growers of all WTO-member countries.[74]

Trade experts have expressed concern that the panel findings could extend beyond cotton to other major field crops, particularly as concerns the potential limits on export credit guarantees. Some trade and market analysts, as well as legislators, have expressed concern that a broad finding against U.S. farm program provisions under the actionable subsidies ruling could necessitate legislative changes to the U.S. farm bill to bring existing program operations into compliance.

Bringing GSM-102 into WTO Compliance

Brazil argued that the fees charged to users of GSM failed to cover the U.S. government's costs (whether a default on the credit or late or partial payment) associated with running the program. This charge was confirmed by the original WTO panel (based on U.S. historical data of GSM- 102 program operations) and upheld on appeal. Thus, a key to bringing the GSM-102 program into compliance would be setting premium rates high enough to cover long-run program operating costs. By the WTO Compliance Panel's own measure, this could be achieved by adopting the minimum premium rates as reported in the OECD *Arrangement on Officially Supported Export Credits*. Further, the rates could be subject to a proviso that, should the GSM-102 program operate at a loss during any given year, then the fees would be adjusted higher by some amount to offset the loss in the subsequent year.

A review of the estimated credit subsidies on CCC export credit guarantees since 2001 suggests that an annual average of $302 million could be saved by adjusting fees upward to more fully cover operating costs. The program net losses have varied annually with changes in the rates of participation and default.

Bringing Price-Contingent Programs into WTO Compliance

The obvious adjustment needed to bring price-contingent cotton programs into compliance involves lowering the support prices (i.e., the loan rate and the target price) until they are more in line with market prices. Depending on the degree to which cotton price triggers are adjusted downward relative to market prices, the average payment rate will decline. By setting trigger prices at a moving average of market prices, payments could approach zero.

CCC outlays to cotton producers under the price-contingent market loan provisions (including loan deficiency payments, marketing loan gains, and certificate exchange gains) and CCP program have, on average, accounted for about 42% of all CCC payments under these programs since 2003 (**Table 4**). During that period, cotton producers received an annual average of over $1.8 billion. Since 2007, cotton receipts have surged to a 66% share of total CCC outlays as high world commodity prices have raised prices for most other major U.S. program crops above their program price triggers.

Table 4. CCC Cotton Outlays under Marketing Loan Benefits and CCP Programs ($ millions)

Fiscal Year	Counter-cyclical Payments	Marketing Loan Benefits[a]	Total	% Share of Total CCC Outlays[b]
2003	$ 1,264	$ 891	$ 2,155	59.5%
2004	$ 217	$ 193	$ 409	24.8%
2005	$ 1,421	$ 1,840	$ 3,261	38.5%
2006	$ 1,410	$ 1,189	$ 2,600	25.1%
2007	$ 1,281	$1,1 18	$ 2,399	55.1%
2008	$ 267	$ 1	$ 268	73.2%
2009	$ 728	$ 885	$ 1,612	9 1.4%
7-year average	$ 941	$ 874	$ 1,815	41.6%

Source: USDA, Farm Service Agency, *CCC Budget Essentials*, "FY 2002 thru FY 2009 CCC Actual Payments" as of March 8, 2010, at http://www.fsa.usda.gov/FSA/webapp?area=about&subject=landing&topic=bap-bu-cc.

a. Sum of loan deficiency payments (LDPs), marketing loan gains, and certificates of exchange.

b. Cotton payments as a share of total USDA, Commodity Credit Corporation outlays for marketing loan benefits and CCP payments.

Direct Payments Classification

Concerns have also been expressed regarding the reclassification of PFC and direct payments away from non-trade-distorting green box support.[75] However, the panel finding that U.S. direct payments do not qualify for WTO exemptions from reduction commitments as fully decoupled income support (i.e., they are not green box compliant) appears to have no further consequences within the context of this case and does not involve any compliance measures. This is because direct payments were deemed "non-price contingent" and were evaluated strictly in terms of the Peace Clause violation.

The panel did not specifically reclassify U.S. PFC and DP payments as "amber box," nor did the panel recommend that the United States should notify such future payments as "amber box." This is a subtle but critical distinction because of the enormity of PFC and DP payments. During FY1996 to FY2007, PFC and DP payments averaged $5.2 billion per year and accounted for 33% of total U.S. farm program outlays. Shifting this amount to amber box could have important implications for future dispute settlement cases, as well as for the United States' ability to meet its WTO amber box commitments.

U.S. cotton industry and government officials are concerned that the specific finding on the apparent failure of U.S. "decoupled" payments to meet WTO green box criteria leaves such programs open to future charges, and that third countries may feel emboldened by knowing how a WTO panel is likely to rule on such matters. The European Union (EU) is also likely to be concerned about this finding since the EU's agricultural program (following agricultural policy reforms of June 2003) relies heavily on "decoupled" payments similar to the those of the U.S. program. These concerns appear to have merit, as both Canada and Brazil have initiated WTO dispute settlement proceedings against the United States charging that the United States has indeed incorrectly notified PFC and DP payments as green box and that their inclusion in the U.S. amber box results in the United States exceeding its WTO-agreed AMS spending limit on several occasions in recent years (**Figure 5**).[76]

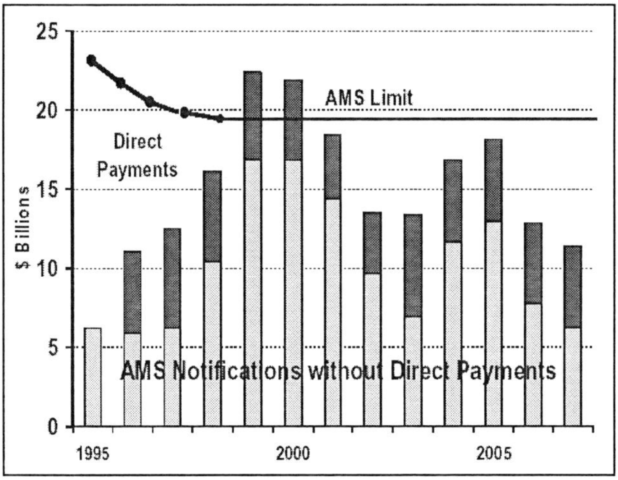

Source: 1995-2007 are U.S. WTO notifications.

Figure 5. U.S. AMS Outlays, as Notified Without Direct Payments versus With Addition of Direct Payments

Other Cotton-Related Trade Issues

Besides Brazil's WTO-initiated dispute settlement case (DS267), U.S. cotton subsidies are being challenged at the WTO on two additional fronts.

- First, the Doha Development Agenda negotiating round has substantial reductions in trade-distorting domestic program support as one of its principal modalities.[77] If realized, a new round of domestic spending limitations could potentially represent a "real" ceiling on U.S. commodity spending and could result in lower program outlays.
- Second, a consortium of four African cotton-producing countries—Benin, Burkina Faso, Chad, and Mali—has submitted a WTO proposal calling for a global agreement to end all production-related support for cotton growers of all WTO-member cotton producing nations.[78] In acknowledgment of the concerns of African cotton-producing countries, the United States—while not agreeing with the African proposal—worked with the African countries on a formulation in the initial agriculture framework (of July 31, 2004) of the WTO's ongoing Doha Round.[79] Although no specific cotton program concessions were mentioned in the framework, the United States committed "to achieve ambitious results expeditiously" under the framework. Further, it is notable that cotton is the only commodity singled out for special mention in the framework.

ROLE OF CONGRESS

Given the importance of cotton in the U.S. agricultural economy and the potential for WTOimposed limitations on U.S. cotton program operations, Congress likely will be closely monitoring developments in the WTO cotton case and the Doha Round of trade negotiations. Both the Senate and House Agriculture Committees regularly hold hearings on agricultural trade negotiations. In addition to congressional hearings, Congress will likely be engaged in consultations with the Administration on the bilateral trade negotiations as well as the Doha Round of WTO trade negotiations. Such consultations will be a major vehicle for Members to express their views on this dispute and on the negotiating issues it raises.

When confronted with a negative WTO dispute settlement ruling, a country has essentially five options to choose from: eliminate the subsidy; reduce the subsidy to diminish its adverse effect; revise the program function to reduce the linkage between the subsidy and the adverse effect (referred to as decoupling); pay a mutually acceptable compensatory payment to offset the adverse effects of the subsidy; or suffer the consequences of trade retaliation.

Ultimately, Congress is responsible for passing farm program legislation that complies with U.S. commitments in international trade agreements. The United States would appear to have already complied with several of the AB 's recommendation concerning "prohibited subsidies" through changes in the 2008 farm bill (P.L. 110-246; Sec. 3 101(a)) by eliminating the Step 2, GSM-103, and SCGP programs, and by removing the fee cap on GSM-102 credit guarantees (i.e., by eliminating the "subsidy" component of export credit guarantees). In addition, by the same 2008 farm bill provision Congress requires that the Secretary of Agriculture, in carrying out the GSM- 102 program, " work with the industry to ensure, to the maximum extent practicable, that risk- based fees associated with the guarantees cover, but do not exceed, the operating costs and losses over the long-term." However, a more explicit definition of "long-term" such as a two-year period would perhaps provide a stronger signal to the Secretary of Agriculture in regard to operating the GSM-102 program with no net losses.

Also, some questions remain as to what extent the 2008 farm bill has addressed the adverse effects charge related to price-contingent subsidies. Instead of eliminating or reducing program triggers, the 2008 farm bill appears to offer higher levels of price and income support that potentially could aggravate the perception (if not the reality) of adverse effects in the marketplace. Several of the proposed changes are specifically relevant to the Brazil cotton case, but also germane to the broader issue of program vulnerability to WTO challenge.[80] For example, the enacted 2008 farm bill:[81]

- extends the counter-cyclical payments (CCP) program and current marketing loan provisions (Sections 1104 and 1201 of P.L. 110-246);
- raises both target prices and loan rates for several commodities, while only lowering (marginally) the target price for upland cotton (Sections 1104 and 1202);
- offers producers the choice (subject to a 30% reduction in marketing loan rates and in lieu of 100% of CCP and 20% of direct payments) of a revenue-based support option under the Average Crop Revenue Election program (ACRE, Section 1105) with potentially higher per-

acre revenue guarantees for several crops than under the previous 2002 farm bill; and

- creates a new cotton-user payment of 4 cents per pound (Section 1207). This payment appears similar to the WTO-illegal Step 2 payment except that cotton from all origins (not just domestic sources) is eligible for the payment. Since the United States imports very little cotton, most payments would still likely go to domestically sourced cotton. As a result, this subtle technical loophole might ultimately be subject to a WTO challenge, but would not be part of the current WTO cotton case.

Table 5. Timeline: U.S.-Brazil WTO Dispute Settlement Case 267

Date	Event
Sept. 27, 2002	Brazil makes a formal "request for consultations" with the United States (WT/DS267/1).
Oct. 2002 to Jan. 2003	Brazil and United States hold three consultations to discuss dispute over U.S. cotton subsidies. The consultations are unsuccessful.
Feb. 7, 2003	Brazil's first request for the establishment of a dispute panel to rule on its complaint is vetoed by the United States (WT/DS267/7).
Mar. 18, 2003	Upon Brazil's second request, the WTO's Dispute Settlement Body (DSB) establishes a panel (WT/DS267/15).
May 19, 2003	Appointment of the panelists by the WTO Director-General. Once formed, a panel normally has six months to hold hearings and gather testimony before issuing its final report to both parties.
July 22, 2003	First meeting with DSB panel. Panel decides to review peace clause issue and Brazil's challenge to U.S. cotton subsidies separately.
Sept. 2003	The panel reverses an earlier procedural decision and states that it will decide both the peace clause issue and Brazil's challenge to U.S. cotton subsidies together.
Nov. 17, 2003	The panel chairman informs the DSB that the panel will not be able to complete its work in six months due to the complexity of the matter. An extension is announced (WT/DS267/16).
Apr. 26, 2004	The panel's interim report is released confidentially to the two parties. Both parties review the interim report and submit written comments by May 10, at which time they have three additional weeks to review each other's comments and

Table 5. (Continued)

Date	Event
	respond. Although the report is released confidentially, news reports suggest at least a partial finding against the United States on each of the five major claims.[83]
June 18, 2004	The panel's final report is released confidentially to the two parties. News reports suggest that the final ruling varies little from the interim ruling against the United States.[84]
Sept. 8, 2004	After translation into English, French, and Portuguese, the final report is delivered to the WTO Dispute Settlement Body (DSB), as well as to the public (WT/DS267/R).
Oct. 18, 2004	The United States notifies its intention to appeal 14 specific points of the final report to the Appellate Body. The 14 points identify certain issues of law covered in the panel's finalreport and certain legal interpretations developed by the panel in the dispute. An appeal cannot reexamine existing evidence or examine new evidence (WT/DS267/17).
Nov. 16, 2004	Several additional countries file a third participant's submission, while others notify their intention to appear at the oral hearing.
Dec. 10, 2004	Due to the extent and complexity of issues under review, both the United States and Brazil agree to an extension to March 3, 2005, for circulation of the Appellate Body's (AB's) final report (WT/DS267/18).
Mar. 3, 2005	The AB issues its report upholding most of the panel's rulings (WT/DS267/ABR). Deadlines of July 1, 2005 for removal of prohibited subsidies, and Sept. 21, 2005, for removal of prejudicial effects from actionable subsidies are announced by AB.
Mar. 21, 2005	The DSB adopts the AB and panel reports, thus initiating a sequence of compliance deadlines (WT/DS267/20).
Apr. 20, 2005	The United States announces to the DSB that it intends to implement the recommendations and rulings of the DSB.
June 30, 2005	USDA announces temporary fix for its export credit guarantee programs, including adoption of risk-based fee structure for GSM-102 and cessation of use of GSM-103 program. In addition, USDA proposes legislation to Congress to repeal the Step 2 cotton program.
July 1, 2005	AB deadline for U.S. removal of prohibited subsidies expires.
July 4, 2005	Brazil requests authorization from WTO to impose $3 billion in retaliatory measures against prohibited U.S. subsidies (WT/DS267/21).
July 5, 2005	USDA proposes statutory changes be made by Congress: remove 1% fee cap on GSM-102 program and terminate GSM-103 program.

Table 5. (Continued)

Date	Event
July 5, 2005	United States objects to the amount of Brazil's proposed sanctions on the prohibited subsidies and requests WTO arbitration (WT/DS267/23). Such arbitration shall be carried out by the original panel and completed within 60 days.
July 14, 2005	The DSB assigns role of arbitration on the prohibited-subsidy sanctions to the original panel (WT/DS267/24).
Aug. 17, 2005	Brazil and United States reach procedural agreement to temporarily suspend arbitration proceedings concerning the prohibited subsidies (WT/DS267/25).
Sept. 1, 2005	AB deadline for U.S. removal of prejudicial effects from actionable subsidies expires.
Oct. 6, 2005	Brazil requests authorization from WTO to impose $1 billion in retaliatory measures against actionable U.S. subsidies to offset their adverse effects (WT/DS267/26).
Oct. 17, 2005	United States objects to the amount of Brazil's proposed sanctions on the actionable subsidies and requests WTO arbitration (WT/DS267/27).
Oct. 18, 2005	The DSB assigns role of arbitration on the actionable-subsidy sanctions to the original panel (WT/DS267/28).
Nov. 21, 2005	Brazil and United States reach procedural agreement to temporarily suspend arbitration proceedings concerning the actionable subsidies (WT/DS267/29).
July 24, 2006	Doha round of WTO trade negotiations suspended indefinitely.[85]
Aug. 1, 2006	Step 2 cotton program eliminated (Sec. 1103, P.L. 109-171; Deficit Reduction Act of 2005).
Aug. 18, 2006	Brazil requests the establishment of a WTO compliance panel to review whether the United States has fully complied with the AB's ruling of March 3, 2005 (WT/DS267/30).
Sept. 28, 2006	The DSB agrees to establish a panel (WT/DS267/31). The panel members are announced on Oct. 25, 2006.
Jan. 9, 2007	The DSB announces that, because of particular circumstances, the compliance panel will not complete its work before July 2007.
July 27, 2007	The WTO compliance panel issues confidential interim ruling to Brazil and the United States. News reports suggest a ruling that the United States has not fully complied with the March 2005 ruling.[86]
Oct. 15, 2007	The WTO compliance panel releases its confidential final report to the United States and Brazilian governments. News reports suggest a ruling that the United States had not fully complied with the March 2005 ruling.

Table 5. (Continued)

Date	Event
Dec. 18, 2007	The WTO compliance panel issues its final ruling publicly (WT/DS267/RW), confirming earlier news reports that the panel has found that the United States is not in full compliance.
Feb. 12, 2008	The United States notifies its intention to appeal certain issues of law covered in the report of the WTO compliance panel (WT/DS267/33).
June 2, 2008	The Appellate Body (AB) issues its report upholding most of the compliance panel's rulings (WT/DS267/ABR).
June 18, 2008	2008 farm bill (P.L. 110-246) enacted, including a provision (3101(a)) that alters the U.S. export credit guarantee program by eliminating the GSM-103 and Supplier Credit Guarantee Programs, and the 1% cap on GSM-102 user fees.
June 25, 2008	The DSB adopts the compliance panel and AB reports.
Aug. 25, 2008	Brazil officially asks the chair of the DSB panel to resume the arbitration proceedings concerning proposed countermeasures for both the prohibited subsidies and the actionable subsidies rulings (WT/DS267/38 and WT/DS267/39).
Oct. 1, 2008	Brazil and the United States agree on the arbitration panelists (WT/DS267/24/Add.1 and WT/DS267/28/Add.1).
Dec. 9, 2008	U.S. written submission in arbitration proceedings.
Jan. 13, 2009	Brazil written submission in arbitration proceedings.
Aug. 31, 2009	WTO arbitrator releases a decision in two parts: WT/DS267/ARB/1, which rules on Brazil's retaliation requests regarding the prohibited subsidies, and WT/DS267/ARB/2, which rules on Brazil's retaliation requests regarding the actionable subsidies.
Nov. 19, 2009	DSB grants authorization to Brazil to impose countermeasures against the United States.
Dec. 21, 2009	Brazil announces authorization by WTO to impose trade retaliation in 2010 against$829.3 million in U.S. goods and services (based on 2008 data), including $268.3 million in cross-retaliation.
Feb. 10, 2010	Brazil's Chamber of Foreign Trade (CAMEX) releases a preliminary list identifying U.S. goods exports that would be subject to retaliatory duties.
March 10, 2010	Brazil announces that it will impose retaliatory tariffs worth $591 million on a list of 102 U.S. products. The new tariffs are set to take effect 30 days after their announcement.

Table 5. (Continued)

Date	Event
March 15, 2010	Brazil announces a preliminary list of U.S. patents and intellectual property rights it could restrict unless both countries reach a settlement. The proposed measures are open to public comment for a period of 20 days and are still subject to public hearings.
April 1, 2010	U.S. negotiating team meets with Brazilian officials to discuss possible resolution of the dispute.
April 5, 2010	The United States floats a proposal to Brazil on a negotiated settlement. After reviewing the proposal, Brazil's Foreign Trade Council (CAMEX) approves a resolution that would postpone until April 22 the implementation of WTO-approved countermeasures by Brazil against U.S. imports.
June 2010	Tentative deadline for completion of ongoing negotiated settlement.

Source: Compiled by CRS from official WTO documents and news sources as cited.

Finally, the 2008 farm bill does not address the issue surrounding the disqualification of direct payments from the WTO's green box exclusion as decoupled payments due to the planting restriction on fruits, vegetables, and wild rice on program base acres. Instead, direct payments are extended with no change to the current planting restriction, except for a small pilot program on 75,000 acres in seven states (Section 1107). This retention of the status quo has important WTO implications for the AMS case being brought against the United States by both Canada and Brazil. The U.S. aggregate measure of support (AMS) has exceeded, on at least two occasions, its total WTO limit if direct payments are included in the AMS calculation (Figure 5).[82]

Additional uncertainty arises from the ongoing Doha Round of trade negotiations, where a successful conclusion could potentially mitigate or end Brazil's interest in continuing its case against the U.S. farm programs. Both agriculture committees (House and Senate) of the 111th Congress will likely continue to monitor developments in the WTO cotton case and the Doha negotiations, as well as the aftermath of the compliance panel's final ruling.

End Notes

[1] Official WTO documents as cited in Table 5 and throughout this chapter are available at http://docsonline.wto.org/ under a simple search using the specific "document symbol" cited, e.g., WT/DS267/1.

[2] "Brazil Releases List of U.S. Goods for Retaliation in Cotton Dispute," *Bridges Weekly Trade News Digest*, vol. 14, no. 9, March 10, 2010.

[3] "U.S. Cotton Dispute—Public Consultations About Measures for the Suspension of Concessions or Obligations vis-à- vis the United States in the Area of Intellectual Property Rights," press release, Press Office of the Brazilian Ministry of External Relations, Brasilia, March 15, 2010.

[4] "Brazil Details Retaliation on U.S. Copyright, Patents," *Reuters*, March 15, 2010.

[5] Ibid.

[6] "U.S., Brazil Agree Upon Path Toward Negotiated Solution of Cotton Dispute," *USDA News Release* No. 0168.10, April 6, 2010.

[7] "U.S. May Float Proposal in Cotton Dispute Today, CAMEX to Hold Meeting," *World Trade Online*, April 5, 2010.

[8] "USDA Amends GSM-102 Credit Guarantees for Fiscal Year 2010," *USDA News Release*, April 6, 2010.

[9] The Step 2 cotton-user payments program was ended on August 1, 2006, by P.L. 109-171. For a description of major farm programs, see CRS Report RL34594, *Farm Commodity Programs in the 2008 Farm Bill*, by Jim Monke.

[10] For more information, see CRS Report RL34053, *Measuring Equity in Farm Support Levels*, by Randy Schnepf.

[11] Ministry of Foreign Affairs [Ministério das Relações Exteriores], Brasilia; "Brazil-U.S.A. Dispute on Subsidies on Upland Cotton," translation from the original in Portuguese, Nota n° 248-18/06/2004; Distribuição 22 e 23.

[12] WTO, *The Legal Texts: The Results of the Uruguay Round of Multilateral Trade Negotiations*, Cambridge Univ. Press, ©World Trade Organization 1999; hereafter referred to as *WTO Legal Texts*. Text of the Agreement on Agriculture is available online at *http://www.wt o.org/english/docs_e/legal_e/14-ag.pdf*.

[13] USDA reports commodity program outlays on a fiscal year (FY) basis. (See Table 1.) However, marketing year data, not fiscal year, must be used in the WTO case. The U.S. cotton marketing year starts August 1 and ends July 31 of the following year, but identifies with the first year, such that MY 1992 starts August 1, 1992, and ends July 31, 1993. The principal period in question, MY 1999-MY2002, corresponds roughly with FY2000-FY2003.

[14] *United States—Subsidies on Upland Cotton*, WT/DS267, "Initial Brief of the United States of America on the Question Posed by the Panel," June 13, 2003; available from the USTR website at http://www.ustr.gov/assets Trade_Agreements/Monitoring_Enforcement/ Dispute_Settlement/WTO/Dispute_Settlement_Listings/ asset_upload_file376_5598.pdf.

[15] WTO, "Annex 2—Domestic Support: The Basis for Exemption from the Reduction Commitments," paragraphs 5 and 6, Agreement on Agriculture, *WTO Legal Texts*.

[16] For more information on these restrictions see USDA, Farm Service Agency, Fact Sheet, *Direct and Counter- Cyclical Payment Program Wild Rice, Fruit, and Vegetable Provisions*, February 2003, at http://www.fsa.usda.gov/pas/ publications/facts/ tml/fav03.htm.

[17] The Step 2 cotton program was eliminated on August 1, 2006 (Sec. 1103, P.L. 109-171).

[18] Only prices for Middling (M) 1-3/32-inch upland cotton are used in the calculation. Also, certain price triggers must be met and held for a specified period of time before payments can be made. For information on the Step 2 program and other U.S. cotton program features, see USDA, ERS, "Cotton Briefing Room," at http://www.ers.usda.gov/ Briefing/Cotton/.

[19] Item (j), Annex I, Agreement on Subsidies and Countervailing Measures, The Legal Texts, The Results of the Uruguay Round of Multilateral Trade Negotiations, World Trade Organization, Cambridge University Press©WTO1999.

[20] GSM-103 and SCGP were eliminated by the 2008 farm bill (P.L. 110-246; Sec. 3101(a)) upon its enactment on June 18, 2008. For information on the U.S. GSM-102 program, see USDA, Foreign Agricultural Service, "Export Credit Guarantee Programs," at *http://www.fas. usda.gov/excredits/default.htm*.

[21] For a list of commodities eligible for export credit guarantees see USDA, Foreign Agricultural Service, *USDA Amends Commodity Eligibility under Credit Guarantee Programs*, News Release, September 24, 2002; available at *http://www.fas.usda.gov/scriptsw /PressRelease/pressrel_dout.asp?Entry=valid&PrNum=0346-02.*

[22] The United States has scheduled export subsidy reduction commitments for the following thirteen commodities: wheat, coarse grains, rice, vegetable oils, butter and butter oil, skim milk powder, cheese, other milk products, bovine meat, pigmeat, poultry meat, live dairy cattle, and eggs.

[23] Those agricultural products which did not receive U.S. farm program support payments, but whose exports were otherwise assisted by export credit guarantee program are excluded from this case; WT/DS267/R, p. 348(d)(ii).

[24] Articles 5(c) and 6.3(b) of the Agreement on Subsidies and Countervailing Measures (SCM) deal with subsidies that result in adverse effects in other WTO-member countries. Brazil specifically identified Argentina, Bangladesh, Colombia, Germany, India, Indonesia, Italy, Portugal, Philippines, Slovenia, South Africa, South Korea, Switzerland, Thailand, and Turkey as the relevant third-country markets. WTO "Communication from Brazil," WT/DS267/9, March 21, 2003.

[25] Text of the Agreement on SCM is available online at *http://www.wto.org/english/ docs_e/legal_e/24-scm.pdf.*

[26] WT/DS267/R, paragraph 7. 1307, p. 307.

[27] *Report of the Panel*, "United States—Subsidies on Upland Cotton," WTO, WT/DS267/R, para 7.1503, September 8, 2004, p. 345; hereafter referred to as WTO, WT/DS267/R.

[28] Ibid.

[29] For more information on DS108, see CRS Report RL32014, *WTO Dispute Settlement: Status of U.S. Compliance in Pending Cases*, by Jeanne J. Grimmett.

[30] Done in accordance with SCM, Article 4.7.

[31] WTO, WT/DS267/R, para. 7. 1503, p. 354.

[32] For details, see *Understanding the WTO: Settling Disputes*, "The Case Has Been Decided, What Next?" at http://www.wto.org/english/thewto_e/whatis_e/tif_e/disp1_e.htm.

[33] Normally a 30-day period is given to respond (DSU, Article 21.3); however, this is halved under SCM, Article 4.12.

[34] U.S. Mission to the United Nations in Geneva, Press Release, "Statements by the U.S. Representative at the meeting of the WTO Dispute Settlement Body," April 20, 2005.

[35] Normally a 20-day period is given (DSU, Article 22.2); however, for disputes involving prohibited subsidies the prescribed time is halved (SCM, Article 4.12).

[36] Normally a 30-day period is given for authorization (DSU, Article 22.6); however, for disputes involving prohibited subsidies the prescribed time is halved (SCM, Article 4.12).

[37] Normally a 60-day period is given for arbitration (DSU, Article 22.6); however, for disputes involving prohibited subsidies the prescribed time is halved (SCM, Article 4.12).

[38] For more information on case DS108, see CRS Report RL32014, *WTO Dispute Settlement: Status of U.S. Compliance in Pending Cases*, by Jeanne J. Grimmett.

[39] In accordance with SCM, Article 7.9.

[40] *Inside U.S. Trade*, "Appellate Body Favors Brazil in Cotton Subsidies Challenge," Vol. 23, No.9, March 4, 2005.

[41] *Congressional Daily*, "Comply Quickly With WTO Ruling, Brazil Urges U.S." March 15, 2005.

[42] NCC, "NCC Statement on WTP Appellate Ruling," March 3, 2005; available at http://www.cotton releases/2005/wtostatement.cfm.

[43] For details, see CRS Report RL32014, *WTO Dispute Settlement: Status of U.S. Compliance in Pending Cases*, by Jeanne J. Grimmett.

[44] Presented in Brazil's written submission to the WTO arbitration panel, January 13, 2009.

[45] WTO official document WT/DS267/24, July 19, 2005. Official WTO documents are accessible online at http://docsonline.wto.org/gen_search.asp?searchmode=simple.

[46] WT/DS267/25, August 18, 2005.

[47] "U.S., Brazil Clash on Cotton Sanctions," International Center for Trade and Sustainable Development (ICTSD), *Bridges*, vol. 12, no. 6, January 2009.

[48] Ibid.

[49] WT/DS267/27, October 18, 2005.

[50] WT/DS267/29, December 7, 2005.

[51] For more information and an update on the status of Doha negotiations, see CRS Report RL33 144, *WTO Doha Round: The Agricultural Negotiations*, by Charles E. Hanrahan and Randy Schnepf.

[52] For more information, see OECD, Trade and Agriculture Directorate, "Arrangement on Export Credits," *at* http://www.oecd.org/department/0,3355,en_2649_34171 1_1_ 1_1_1 ,00.html.

[53] *United States—Subsidies on Upland Cotton (WT/DS267)*, written submissions of the United States, December 9, 2008; and *United States—Subsidies on Upland Cotton (WT/DS267)*, written submission of Brazil, January 13, 2009.

[54] *United States—Subsidies on Upland Cotton (WT/DS267)*, written submissions of the United States, Dec. 9, 2008.

[55] Ibid., paragraph 312, p. 99.

[56] *United States—Subsidies on Upland Cotton: Recourse to Arbitration by the United States under Article 22.6 of the DSU and Article 4.11 of the SCM Agreement*, WT/DS267/ARB/1, WTO, August 31, 2009; and *United States— Subsidies on Upland Cotton: Recourse to Arbitration by the United States under Article 22.6 of the DSU and Article 7.10 of the SCM Agreement*, WT/DS267/ARB/2, WTO, August 31, 2009.

[57] "WTO Arbitration Panel Decision Falls Short of Brazilian Demands," *Inside U.S. Trades' World Trade Online*, Daily News, August 31, 2009.

[58] The actual total is $5.9 billion including the $5.5 billion allowed under the 2008 farm bill plus $465 million in re- announcement of unutilized programs or cancelled guarantees from earlier in FY2009; available at http://www.fas.usda.gov/excredits/ecgp.asp.

[59] "USTR Statement on Awards in Brazil Cotton Dispute," U.S.T.R., August 31, 2009; available at http://www.ustr.gov/about-us/press-office/press-releases/2009/august/ustr-statement-awards-brazil-cotton

[60] "WTO Arbitration Panel Ruling Fails to Recognize Changes to GSM Program; Punishes USA Despite Compliance with WTO," NCC news release, September 2, 2009; at http://www.cotton

[61] "NCC Statement—Arbitration Determination," NCC news release, August 31, 2009; at http://www.cotton

[62] *BNA, International Trade Reporter*, "Brazil Says Entitled to Impose $829 Million in Annual Sanctions on U.S. in Cotton Case," December 24, 2009.

[63] Notes from the WTO DSB meeting of November 19, 2009, at *http://www.wto.org/english/news_e/news09_e/* dsb_19nov09_e.htm.

[64] *BNA, International Trade Reporter*, "Brazil Delays Final List of U.S. Goods to Be Sanctioned in WTO Cotton Dispute," December 24, 2009.

[65] "Brazil Releases List of U.S. Goods for Retaliation in Cotton Dispute," *Bridges Weekly Trade News Digest*, vol. 14, no. 9, March 10, 2010.

[66] "U.S. Cotton Dispute—Public Consultations About Measures for the Suspension of Concessions or Obligations vis- à-vis the United States in the Area of Intellectual Property Rights," press release, Press Office of the Brazilian Ministry of External Relations, Brasilia, March 15, 2010.

[67] "Brazil Details Retaliation on U.S. Copyright, Patents," *Reuters*, March 15, 2010.

[68] Ibid.

[69] "Brazil Holds Off on Goods Retaliation List; U.S. Industries Press for Settlement," *Inside U.S. Trade*, Feb. 12, 2010.

[70] Ibid.

[71] "U.S., Brazil Agree Upon Path Toward Negotiated Solution of Cotton Dispute," *USDA News Release* No. 0168.10 April 6, 2010.

[72] "U.S. May Float Proposal in Cotton Dispute Today, CAMEX to Hold Meeting," *World Trade Online*, April 5, 2010.

[73] "USDA Amends GSM-102 Credit Guarantees for Fiscal Year 2010," *USDA News Release*, April 6, 2010.

[74] For more information, see CRS Report RS21712, *The African Cotton Initiative and WTO Agriculture Negotiations*, by Charles E. Hanrahan.

[75] "Brazil Wins Key Points in Interim WTO Panel on U.S. Cotton Subsidies," *Inside U.S. Trade*, April 30, 2004.

[76] See CRS Report RL34351, *Brazil's and Canada's WTO Cases Against U.S. Agricultural Direct Payments*, by Randy Schnepf.

[77] WTO, Doha Ministerial Declaration, WT/MIN(01)/DEC/1, November 20, 2001.

[78] For more information, see CRS Report RS21712, *The African Cotton Initiative and WTO Agriculture Negotiations*, by Charles E. Hanrahan.

[79] For more information, see CRS Report RS21905, *Agriculture in the WTO Doha Round: The Framework Agreement and Next Steps*, by Charles E. Hanrahan.

[80] For more information on this issue, see CRS Report RS22522, *Potential Challenges to U.S. Farm Subsidies in the WTO: A Brief Overview*, by Randy Schnepf.

[81] See CRS Report RL34696, *The 2008 Farm Bill: Major Provisions and Legislative Action*, coordinated by Renée Johnson.

[82] See CRS Report RL3435 1, *Brazil's and Canada's WTO Cases Against U.S. Agricultural Direct Payments*, by Randy Schnepf.

[83] "Brazil Wins Key Points in Interim WTO Panel on U.S. Cotton Subsidies," *Inside U.S. Trade*, April 30, 2004; "WTO Panel Backs Brazil in Complaint Against U.S. Over Cotton Subsidies," *International Trade Reporter*, Vol. 21, No. 18, April 29, 2004; and "WTO Panel Reportedly Rules Direct Payments are Trade Distorting and Thus 'Amber Box,'" *AgWeb.com*, April 30, 2004.

[84] "WTO Ruling Against U.S. Cotton Subsidies is Not Limited to Cotton," *AgWeb.com*, June 29, 2004; and "WTO Issues Final Ruling Condemning U.S. Cotton Subsidies; U.S. Plans Appeal," *International Trade Reporter*, Vol. 21, No. 26, June 24, 2004.

[85] For more information, see CRS Report RL33 144, *WTO Doha Round: The Agricultural Negotiations*, by Charles E. Hanrahan and Randy Schnepf.

[86] For example, see *Financial Times*, "Brazil Claims WTO Cotton Victory," July 27, 2007.

In: Disputed WTO Cases Involving the United… ISBN: 978-1-61761-433-0
Editors: Jacqueline P. Daniels

Chapter 3

BRAZIL'S AND CANADA'S WTO CASES AGAINST U.S. AGRICULTURAL DIRECT PAYMENTS*

Randy Schnepf

SUMMARY

In 2007, Brazil and Canada, independently of each other, requested consultations with the United States under the auspices of the World Trade Organization's (WTO's) Dispute Settlement process concerning similar grievances regarding U.S. domestic agricultural support programs and the U.S. export credit guarantee program. After consultations failed to resolve their concerns, both countries (again acting independently) requested the establishment of a WTO panel to rule on their complaints. The WTO's Dispute Settlement Body, on December 17, 2007, established a single panel to consider both cases. In late April 2008, Brazil and Canada informally agreed to postpone proceeding with their joint World Trade Organization (WTO) dispute settlement case challenging certain U.S. agricultural subsidies. At the time of the postponement, the three parties involved in the dispute had been unable to agree on panel membership.

---

* This is an edited, reformatted and augmented edition of a United States Congressional Research Service publication, Report RL34351, dated January 27, 2010.

The postponement was thought to be provisional based on success in achieving further disciplines on domestic support in the current Doha Round of WTO trade negotiations. However, the Doha Round negotiations failed to complete an agreement in 2009. As of early 2010 there are no prospects for revival of Doha Round negotiations. Nor have Brazil and Canada given any indication that they will revive their pursuit of their joint case. It is not clear how long the postponement will persist. If resumed, the first order of business will be the formation of a panel.

The joint case combines two separate but similar cases: DS357, brought by Canada, and DS365, brought by Brazil. Both cases make two charges against U.S. farm programs—first, that the United States has exceeded its annual WTO commitment levels for total aggregate measurement of support (AMS) for agriculture in each of the years 1999, 2000, 2001, 2002, 2004, and 2005, and second, that the U.S. export credit guarantee program for agricultural commodities operates as a WTO-illegal export subsidy. Both charges stem, in large part, from a previous negative ruling against U.S. farm programs in a case (DS267) brought by Brazil against the U.S. cotton program. In that case, a WTO panel ruled (the ruling subsequently was upheld by a WTO Appellate Body), first, that direct payments made under U.S. farm programs do not qualify for green box exemption status because of a restriction prohibiting the planting of fruits, vegetables, or wild rice on payment acres; and second, that the U.S. export credit guarantee program operates as a prohibited export subsidy program because the financial benefits returned by these programs failed to cover their long-run operating costs. As a result of the ruling, U.S. export credit guarantees became subject to previously scheduled export subsidy commitments. For more information, see CRS Report RL32571, *Brazil's WTO Case Against the U.S. Cotton Program*, by Randy Schnepf.

Canada and Brazil claim that, since they fail to qualify for inclusion in the green box, U.S. direct payments should be added to its AMS when calculating total domestic support. In addition, they also charge that the United States has improperly notified several of its farm support programs as exempt from the AMS limit, while several other programs were improperly excluded from U.S. notifications. Canada and Brazil claim that when all of the outlays from these allegedly misnotified programs are included, then the U.S. AMS total exceeds its WTO commitment level.

Should a panel be formed and eventually rule on this case, any changes in U.S. farm policy needed to comply with a WTO ruling against the United States would likely involve action by Congress to produce new legislation.This chapter provides background and details, as well as the current status of the two WTO dispute settlement cases. In addition, it discusses the role of Congress in responding to developments.

INTRODUCTION

In 2007, Canada and Brazil initiated separate but similar WTO cases against certain U.S. farm programs as they relate to U.S. commitments made to the World Trade Organization (WTO). Both Canada's (DS357) and Brazil's (DS365) cases make two broad charges. First, they contend that the United States has exceeded the subsidy spending limit it committed to for domestic agricultural support programs. Second, they charge that the United States operates its agricultural export credit guarantee program in such a manner as to provide prohibited subsidies to those exports made under the programs.

On December 17, 2007, the WTO's Dispute Settlement Body (DSB) announced the establishment of a single panel to hear both cases against U.S. farm programs. Panel membership is based on mutual agreement of the parties involved—Brazil, Canada, and the United States. However, by late February 2008 the case had stalled due to the inability of the three parties to agree on a panel of arbitrators to preside over the case.[1] Under WTO rules, Brazil is legally entitled to ask the WTO director-general to compose the panel if the parties are unable to agree on the members within 20 days after the establishment of a panel. However, Brazil did not pursue this course of action. Then, in late April 2008, Brazil and Canada informally agreed to postpone proceeding with their case pending the U.S. offer to substantially cut domestic agricultural subsidies as part of the Doha Round of WTO trade negotiations.[2]

Presently, no date has been announced for the resumption of the case. If resumed, the first order of business will be the formation of a panel. Should a panel be formed, it would then have six months to rule on this case. Subsequent appeals of any negative ruling and disagreement over appropriate retaliatory levels, etc., could push resolution of the dispute well into the future. However, the importance of the case is not diminished to the U.S. agricultural community. U.S. agriculture depends heavily on international markets to sell its surpluses. In FY2008, U.S. agricultural exports were a record $115.5 billion and represented 30% of gross farm income.[3]

This chapter begins with background on the evolution of the Canadian and Brazilian WTO cases. This is followed by a section that describes in detail the nature of the two major charges made against U.S. farm programs in the two cases and the U.S. response to those charges. Finally, the report briefly discusses the implications of the case and the potential role of Congress.

Table 1 . Time Line of the WTO Dispute Settlement Cases DS357 (Canada) and DS365 (Brazil) Against the United States

Date	Event
Jan. 8, 2007	Canada makes a formal "request for consultations" with the United States (WT/DS357/1) to discuss three charges: (1) U.S. export credit guarantee programs operate as prohibited export subsidies; (2) the United States provides total AMS support in excess of its commitment levels; and (3) U.S. support programs provided to U.S. corn producers result in adverse effects in the form of serious prejudice to the interests of Canada during the 1996 to 2006 period in violation of Articles 5(c) and 6.3(c) of the WTO's Agreement on Subsidies and Countervailing Measures (SCM Agreement).[a]
Jan. 22, 2007, To Jan. 24, 2007	Several additional WTO members—Australia, Argentina, Australia, Brazil, the European Communities, Guatemala, Nicaragua, Thailand, and Uruguay—officially request to join the consultations as interested third parties in accordance with Article 4.11 of the Dispute Settlement Memorandum of Understanding (DSU).[b]
Feb. 7, 2007	Canada and the United States hold consultations to discuss Canada's allegations. The consultations fail to resolve the dispute.
June 7, 2007	Canada requests (WT/DS357/11) that the establishment of a dispute panel to rule on its complaint in case DS357 be included on the Dispute Settlement Body's (DSB's) agenda for its next monthly meeting. Canada drops its "serious prejudice" charge against U.S. corn subsidies, but retains the two other charges identified in its Jan. 8, 2007, consultations request.
June 21, 2007	Canada's first request for the establishment of a dispute panel to rule on its complaint is vetoed by the United States at the DSB's monthly meeting.
July 11, 2007	Brazil makes a formal "request for consultations" with the United States (WT/DS365/1) to discuss two charges: (1) U.S. export credit guarantee programs operate as prohibited export subsidies; and (2) the United States provides total AMS support in excess of its commitment levels.
July 24, 2007 To Aug. 1, 2007	Several additional WTO members—Canada, Guatemala, Costa Rica, the European Communities (EC), Mexico, Australia, Argentina, Thailand, India, and Nicaragua—officially request to join the consultations as interested third parties.[c]

Aug. 22, 2007	Brazil and the United States hold consultations to consultations fail to resolve the dispute.
Oct. 8, 2007	The United States notifies data to the WTO for domestic support for the marketing years 2002, 2003, 2004, and 2005.
Nov. 8, 2007	Brazil (WT/DS365/13) and Canada (WT/DS357/12) request that the establishment of a dispute panel to rule on their complaints against the United States be included on the DSB agenda for its next monthly meeting.
Nov. 27, 2007	At the DSB meeting, both Canada's and Brazil's requests for a panel on cases DS357 and DS365 were blocked by the United States,.
Dec. 17, 2007	The DSB, at its monthly meeting, announced the establishment of a single panel to examine jointly Brazil's and Canada's charges against U.S. farm subsidies and domestic support.
Feb. 2008	The case stalls over the inability to agree on panel members.
Apr. 2008	Brazil and Canada informally agree to postpone proceeding with the case pending Doha negotiations. No resumption date is announced.
See **Table 2** for a WTO Dispute Settlement process timeline; and **Table 3** for a timeline of a panel's work stages.	

Source: Compiled by CRS from official WTO documents and news sources as cited. All WTO official documents for each of these cases are available at the WTO Documents Online gateway and may be accessed by a simple search on the respective case number, DS357 or DS365, at http://docsonline.wto.org/gen_search.asp?searchmode=simple.

a. For a description and interpretation of Articles 5(c) and 6.3(c) of the SCM Agreement, see CRS Report RL33697, *Potential Challenges to U.S. Farm Subsidies in the WTO*, by Randy Schnepf.

b.Official WTO documents are Australia, WT/DS357/2; Guatemala, WT/DS357/3; Brazil, WT/DS357/4; Argentina, WT/DS357/5; the EC, WT/DS357/6; Uruguay, WT/DS357/7; Nicaragua, WT/DS357/8; and Thailand, WT/DS357/9.

c.Official WTO documents are Canada, WT/DS365/2; Guatemala, WT/DS365/3; Costa Rica, WT/DS365/4; the EC, WT/DS365/5; Mexico, WT/DS365/6; Australia, WT/DS365/7; Argentina, WT/DS365/8; Thailand, WT/DS365/9; India, WT/DS365/10; and Nicaragua, WT/DS365/11.

Each of these sections may be read independent of the other; thus, readers only interested in the specific charges and their implications may proceed directly to those sections of the report.

Background on the Evolution of the Two Cases

This section provides a historical record of the evolution of both Canada's and Brazil's WTO cases against U.S. farm programs. It includes a timeline (Table 1) of the official events as well as a descriptive narrative of the likely motivations and circumstances behind each country's case.

Origins of Canada's WTO Case

Canada and the United States have a history of commodity trade disputes, traditionally focused on various wheat support programs and trade practices.[4] In 2005, after several years of wrangling over wheat trade issues, Canada extended its disagreement with U.S. farm programs to the corn sector when Canadian corn producers sought legal action for alleged unfair subsidization and dumping of U.S. corn in Canadian markets. Canada's International Trade Tribunal (CITT) ultimately ruled on the 2005 anti-dumping and countervailing (AD/CV) duty case in favor of the United States.[5] However, Canadian corn producers continued to press their concerns upon the Canadian government about perceived unfair subsidization of U.S. corn.

In January 2007, Canada requested consultations with the United States to discuss three specific charges against U.S. farm programs: (1) U.S. farm support resulted in serious prejudice against Canadian corn producers, (2) U.S. domestic support exceeded its WTO commitments; and (3) U.S. export credit guarantee programs contained implicit WTO-illegal subsidies. Canada's first allegation in its WTO case built upon previous trade complaints against the United States initiated by Canadian corn producers starting in 2005, while the latter two allegations were based on a previous WTO ruling in a case (WTO case DS267) brought by Brazil against the U.S. cotton program. [6]

Another potential factor motivating Canada to bring its case against U.S. farm subsidies was Canadian domestic political concerns emanating from a weak coalition government responding to pressure from corn-producing interests following the unfavorable CITT AD/CV corn duty ruling. In addition, Canada had a general interest in influencing the 2007 U.S. farm bill debate in favor of lower amber-box-type support.[7] A news report suggested that two additional factors motivating Canada's case included the temporary suspension of Doha Round negotiations (July 24, 2006), which indefinitely postponed the possibility of U.S. farm program reforms under multilateral trade negotiations, and the settlement of a softwood lumber dispute between Canada and the United States, which freed up Canadian government trade attorneys to refocus on the WTO litigation against U.S. farm programs.[8]

The request for consultations represented the first step in instituting a WTO dispute settlement case against the United States—the assigning of an official dispute settlement case number (DS357)—thus setting in motion the explicit rules and timetables of the WTO DSU process.[9] Following Canada's request for consultations, several other WTO members—Argentina, Australia, Brazil, the European Communities, Guatemala, Nicaragua, Thailand, and Uruguay— officially requested to join the consultations as interested third parties.

On February 7, 2007, Canada and the United States held consultations concerning the three charges raised by Canada. Under WTO rules, for subsidy complaints alleging adverse effects, a minimum 60-day consultation period is required before a country can ask the WTO to establish a dispute settlement panel.[10] Although the consultations failed to resolve the dispute, the Canadian International Trade Minister, David Emerson, announced on May 2, 2007, that the Canadian government would temporarily hold off on taking any further action in its WTO dispute settlement proceeding (DS3 57) against U.S. corn subsidies until at least the end of the year, pending the outcome of Doha Round trade negotiations.[11]

However, in June 2007, Canada requested that the establishment of a WTO dispute settlement panel to hear its case against U.S. farm programs be included on the agenda of the next meeting of the WTO's Dispute Settlement Body (DSB). In its panel request, Canada dropped the serious prejudice charge against U.S. corn subsidies, probably in large part because corn market prices had risen so dramatically since mid-2006 and were projected to remain high for at least the next ten years.[12] The United States blocked Canada's request at the June 21, 2007, DSB meeting. According to WTO rules, a panel can be blocked only once, implying that a second request by Canada, if made at one of the subsequent DSB meetings, would have to be honored. However, Canada refrained from pursuing the establishment of a panel to hear the case at the next several DSB meetings.

Origins of Brazil's WTO Case

Brazil—which has already won a series of WTO dispute settlement rulings against U.S. cotton programs [13]—introduced its new challenge against

U.S. farm programs on July 11, 2007, when it requested consultations with the United States to discuss the same two charges against U.S. farm programs as in Canada's case (DS357).

The context for Brazil's new challenge of U.S. farm programs is significant. First, the new challenge builds on panel rulings from Brazil's successful case (DS267) against certain aspects of the U.S. cotton program. Previous findings in the case, although not part of the final recommendations, appear to have set legal precedent and could facilitate Brazil's new claims. Second, the Doha Round of WTO trade negotiations continues to make very little apparent progress after having resumed in September 2007, possibly providing further incentive to seek legal recourse under WTO's dispute settlement process rather than via negotiation. [14] Third, the U.S. Congress is presently revisiting omnibus farm legislation. Brazil has a general interest in influencing the U.S. farm bill debate in favor of lower amber-box-type support. Fourth, Canada had already initiated a similar case. Brazil initially joined Canada's case as an "interested third party"; however, Brazil has since chosen to pursue its own separate but similar case. News sources speculate that Brazil did this in order to have a "greater voice" in the WTO dispute settlement process.[15] Furthermore, Brazil's case appears to be more comprehensive than Canada's WTO case in terms of the level of detail of program support activity that is alleged to have been incorrectly notified as exempt or excluded from the AMS spending limit.

Following Brazil's request for consultations, several other WTO members—Canada, Guatemala, Costa Rica, the European Communities (EC), Mexico, Australia, Argentina, Thailand, India, and Nicaragua—officially requested to join the consultations as interested third parties. As with Canada's case, Brazil was assigned an official dispute settlement case number (DS365)—thus setting in motion the explicit rules and timetables of the WTO dispute settlement process.[16] Consultations between Brazil and the United States were held on August 22, 2007, but failed to resolve the dispute.

Status of the Two Cases

By late 2007, Canada and Brazil appear to have coordinated their efforts as both countries submitted official requests on November 8, 2007, for the DSB to add the establishment of a panel to its next meeting agenda. Again, according to the WTO rules, the United States blocked this new panel request at the November 27, 2007, DSB meeting. However, at its next meeting on

December 17, the DSB announced the establishment of a single panel to jointly hear both cases brought by Canada (DS357) and Brazil (DS365) against U.S. farm programs. In their requests, Brazil and Canada asked for a single panel to be established to consider both cases jointly. The United States did not object to this proposal. [17] All three countries involved—the United States, Canada, and Brazil—have agreed that the meeting of the panel would be open to the public.

However, by late February 2008 the case had stalled due to the inability of the three parties to agree on a panel of arbitrators to preside over the case.[18] Under WTO rules, Brazil is legally entitled to ask the WTO director-general to compose the panel if the parties are unable to agree on the members within 20 days after the establishment of a panel.[19] However, Brazil did not pursue this course of action. Then, in late April 2008, Brazil and Canada informally agreed to postpone proceeding with their case.[20] The postponement was thought to be provisional and based on success in achieving further disciplines on domestic support measures in the current Doha Round of WTO trade negotiations. As part of the Doha trade negotiations, U.S. officials had offered to substantially cut domestic agricultural subsidies.[21]

It is not clear how long the postponement will persist. If resumed, the first order of business will be the formation of a panel. In accordance with the DSU, once the establishment of a panel has been announced the DSB has up to 45 days for a panel to be appointed, plus six months for the panel to conclude its work.

Major Charges against U.S. Farm Programs

Both the Canadian (DS357) and Brazilian (DS365) cases raise two principal charges against U.S. farm programs. Each of these is discussed below.

First Allegation: U.S. Total Domestic Agricultural Support Exceeds Its WTO Limit

In accordance with WTO commitments, all WTO members have agreed to submit annual notifications of their farm program outlays to the WTO, and these outlays are subject to specific limits. For the United States, its total spending limit for "amber box" programs (i.e., programs that are trade- and market-distorting) was $19.9 billion in 1999 and $19.1 billion in all subsequent years.[22] To date, the United States has notified details of its farm program outlays through 2005.[23] According to U.S. farm program spending notifications to the WTO, U.S. domestic support outlays have remained well within U.S. WTO spending commitments.[24] However, Canada and Brazil argue that several U.S. program payments were either omitted from the notification data, or incorrectly notified either as green box or as non-product-specific AMS (where they would more easily qualify for exclusion from amber box limits under the non-product-specific *de minimis* exemption). Canada and Brazil contend that when all of the disputed payments and other subsidies are included in the U.S. AMS calculation, then the total outlays would exceed the spending commitment in each of 1999, 2000, 2001, 2002, 2004, and 2005.

The claim that the United States has exceeded its total spending limits hinges largely on a previous ruling from the U.S.-Brazil cotton case in which a WTO panel found that U.S. payments made under the Production Flexibility Contract (PFC) and Direct Payment (DP) programs do not qualify for the WTO's green box exemption category because of their prohibition on planting fruits, vegetables, and wild rice on covered program acreage.[25] However, the panel did not make the extension that PFC and DP payments should therefore be counted as amber box programs, but instead was mute on this point. In its WTO notifications, the United States has notified its PFC payments as fully decoupled and green box compliant.[26] This is an important distinction because the green box contains only non-distorting program payments and is not subject to any limit. Canada and Brazil argue that, because of the previous panel ruling, PFC and DP payments do not conform with WTO green-box rules and should be included with U.S. amber box payments.

Furthermore, Canada and Brazil argue that several other U.S. program payments were incorrectly notified as exempt from the U.S. AMS limit. These include:

- Production Flexibility Contract (PFC) and Direct Payment (DP) programs whose payments were notified as green box under "decoupled income" payments;
- Non-insured Crop Disaster Assistance Program (NAP) payments, Crop Disaster Assistance, Emergency Feed, Livestock Indemnity, and Tree Assistance programs that were notified as green box under "payments for relief from natural disasters;" and

- emergency "crop market loss assistance" payments from the early 2000s that were notified as non-product-specific AMS, but which Brazil and Canada contend would be more correctly notified as product-specific AMS outlays.

In addition, both Canada and Brazil argue that CCP payments (established under the 2002 Farm Act [P.L. 107-171]) should similarly be counted against the U.S. amber box spending limit of $19.1 billion. In contrast, the United States has notified CCP payments as exempt from AMS limits under the non-product specific de minimis exemption. In addition, as part of its Doha policy reform proposal the United States recommends that CCP payments be eligible for the blue box, where they would be subject to a different limit than the amber box.[27]

Unlike Canada's case, Brazil cited several additional U.S. farm support programs that it claims were simply not notified (i.e., they were omitted from inclusion in the U.S. AMS total). These include:

- both direct and guaranteed loans, and USDA farm loan programs;
- programs exempting on-farm use of gasoline and diesel fuel from payment of various excise and sales taxes;
- programs exempting U.S. farmers from taxes based on overall farm income— e.g., deductions from taxable income from farming; farm marketing and purchasing cooperatives; and export transactions of agricultural commodities; and
- subsidies related to the operation and maintenance of irrigation works by the U.S. Department of the Interior.

Canada and Brazil charge that, when PFC, DP, and CCP payments for all covered crops—wheat, corn, grain sorghum, barley, oats, upland cotton, rice, soybeans, and other oilseeds—as well as the additional program outlays that were excluded from U.S. notifications are included in the U.S.'s amber box, then the total outlays would exceed the spending commitment in each of 1999, 2000, 2001, 2002, 2004, and 2005. However, neither Canada nor Brazil provide the specific details on its year-by-year determinations, so direct comparisons are not possible.

CRS calculations based on U.S. notifications and available USDA data suggest that, with the inclusion of the otherwise excluded PFC and DP payments, the U.S. AMS total would exceed the spending limit in two of the years indicated (Figure 1). The further inclusion of both market loss assistance and CCP payments as product specific amber box payments to the U.S. AMS total suggests that the spending limit would be exceeded in five of the years indicated (Figure 2).

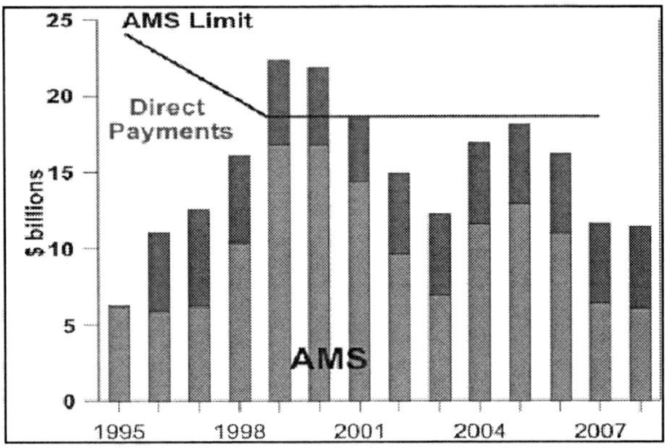

Source: Data for 1995-2005 are from U.S. WTO notifications, and 2006-2008 are CRS calculations based on USDA data.

Note: Direct payments include PFC and DP payments.

Figure 1. U.S. AMS Outlays and Direct Payments

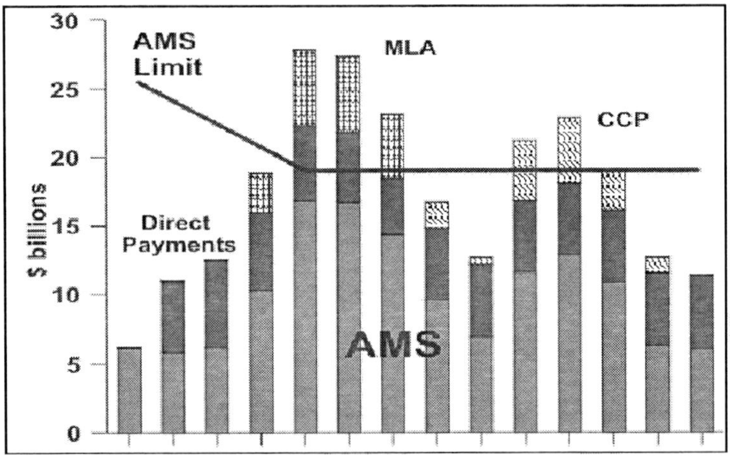

Source: Data for 1995-2005 are from U.S. WTO notifications, and 2006-2008 are CRS calculations based on USDA data.

Note: DP includes PFC and DP payments; MLA (1998-2001); CCP (2002-2008).

Figure 2. U.S. Outlays for AMS, Direct Payments (DP), Market Loss Assistance (MLA), and Counter-Cyclical Payments (CCP)

Second Allegation: U.S. Export Credit Guarantees Are WTO-Illegal Export Subsidies

Canada and Brazil argue that the U.S. export credit guarantee program operates as a WTO-illegal export subsidy. In the U.S.-Brazil cotton case (DS267), a WTO panel found that U.S. export credit guarantees effectively function as export subsidies because the financial benefits returned by these programs failed to cover their long-run operating costs.[28] Furthermore, the panel found that this applies not just to cotton, but to all commodities that benefit from U.S. commodity support programs and receive export credit guarantees. As a result, export credit guarantees for any recipient commodity are subject to previously scheduled WTO spending limits. The panel recommended (and was upheld on appeal) that these prohibited subsidies be removed by July 1, 2005. On December 18, 2007, a compliance panel found that the United States had not yet fully complied with the panel ruling.

U.S. Response

In response to Canada's request for consultations on U.S. subsidies, then-U.S. Secretary of Agriculture Mike Johanns declared in early 2007 that the United States would vigorously defend U.S. farm programs against any possible WTO challenge by Canada.[29] A spokesman for the U.S. Trade Representative (USTR) declared that this dispute was an unnecessary diversion of resources and time from the Doha Round negotiations. The official also stated that U.S. farm programs were designed to be in compliance with its WTO obligations and believed that the panel would agree. The official also added that some measures identified by Canada and Brazil had ceased to exist prior to the 2002 farm bill, and that others were not part of the consultations with Canada.

With respect to the ruling that export credit guarantees operate like illegal export subsidies, provisions in the 2008 farm bill (P.L. 110-246; Section 3101(a)), enacted into law on June 18, 2008, would appear to have brought the export credit guarantee program into compliance with WTO rules by eliminating the "subsidy" component of export credit guarantees. This includes repeal of authority for both the GSM-103 program (which guaranteed longer-term—3-10 years— financing) and the Supplier Credit Guarantee Program (which guaranteed very short-term—up to 1 year—financing of exports), as well as repeal of the 1% cap on loan origination fees for the GSM-102 program (which guaranteed intermediate-term—up to 3 years—financing). The 1% fee cap had prevented charging market-based fees and had contributed to the export credit program operating as a WTO-illegal export subsidy. The new farm bill (Sec. 3101(b)) also caps the credit subsidy for the program at $40 million annually.[30]

However, the 2008 farm bill did not address the issue surrounding the disqualification of direct payments from the WTO's green box AMS exclusion due to the planting restriction on fruits, vegetables, and wild rice on program base acres. Instead, direct payments are extended (Sec. 1103) with no change to the current planting restriction, except for 84,000 acres of pilot programs in seven states (Sec. 1107(d)). This retention of the status quo in the face of the cotton panel's ruling and recommendation has important WTO implications, as it would appear to favor the charge that the United States has exceeded its total AMS limit in at least two years (1999 and 2000) if direct payments are included in the AMS calculation (Figure 1).

Potential Implications and Role of Congress

Many market analysts suggest that these two cases brought by Brazil and Canada are harbingers of future challenges to U.S. commodity programs. If either country were to successfully pursue its case, it could affect most U.S. program commodities, since the charges against the U.S. export credit guarantee program and AMS limit extend to all major program crops. Should any eventual changes in U.S. farm policy be needed to comply with a WTO ruling, Congress likely would be called upon to address this issue (including adjustment, if not full removal, of the planting restriction on base acres receiving direct payments).

Ultimately, Congress is responsible for passing farm program legislation that complies with U.S. commitments in international trade agreements. When confronted with a negative WTO dispute settlement ruling, a country has essentially five options to choose from: eliminate the subsidy; reduce the subsidy to diminish its adverse effect; revise the program function to reduce the linkage between the subsidy and the adverse effect (referred to as decoupling); pay a mutually acceptable compensatory payment to offset the adverse effects of the subsidy; or suffer the consequences of trade retaliation.

While a WTO case can result in punitive sanctions being authorized, the proceedings of a formal case can take many months, and sometimes years, to reach a conclusion.[31] For example, the U.S.- Brazil cotton case was initiated by Brazil's request for WTO consultations on September 27, 2002. A panel was established nearly six months later on March 18, 2003. The panel's final report was delivered to the DSB on September 8, 2004. The case was appealed and the Appellate Body's final report was adopted by the DSB on March 21, 2005, nearly 30 months after the initial request for consultations.[32] Subsequently, Brazil requested a WTO compliance panel to review whether the United States had fully complied with the panel's rulings. The WTO compliance panel issued its final ruling on December 18, 2007, thus extending the length of the U.S.-Brazil cotton case to over five years.

Many market watchers question the relevance of expending legal resources to establish an historical AMS violation in light of the high commodity prices that have persisted since mid- 2007. U.S. farm program payments made under the marketing loan provisions and CCP program have to be triggered by low commodity prices before payments are made. Most long-run commodity market projections predict high commodity prices and low government program support to persist well into the future, thus, keeping U.S. domestic support outlays well within current AMS limits without any further changes to the programs. Additional uncertainty arises from the ongoing Doha Round of trade negotiations, where a successful conclusion could potentially mitigate or end Canada's and Brazil's interest in continuing its case against the U.S. farm programs.

Given the importance of agricultural trade in the U.S. agricultural economy, Congress will likely be monitoring developments in the WTO AMS dispute. The House and Senate Agriculture Committees regularly hold hearings on agricultural trade negotiations. If the ongoing Doha Round of WTO trade negotiations were to successfully conclude with a text for further multilateral trade reform, it is likely that Congress would hold hearings and consult with the Administration concerning the possible renewal of fast-track, or Trade Promotion Authority (TPA), legislation, which expired on July 1, 2007.[33] Such hearings and consultations would be a major vehicle for Members to express their views on the U.S.-Brazil/Canada AMS trade dispute, on the negotiating issues that it raises, and on the potential implications for U.S. farm policy.

Table 2. WTO Time Line for Dispute Settlement

Time Allowed[a]	Activity
60 days	Consultations, mediation, etc.
45 days	Panel set up and panelists appointed
6 months	Final panel report to parties
3 weeks	Final panel report to WTO members
60 days	Dispute Settlement Body adopts report (if no appeal)
Total = 1 year	**Without Appeal**
60 to 90 days	Appeals report
30 days	Dispute Settlement Body adopts appeals report
Grand Total = 1 year 3 months	**With Appeal**

Source: WTO Dispute Settlement online resources; available at http://www.wto.org/english/tratop_e/dispu_e/ dispu_e.htm.

Note: These approximate periods for each stage of a dispute settlement procedure are target figures—the agreement is flexible. In addition, the countries can settle their dispute themselves at any stage. Totals are also approximate.

a. Time period begins when the official request for consultations is received by the WTO Dispute Settlement Body (DSB).

Table 3. The Main Stages of a WTO Panel's Work

Timing	Activity
Establishment of Panel	The Dispute Settlement Body (DSB) has 45 days to appoint members to the panel.
Panel Members Appointed	The panel has 6 months to finish hearings, rebuttals, and expert testimony, to review the evidence, and to produce a final report on the case.
Before the first hearing	Each side in the dispute presents its case in writing to the panel.
First hearing	The case for the complaining country and the defense. The complaining country or countries, the responding country, and those that have announced they have an interest in the dispute, make their case at the panel's first hearing.
Rebuttals	The countries involved submit written rebuttals and present oral arguments at the panel's second meeting.
Experts	If one side raises scientific or other technical matters, the panel may consult experts or appoint an expert review group to prepare an advisory report.

Table 3. (Continued)

Timing	Activity
First draft	The panel submits the descriptive (factual and argument) sections of its report to the two sides, giving them two weeks to comment (this chapter does not include findings and conclusions).
Interim report	The panel then submits an interim report, including its findings and conclusions, to the two sides, giving them one week to ask for a review.
Review	The period of review must not exceed two weeks (during that time, the panel may hold additional meetings with the two sides).
Final report	A final report is submitted to the two sides and three weeks later, it is circulated to all WTO members. If the panel decides that the disputed trade measure does break a WTO agreement or an obligation, it recommends that the measure be made to conform with WTO rules. The panel may suggest how this could be done.
The report becomes a ruling	The report becomes the DSB's ruling or ecommendation within 60 days unless a consensus rejects it. Both sides can appeal the report (and in some cases both sides do).

Source: WTO Dispute Settlement online resources; available at *http://www.wto.org* /english/tratop_e/dispu_e/ dispu_e.htm.

End Notes

[1] "Brazil, Canada Subsidies Challenge Stalled Over WTO Panel Selection," *Inside U.S. Trade*, February 29, 2008.

[2] "Brazil, Canada Put WTO Subsidies Challenge on Temporary Hold," *Inside U.S. Trade*, April 25, 2008.

[3] *Outlook for U.S. Agricultural Trade*, AES-60, USDA, ERS, December 1, 2008; and *Agricultural Income and Finance Outlook*, AIS-86, USDA, ERS, December 2008.

[4] For more information see CRS Report RL32426, *U.S.-Canada Wheat Trade Dispute*, by Randy Schnepf.

[5] CITT, *Dumping and Subsidizing: Finding*, Inquiry No. NQ-2005-001, Unprocessed Grain Corn, April 18, 2006, at http://www.citt-tcce.gc.ca/dumping

[6] For more information, see CRS Report RL32571, *Brazil's WTO Case Against the U.S. Cotton Program*, by Randy Schnepf.

[7] The amber box includes those policies that result in market-distorting support. For a discussion of proposed reductions in WTO domestic support commitments, see CRS Report RL33 144, *WTO Doha Round: The Agricultural Negotiations*, by Charles E. Hanrahan and Randy Schnepf.

[8] *Inside U.S. Trade*, "Johanns Says U.S. Will Defend Farm Programs from Canadian Challenge," January 12, 2007.

[9] For more information, see CRS Report RS20088, *Dispute Settlement in the World Trade Organization (WTO): An Overview*, by Jeanne J. Grimmett.

[10] Article 7.4, SCM Agreement.

[11] "Holding Up on the US Corn WTO Case," *Washington Trade Daily*, Vol. 16, No. 88, May 3, 2007.

[12] For long-run commodity price projections, see USDA's Agricultural Baseline Projections; available at http://www.ers.usda.gov/Briefing/Baseline/.

[13] For more information, see CRS Report RL32571, *Brazil's WTO Case Against the U.S. Cotton Program*, by Randy Schnepf.

[14] Doha Round talks were indefinitely suspended on July 24, 2007, but restarted the following September. For more information, see CRS Report RL33 144, *WTO Doha Round: The Agricultural Negotiations*, by Charles E. Hanrahan and Randy Schnepf.

[15] "Brazil Changes Course by Filing Separate Case Rather than Joining Canada," Jim Wiesemeyer, *AgWeb.com*, July 12, 2007.

[16] For more information, see CRS Report RS20088, *Dispute Settlement in the World Trade Organization (WTO): An Overview*, by Jeanne J. Grimmett.

[17] WTO Dispute Settlement Body monthly news release, December 17, 2007, available at http://www.wto.org/english/ news _e/news07 _e/dsb _17dec07 _e.htm.

[18] "Brazil, Canada Subsidies Challenge Stalled Over WTO Panel Selection," *Inside U.S. Trade*, February 29, 2008.

[19] Article 8.7, Understanding on Rules and Procedures Governing the Settlement of Disputes, WTO *Legal Texts*, Annex 2—Dispute Settlement Understanding (DSU); available at http://www.wto.org/english/docs_e/legal_e/legal_e.htm.

[20] "Brazil, Canada Put WTO Subsidies Challenge on Temporary Hold," *Inside U.S. Trade*, April 25, 2008.

[21] For more information on the Doha Round of WTO trade negotiations and specific offers by major negotiating parties, see CRS Report RL33 144, *WTO Doha Round: The Agricultural Negotiations*, by Charles E. Hanrahan and Randy Schnepf.

[22] Amber box outlays are actually a residual category comprised of the total Aggregate Measure of Support (i.e., a total of all market and trade distorting support) less those outlays that are exempt from any limit under four possible exclusion classifications: green box, blue box, and product- or non-product-specific de minimis exclusions. For more information on WTO support classifications see CRS Report RS20840, *Agriculture in the WTO: Limits on Domestic Support*, by Randy Schnepf.

[23] At the time that both Canada and Brazil initiated their cases (DS357 and DS365), the United States had only notified its domestic support data through marketing year 2001. The United States notified for the marketing years 2002, 2003, 2004, and 2005 on October 8, 2007.

[24] For more information on WTO commitments and actual outlays, see CRS Report RL30612, *Agriculture in the WTO: Member Spending on Domestic Support*, by Randy Schnepf, and CRS Report RL32916, *Agriculture in the WTO: Policy Commitments Made Under the Agreement on Agriculture*, by Randy Schnepf.

[25] For more information on these restrictions see USDA, Farm Service Agency, Fact Sheet, *Direct and Counter- Cyclical Payment Program Wild Rice, Fruit, and Vegetable Provisions*, February 2003, at http://www.fsa.usda.gov/pas/publications/ facts/html/fav03.htm.

[26] Decoupled means it has no influence on producer's decision-making process; green box compliant means it adheres to the terms and conditions of Annex 2 of the Agreement on Agriculture.

[27] Blue box payments are defined as "production-limiting" types of payments. For more information see CRS Report RL33 144, *WTO Doha Round: The Agricultural Negotiations*, by Charles E. Hanrahan and Randy Schnepf.

[28] For more detail, see CRS Report RL32571, *Brazil's WTO Case Against the U.S. Cotton Program*, by Randy Schnepf.

[29] *Inside U.S. Trade*, "Johanns Says U.S. Will Defend Farm Programs from Canadian Challenge," January 12, 2007.

[30] The credit subsidy is the available budget authority for the cost of the program.

[31] For more information, see CRS Report RS20088, *Dispute Settlement in the World Trade Organization (WTO): An Overview*, by Jeanne J. Grimmett.

[32] This timeline is discussed in more detail in CRS Report RL32571, *Brazil's WTO Case Against the U.S. Cotton Program*, by Randy Schnepf.

[33] For more information, see CRS Report RL33743, *Trade Promotion Authority (TPA): Issues, Options, and Prospects for Renewal*, by J. F. Hornbeck and William H. Cooper.

In: Disputed WTO Cases Involving the United... ISBN: 978-1-61761-433-0
Editors: Jacqueline P. Daniels

Chapter 4

DISPUTE SETTLEMENT IN THE WORLD TRADE ORGANIZATION (WTO): AN OVERVIEW*

Jeanne J. Grimmett

SUMMARY

Dispute settlement in the World Trade Organization (WTO) is carried out under the WTO Understanding on Rules and Procedures Governing the Settlement of Disputes (DSU). In effect since January 1995, the DSU provides for consultations between disputing parties, panels and appeals, and possible retaliation if a defending party fails to comply with a WTO decision by an established deadline. Automatic establishment of panels, adoption of panel and appellate reports, and authorization of requests to retaliate, along with deadlines and improved multilateral oversight of compliance, are aimed at producing a more expeditious and effective system than had existed under the General Agreement on Tariffs and Trade (GATT). To date, 405 complaints have been filed, approximately half involving the United States as complainant or defendant.

* This is an edited, reformatted and augmented edition of a United States Congressional Research Service publication, Report RS20088, dated April 8, 2010.

Expressing dissatisfaction with WTO dispute settlement results in the trade remedy area, Congress, in the Trade Act of 2002, directed the executive branch to address dispute settlement in WTO negotiations. WTO Members have been negotiating DSU revisions in the currently stalled Doha Development Round of trade negotiations but no final agreement on the DSU has been reached. Use of the DSU has revealed procedural gaps, particularly affecting the compliance phase of a dispute. These include a failure to coordinate procedures for requesting retaliation with procedures for tasking a WTO panel with determining whether a defending Member has complied in a case and the absence of a procedure for withdrawing trade sanctions imposed by a complaining Member where the defending Member believes it has fulfilled its WTO obligations. As a result, disputing Members have entered into bilateral agreements permitting retaliation and compliance panel processes to progress on an agreed schedule and have initiated new dispute proceedings aimed at removing retaliatory measures.

Where a U.S. law or regulation is at issue in a WTO case, the adoption by the WTO of a panel or Appellate Body report finding that the measure violates a WTO agreement does not give the report direct legal effect in this country; thus federal law is not affected until Congress or the executive branch, as the case may be, takes action to remove the offending measure. Where a restrictive foreign trade practice is at issue, Section 301 of the Trade Act of 1974 provides a mechanism by which the United States Trade Representative (USTR) may challenge the measure in a WTO dispute settlement proceeding and authorizes the USTR to take retaliatory action if the defending Member has not complied with the resulting WTO decision. Although Section 301 was challenged in the WTO on the ground that it requires the USTR to act unilaterally in WTO-related trade disputes in violation of DSU provisions requiring resort to multilateral WTO dispute settlement, the United States was ultimately found not to be in violation of its DSU obligations.

H.R. 496 (Rangel) would create an Office of the Congressional Trade Enforcer that would, inter alia, investigate restrictive foreign trade practices in light of WTO obligations and call on the USTR to pursue WTO cases where alleged violations are found; express congressional dissatisfaction with WTO decisions; and restrict implementation of a revised methodology for calculating dumping margins adopted by the Commerce Department in 2007 in response to adverse WTO decisions. S. 363 (Snowe) would grant the U.S. Court of International Trade exclusive jurisdiction to review *de novo* certain USTR determinations under Section 301 of the Trade Act of 1974, which may in some cases involve the initiation and conduct of WTO disputes, and would amend various Section 301 authorities themselves. S. 1466 (Stabenow) and S. 1982 (Brown) would establish mechanisms under the Trade Act of 1974 requiring the USTR to identify particularly harmful foreign trade practices and, where appropriate, to initiate WTO cases to remedy these practices.

BACKGROUND

From its inception in 1947, the General Agreement on Tariffs and Trade (GATT), signed by the United States and ultimately by a total of 128 countries, provided for consultations and dispute resolution, allowing a GATT Party to invoke GATT dispute settlement articles if it believes that another Party's measure, whether violative of the GATT or not, caused it trade injury. Because the GATT did not set out a dispute procedure with great specificity, GATT Parties developed a more detailed process including ad hoc panels and other practices. The procedure was perceived to have certain deficiencies, however, among them a lack of deadlines, a consensus decision-making process that allowed a GATT Party against whom a dispute was filed to block the establishment of a dispute panel and the adoption of a panel report by the GATT Parties as a whole, and laxity in surveillance and implementation of panel reports even when reports were adopted and had the status of an official GATT decision.

Congress made reform of the GATT dispute process a principal U.S. goal in the GATT Uruguay Round of Multilateral Trade Negotiations, begun in 1986 and concluded in 1994 with the signing of the Marrakesh Agreement Establishing the World Trade Organization (WTO Agreement). The WTO Agreement requires any country that wishes to be a WTO Member to accept all of the multilateral trade agreements negotiated during the Round, including the General Agreement on Tariffs and Trade 1994, an updated version of the GATT adopted in 1947, as well as the Understanding on Rules and Procedures Governing the Settlement of Disputes, applicable to disputes arising under virtually all WTO agreements.

The Uruguay Round package of agreements not only carries forward original GATT obligations, such as according goods of other parties nondiscriminatory treatment, not placing tariffs on goods that exceed negotiated or "bound" rates, generally refraining from imposing quantitative restrictions such as quotas and embargoes on imports and exports, and avoiding injurious subsidies, but also expands on these obligations in new agreements such as the Agreement on Agriculture, the Agreement on the Application of Sanitary and Phytosanitary Measures, the Agreement on Antidumping, and the Agreement on Subsidies and Countervailing Measures.

Congress approved and implemented the WTO Agreement and the other agreements negotiated in the Uruguay Round in the Uruguay Round Agreement Act, P.L. 103-465. The agreements entered into force on January 1, 1995.

WTO Dispute Settlement Understanding

The Understanding on Rules and Procedures Governing the Settlement of Disputes (DSU) continues past GATT dispute practice, but also contains features aimed at strengthening the prior system.[1] The DSU provides for integrated dispute settlement under which the same rules apply to disputes under virtually all WTO agreements, subject to any special or additional rules in an individual agreement.

The WTO Dispute Settlement Body (DSB), created under the DSU and consisting of representatives of all WTO Members, administers WTO dispute settlement proceedings. While the DSB ordinarily operates by consensus (i.e., without objection), the DSU reverses past consensus practice at fundamental stages of the process. Thus, unless it decides by consensus *not* to do so, the DSB will establish panels; adopt panel and appellate reports; and, where WTO rulings have not been implemented and if requested by a prevailing party, authorize the party to impose a retaliatory measure. The DSU also sets forth deadlines for various stages of the proceedings and improves multilateral monitoring of the implementation of adopted rulings.

Given that panel reports would otherwise be adopted automatically, WTO Members have a right to appeal a panel report on legal issues. The DSU creates a standing Appellate Body to carry out this added appellate function. The Appellate Body has seven members, three of whom serve on any one case.

Dispute settlement under the WTO is primarily Member-driven, that is, it is up to the parties to a dispute to decide whether or not to take particular actions available to them, e.g., to request a panel if consultations fail, to request authorization to impose countermeasures against a noncomplying member, or to impose such measures even if the DSB has authorized them. As stated in Article 3.7 of the DSU, the preferred outcome of a dispute is "a solution mutually acceptable to the parties and consistent with the covered agreements." Absent this, the primary objective of the process is withdrawal of a violative measure, with compensation and retaliation being avenues of last resort.

As of the date of this chapter, 405 complaints have been filed under the DSU, with approximately one-half of these resulting in the establishment of a panel. In some of these proceedings, however, the panel process was discontinued due to a settlement of the dispute or for other reasons. To date, 131 original panel reports have been publicly circulated. Some panels have also issued an additional report or reports under Article 21.5 of the DSU determining whether the defending Member complied in a particular dispute. About two-thirds of the original panel reports were appealed.

Approximately one-half of the 405 WTO complaints involve the United States as complaining party or defendant. The United States Trade Representative (USTR) manages U.S. participation and is the chief representative of the United States in the WTO, including in WTO disputes.[2]

The DSU was scrutinized by WTO Members under a Uruguay Round Declaration, which called for completion of a review within four years after the WTO Agreement entered into force (i.e., by January 1999). Members did not agree on any revisions in the initial review and continued to negotiate on dispute settlement issues during the current WTO Doha Development Round of multilateral trade negotiations, doing so on a separate track permitting an agreement to be adopted apart from any overall Doha Round accord. In 2008, the chairman of the dispute settlement negotiations prepared a consolidated draft legal text based mainly on Member proposals, which Members agreed to use in their negotiations.[3] The United States has proposed such revisions as greater Member control over the process, guidelines for WTO adjudicative bodies, and increased transparency, e.g., open meetings and timely access to submissions and final reports.[4] Other Member proposals include, inter alia, a permanent roster of panelists, enabling the Appellate Body to remand decisions to panels for further proceedings, rules for sequencing and the termination of retaliatory measures (see below), tightened time frames, enhanced third-party rights, and special treatment for developing country disputants.[5]

Steps in a WTO Dispute

Following are the stages in a DSU proceeding, with the applicable DSU articles for each:

Consultations (Article 4)

The DSU permits a WTO Member to consult with another Member regarding "measures affecting the operation of any covered agreement taken within the territory" of the latter. If a WTO Member requests consultations with another Member under a WTO agreement, the latter Member must enter into consultations with the former within 30 days.[6]

If the dispute is not resolved within 60 days, the complaining party may request a panel. The complainant may request a panel before this period ends if the other Member has failed to enter into consultations or if the disputants agree that consultations have been unsuccessful.

Establishing a Dispute Panel (Articles 6, 8)

A panel request, which must be made in writing, must "identify the specific measures at issue and provide a brief summary of the legal basis for the complaint sufficient to present the problem clearly" (Art. 6.2). Under GATT and now WTO dispute settlement practice, a Member may challenge a measure of another Member "as such," "as applied," or both.[7] An "as such" claim challenges the measure independent of its application in a specific situation and, as described by the WTO Appellate Body, seeks to prevent the defending Member from engaging in identified conduct before the fact.[8]

If a panel is requested, the DSB must establish it at the second DSB meeting at which the request appears as an agenda item, unless it decides by consensus not to do so. Thus, while a defending Member may block the establishment of a panel the first time the complaining Member makes its request at a DSB meeting, the panel will be established, virtually automatically, the second time such a request is placed on the DSB's agenda. While DSB ordinarily meets once a month, the complaining Member may request that the DSB convene for the sole purpose of considering the panel request. Any such meeting must be held within 15 days after the complaining Member requests that the meeting be held.

The panel is ordinarily composed of three persons. The WTO Secretariat proposes the names of panelists to the disputing parties, who may not oppose them except for "compelling reasons" (Art. 8.6). If there is no agreement on panelists within 20 days from the date that the panel is established, either disputing party may request the WTO Director-General to appoint the panel members.

Panel Proceedings (Articles 12, 15, Appendix 3)

After considering written and oral arguments, the panel issues the descriptive part of its report (facts and argument) to the disputing parties. After considering any comments, the panel submits this portion along with its findings and conclusions to the disputants as an interim report. Following a review period, a final report is issued to the disputing parties and later circulated to all WTO Members. A panel must generally provide its final report to disputants within six months after the panel is composed, but may take longer if needed; extensions are usual in complex cases. The period from panel establishment to circulation of a panel report to WTO Members should not exceed nine months. In practice, panels have been found to take more than 13 months on average to publicly circulate reports.[9]

Adoption of Panel Reports/Appellate Review (Articles 16, 17, 20)

Within 60 days after a panel report is circulated to WTO Members, the report is to be adopted at a DSB meeting unless a disputing party appeals it or the DSB decides by consensus not to adopt it. Within 60 days of being notified of an appeal (extendable to 90 days), the Appellate Body (AB) must issue a report that upholds, reverses, or modifies the panel report. The AB report is to be adopted by the DSB, and unconditionally accepted by the disputing parties, unless the DSB decides by consensus not to adopt it within 30 days after circulation to Members. The period of time from the date the panel is established to the date the DSB considers the panel report for adoption is not to exceed nine months (12 months where the report is appealed) unless otherwise agreed by the disputing parties.

Implementation of Panel and Appellate Body Reports (Article 21)

In the event that the WTO decision finds the defending Member has violated an obligation under a WTO agreement, the Member must inform the DSB of its implementation plans within 30 days after the panel report and any AB report are adopted. If it is "impracticable" for the Member to comply immediately, the Member will have a "reasonable period of time" to do so. The Member is expected to implement the WTO decision fully by the end of this period and to act consistently with the decision after the period expires. [10] Compliance may be achieved by withdrawing the WTO-inconsistent measure or, alternatively, by issuing a revised measure that modifies or replaces it.[11]

Under the DSU, the "reasonable period of time" is: (1) that proposed by the Member and approved by the DSB; (2) absent approval, the period mutually agreed by the disputants within 45 days after the report or reports are adopted by the DSB; or (3) failing agreement, the period determined by binding arbitration. Arbitration is to be completed within 90 days after adoption of the reports. To aid the arbitrator in determining the length of the compliance period, the DSU provides a non-binding guideline of 15 months from the date of adoption. Arbitrated compliance periods have ranged from six months to 15 months and one week. The DSU envisions that a maximum 18 months will elapse from the date a panel is established until the reasonable period of time is determined.

Compliance Panels (Article 21.5)

Where there is disagreement as to whether a Member has complied—i.e., whether a compliance measure exists, or whether a measure that has been taken is consistent with the WTO decision in the case—either disputing party may request that a compliance panel be convened under Article 21.5. A compliance panel is expected to issue its report within 90 days after the dispute is referred to it, but it may extend this time period if needed. Compliance panel reports may be appealed to the WTO Appellate Body and both reports are subject to adoption by the DSB.[12]

Compensation and Suspension of Concessions (Article 22)

If the defending Member fails to comply with the WTO decision within the established compliance period, the prevailing Member may request that the defending Member negotiate a compensation agreement. If such a request is made and agreement is not reached within 20 days after the compliance deadline expires, or if negotiations have not been requested, the prevailing Member may request authorization from the DSB to retaliate, i.e., suspend concessions or obligations owed the non-complying Member under a WTO agreement.

Generally, a Member should first try to suspend concessions or obligations in the same trade sector as the one at issue in the dispute (Art. 22.3(a)). If this is "not practicable or effective," the Member may then seek to suspend concessions in another sector under the same WTO agreement (Art. 22.3(b)). If, however, suspending concessions in other sectors under the same agreement is not "practicable or effective" and "the circumstances are serious enough," the Member may seek to suspend concessions or obligations under another WTO agreement, or "cross-retaliate" (Art. 22.3(c)).

Retaliation most often involves the suspension of GATT tariff concessions, i.e., the imposition of tariff surcharges, on selected products from the non-complying Member. In some cases, however, the non-compliant Member may not be a major exporter of goods to the prevailing Member or some or all of the goods that are exported are considered to be critical to the prevailing Member's economy. In such case, if firms of the non-compliant Member are active service providers or exercise significant intellectual property rights in the prevailing Member's territory, the prevailing Member may seek to suspend market access obligations under the General Agreement on Trade in Services (GATS) or obligations under the Agreement on Trade-Related Aspects of Intellectual Property Rights (Agreement on TRIPS).

The DSB is to grant a retaliation request within 30 days after the compliance deadline expires unless it decides by consensus not to do so, or the defending Member requests that the retaliation proposal be arbitrated. Depending on the contents of the proposal, the defending Member may object to the level of the proposed retaliation, i.e., that it is not equivalent to the level of trade injury in the dispute, claim that DSU principles and procedures for requesting cross-retaliation have not been followed, or both.[13] Once requested, arbitration is automatic and is to be completed within 60 days after the compliance period ends. An arbitral decision is considered final.

After the arbitral decision is issued, the prevailing party may request that the DSB approve its proposal, subject to any modification by the arbitrator. The prevailing Member is not required to request authorization, however, nor is the Member required to do so by a given date if it chooses to pursue such a request. If imposed, retaliation is permitted to remain in effect only until the offending measure is removed or the disputing parties otherwise resolve the dispute.

USE OF MULTILATERAL DISPUTE SETTLEMENT PROCEDURES

Article 23 of the DSU requires that WTO Members invoke DSU procedures in disputes involving WTO agreements and that they act in accordance with the DSU (i.e., not unilaterally) when determining if another Member has violated a WTO agreement, determining a date by which the Member must comply with a WTO decision, and taking any retaliatory action against a noncomplying Member. Whether U.S. trade remedy law, specifically Section 301 of the Trade Act of 1974, requires the United States to act in violation of Section 23 of the DSU was at issue in an early WTO case, *United States—Sections 301-310 of the Trade Act of 1974*, discussed below.

COMPLIANCE ISSUES

"Sequencing"

Although many WTO rulings have been satisfactorily implemented, difficult cases have tested DSU implementation articles, highlighting deficiencies in the system and prompting suggestions for reform. For example, gaps in the DSU have resulted in the problem of "sequencing," which first manifested itself in 1998-1999 during the compliance phase of the successful U.S. challenge of the European Union's banana import regime. Article 22 allows a prevailing party to request authorization to retaliate within 30 days after a compliance period ends, while Article 21.5 provides that disagreements over the existence or adequacy of compliance measures are to be decided using WTO dispute procedures, including resort to panels. A compliance panel's report is due within 90 days after the dispute is referred to it and may be appealed. The DSU does not integrate an Article 21.5 procedure into the 30-day Article 22 deadline, nor does it expressly state how compliance is to be determined so that a prevailing party may pursue action under Article 22. Absent the adoption of multilateral rules on the matter, disputing parties have entered into ad hoc procedural agreements in individual disputes.

Removal of Retaliatory Measures

The DSU is also silent on how authorized retaliation is to be terminated in the event a defending Member believes that it has complied in a dispute. This issue has been the subject of *United States - Continued Suspension of Obligations in the EC—Hormones Dispute* (DS320), a dispute initiated by the European Union (EU)[14] against the United States in 2004 for continuing to maintain increased, i.e., 100% *ad valorem*, tariffs on EU goods first imposed in 1999 in retaliation for the EU's failure to comply with the adverse WTO ruling on the EU's ban on hormone-treated beef. The EU also initiated a separate case against Canada on the same basis.[15] The Appellate Body and modified panel reports in the underlying beef hormone case, *EC -Hormones*,[16] found that an EU ban on imports of meat and meat products from cattle produced from six specific growth-promotion hormones violated the Agreement on the Application of Sanitary and Phytosanitary Measures (SPS Agreement); the reports were adopted by the WTO in February 1998.

Claiming that a 2003 European Union Directive rendered it WTO-compliant, the EU argued that the defending Members, by maintaining their increased tariffs on EU products, were violating the following WTO obligations: (1) the GATT most-favored-nation article; (2) the GATT prohibition on tariff surcharges; and (3) various DSU provisions, including Article 23, which requires WTO Members to invoke WTO dispute settlement for disputes arising under WTO agreements and precludes certain unilateral actions in trade disputes, and Article 22.8, which permits sanctions to be imposed only until the defending Member's WTO-inconsistent measures have been removed or the dispute is mutually resolved.

In separate panel reports issued March 31, 2008, the WTO panel found that the EU was maintaining bans on certain hormones without a sufficient scientific basis in violation of the SPS Agreement, and that United States and Canada had breached Article 23 requirements to resort to WTO dispute settlement and to refrain from unilateral actions by (1) not initiating a WTO proceeding to resolve the EU compliance issue and (2) determining unilaterally that the EU was still in violation of the *EC - Hormones* decision. The panel also found, however, that to the extent that the challenged EU measure had not been removed, the United States and Canada had not violated Article 22.8, which requires that sanctions be removed once the offending measure is withdrawn.[17] The panel noted that it had functioned similarly to a compliance panel for the sole purpose of determining whether Article 22.8 was violated and, because it did not have jurisdiction to make a definitive determination in this regard, it suggested that the United States and Canada initiate a compliance panel proceeding against the EU under Article 21.5 in order to comply with their DSU obligations and to promptly resolve the dispute.

The Appellate Body, in separate reports issued October 16, 2008, reversed the panel's findings that the U.S. and Canada were in breach of the DSU as well as the panel's findings that the EU was still in violation of the SPS Agreement. [18] Because the Appellate Body could not complete the analysis needed to determine whether the contested EU measure had been withdrawn, however, it recommended that the parties initiate an Article 21.5 compliance panel proceeding to resolve their disagreement as to whether the EU is in compliance with the *EC—Hormones* decision and thus whether the U.S. and Canadian countermeasures have a legal basis. The AB and modified panel reports were adopted November 14, 2008.

The EU requested consultations under Article 21.5 in December 2008,[19] but the proceeding involving the United States has been suspended under a bilateral agreement. In a May 2009 memorandum of understanding (MOU) intended to resolve the underlying beef hormone dispute, the United States and the EU agreed, inter alia, that the EU will expand market access for exports of U.S. beef in three phases. In the first phase, the United States may maintain retaliatory tariffs currently applied to EU products and will not impose the new duties that it announced in January 2009 under its "carousel" retaliation provision (see below). The two parties also agreed that they will suspend WTO litigation, i.e., not request a compliance panel, for the first 18 months of the agreement.[20] The USTR delayed the imposition of the additional duties on new items until September 19, 2009, and officially terminated these duties as of this date.[21] As a result of these actions, the duties were never imposed.

WTO DISPUTE SETTLEMENT AND U.S. LAW

Legal Effect of WTO Decisions

The adoption by the WTO Dispute Settlement Body of a panel or Appellate Body report finding that a U.S. law, regulation, or practice violates a WTO agreement does not give the report direct legal effect in this country. Thus, federal law is not affected until Congress or the executive branch, as the case may be, changes the law or administrative measure at issue.[22] Procedures for executive branch compliance with adverse decisions are set out in § § 123(g) and 129 of the Uruguay Round Agreements Act, P.L. 103-465, 19 U.S.C. §§ 3533(g), 3538. Only the federal government may bring suit against a state or locality to declare a state or local law invalid because of inconsistency with a WTO agreement; private remedies based on WTO obligations are also precluded.[23] Federal courts have held that WTO panel and Appellate Body reports are not binding on the judiciary[24] and have treated determinations involving "whether, when, and how" to comply with a WTO decision as falling within the province of the executive rather than the judicial branch.[25]

Section 301 of the Trade Act

Sections 301-310 of the Trade Act of 1974 (referred to collectively as Section 301), 19 U.S.C. § § 2411 *et seq.*, provide a mechanism for private parties to petition the United States Trade Representative (USTR) to take action regarding harmful foreign trade practices. If the USTR decides to initiate an investigation, whether by petition or the USTR's own motion, regarding a foreign measure that allegedly violates a WTO agreement, the USTR must invoke the WTO dispute process to seek resolution of the problem. Section 301 authorizes the USTR to impose retaliatory measures to remedy an uncorrected foreign practice, some of which may involve suspending a WTO obligation (e.g., imposing a tariff increase on a product in excess of the rate negotiated in the WTO or the "bound" rate). The USTR may terminate a Section 301 case if the dispute is settled, but, under § 306 of the act, the USTR must monitor foreign compliance and may take further retaliatory action if compliance measures are unsatisfactory.

If the USTR has taken action against the goods of another country for its failure to comply with a WTO decision, § 306(b)(2)(B)-(F), of the Trade Act, 19 U.S.C. § 241 6(b)(2)(B)-(F), directs the USTR periodically to revise the list of imported products subject to retaliation, unless the USTR finds that implementation of WTO obligations is imminent or the USTR and the petitioner agree that revision is unnecessary. This authority to rotate the products subject to retaliatory action is often referred to as "carousel retaliation." The European Union filed a WTO complaint challenging the statutory provision shortly after its enactment in 2000, alleging that the statute mandates unilateral action and the taking of retaliatory action other than that which had been authorized by the WTO in violation of the DSU.[26] Because the United States had not invoked the provision, the EU refrained from seeking a panel in the case.

In December 2008, however, the United States exercised "carousel" authorities to propose modifications to the list of EU products subject to the WTO-authorized tariff surcharges that it had originally imposed in *EC—Hormones*, discussed earlier. A final modified list was published in January 2009.[27] Originally applicable to all covered goods entering the United States on or after March 23, 2009, the revisions include removal of some products from the original list of covered products, the addition of new products to the list, modified coverage with regard to certain EU member states, and an increase to 300% *ad valorem* of duties on one product, Roquefort cheese. The EU announced on January 15, 2009, that it had decided to "start preparations" to pursue WTO dispute settlement regarding the carousel statute, stating that it "breaches the WTO requirement of equivalence between the damage caused by the sanction or ban and the retaliation proposed."[28] As noted above, under an MOU with the EU aimed at settling the beef hormone dispute, the United States has agreed not to impose the announced tariff increases on new items and officially terminated these additional duties as of September 19, 2009.[29]

The EU filed a broader challenge to Section 301 in 1998 based on various obligations in Article 23 of the DSU, which, as noted earlier, precludes certain unilateral actions in trade disputes involving WTO agreements. Section 301 may generally be used consistently with the DSU, though some U.S. trading partners have complained that the statute allows unilateral action and forces negotiations through its threat of sanctions. The WTO panel found that the language of § 304, which requires the USTR to determine the legality of a foreign practice by a given date, is *prima facie* inconsistent with Article 23 because in some cases it mandates a USTR determination—and statutorily reserves a right for the USTR to determine that a practice is WTO-inconsistent—before DSU procedures are completed. [30] The panel also found, however, that the serious threat of violative determinations and consequently the *prima facie* inconsistency was removed because of U.S. undertakings, as set forth in the Uruguay Round Statement of Administrative Action (H.Doc. 103-316), a document submitted to Congress along with the Uruguay Round agreements, and U.S. undertakings made before the panel, that the USTR would use its statutory discretion to implement Section 301 in conformity with WTO obligations. Moreover, the panel could not find that the DSU was violated by § 306 of the Trade Act of 1974, which directs USTR to make a determination as to imposing retaliatory measures by a given date, given differing good faith interpretations of the "sequencing" ambiguities in the DSU. The panel report, which was not appealed, was adopted in January 2000.

111TH CONGRESS LEGISLATION

Legislation introduced in the 111th Congress generally reflects congressional concerns that the executive branch has not challenged restrictive foreign trade practices in the WTO to a sufficient degree and that, where WTO decisions have been adverse to the United States, the executive branch has too readily used existing statutory authorities to comply with these decisions, particularly where U.S. trade remedies are involved. A particular concern has been U.S. compliance with WTO decisions faulting the use of "zeroing," a practice employed by the Department of Commerce in antidumping proceedings to determine the applicable dumping margin, i.e., the amount by which the price of an import when sold in the United States falls below the fair value of the product, generally the price in the exporting country. The amount of antidumping duties finally imposed on an imported product is based on this margin. "Zeroing" is a practice under which sales above fair value are disregarded or given a "zero" value, thus allowing the dumping margin to be determined solely on the basis of less than fair value sales and, as alleged by some, improperly inflating the dumping margin. The Commerce Department abandoned the use of "zeroing" in original antidumping investigations in early 2007, but has not yet responded to WTO decisions rejecting U.S. use of the practice in later stages of U.S. antidumping proceedings.

H.R. 496 (Rangel) would create an Office of the Congressional Trade Enforcer (CTE), which, inter alia, would investigate restrictive foreign trade practices in light of WTO obligations and call on the United States Trade Representative (USTR) to initiate WTO dispute proceedings where the CTE finds that practices violate such obligations; express congressional dissatisfaction with WTO dispute settlement decisions finding that the U.S. practice of "zeroing" violates the WTO Antidumping Agreement and with decisions of the WTO Appellate Body generally; and place restrictions on the Department of Commerce in implementing the revised zeroing practice that it adopted in 2007 in response to adverse WTO decisions.

S. 363 (Snowe) would give the U.S. Court of International Trade, the specialized federal trade court based in New York City, exclusive jurisdiction to review *de novo* certain USTR determinations under Section 301 of the Trade Act of 1974, including in some cases determinations that may involve the initiation and conduct of WTO disputes, and would amend various Section 301 authorities themselves.

S. 1466 (Stabenow) and **S. 1982** (Brown) would establish mechanisms under the Trade Act of 1974 requiring the USTR to identify particularly harmful foreign trade practices and, where appropriate, to initiate WTO cases to remedy these practices.

End Notes

[1] The text of the DSU, panel and Appellate Body reports, and information on the WTO dispute process are available at http://www.wto.org/english/tratop_e/dispu_e/dispu_e.htm. WTO disputes are listed and summarized by the WTO Secretariat in its "Update of WTO Dispute Settlement Cases," available at the WTO website, above. Information on WTO disputes involving the United States, including the text of U.S. written submissions to WTO panels, may be found at the USTR website, at *http://www.ustr.gov/trade-topics/enforcement*. For the status of current cases in which the United States has been successfully challenged, see CRS Report RL32014, *WTO Dispute Settlement: Status of U.S. Compliance in Pending Cases*, by Jeanne J. Grimmett.

[2] Trade Act of 1974, P.L. 93-618, § 141(c)(1)(C),(D), 19 U.S.C. § 2171(c)(1)(C),(D). See also Uruguay Round Agreements Act, P.L. 103-465, §§ 123, 127, 129, 19 U.S.C. § 3533, 3537, 3538.

[3] Special Session of the Dispute Settlement Body, *Report by the Chairman to the Trade Negotiations Committee*, TN/DS/23 (December 5, 2008).

[4] See, e.g., WTO documents TN/DS/W/79 (July 13, 2005), TN/DS/W/82 (Oct. 24, 2005), TN/DS/W/82/Add. 1 (Oct. 25, 2005), as corrected, and TN/DSW/86 (Apr. 21, 2006). See also documents posted on the USTR website, at http://www.ustr.gov/trade-topics/enforcement

[5] For further information on proposals, see Institute of International Economic Law, *DSU Review*, at http://www.law.georgetown.edu/iiel/research/projects/dsureview/synopsis.html.

[6] Once the WTO is notified that a request for consultations has been made, the dispute will be assigned a number. Disputes are numbered in chronological order. The prefix WT/DS, followed by the assigned number, is then used to designate WTO documents issued in connection with the dispute. For example, the pending dispute between the United States and China, *China—Measures Affecting Trading Rights and Distribution Services for Certain Publications and Audio Entertainment Products* is DS363, with the U.S. request for consultations sent to China on August 10, 2007, numbered WT/DS363/1, and the WTO Appellate Body report issued on December 21, 2009, numbered WT/DS363/AB/R.

[7] Appellate Body Report, *United States—Anti-dumping Act of 1916*, paras. 60-61, WT/DS136/AB/R, WT/DS162/AB/R (Aug. 28, 2000).

[8] Appellate Body Report, *United States—Sunset Review of Anti-Dumping Measures on Oil Country Tubular Goods from Argentina*, para. 172, WT/DS268/AB/R (Nov. 29, 2004). The Appellate Body further described "as such" claims as follows:

By definition, an "as such" claim challenges laws, regulations, or other instruments of a Member that have general and prospective application, asserting that a Member's conduct—not only in a particular instance that has occurred, but in future situations as well—will necessarily be inconsistent with that Member's WTO obligations. In essence, complaining parties bringing "as such" challenges seek to prevent Members *ex ante* from engaging in certain conduct. The implications of such challenges are obviously more far-reaching than "as applied" claims.

[9] See, e.g., Henrik Horn & Petros C. Mavroidis, The WTO Dispute Settlement System 1995-2006: Some descriptive statistics, at 28-29 (Mar. 14, 2008), at *http://siteresources.worldbank.org/INTRES/Resources/469232-1107449512766/* DescriptiveStatistics_03 1408 .pdf.

[10] E.g., Report of the Appellate Body, *United States—Measures Relating to Zeroing and Sunset Reviews, Recourse to Article 21.5 of the DSU by Japan*, paras. 153-158, WT/DS322/AB/RW (Aug. 18, 2009).

[11] *Id.* para. 154.

[12] As of the date of this chapter, there have been 29 compliance panel proceedings, 13 of which involved the United States. Nineteen of the 29 panel reports were appealed, including 11 appeals by the United States.

[13] See Decision by the Arbitrator, *United States—Subsidies on Upland Cotton, Recourse to Arbitration by the United States under Article 22.6 of the DSU and Article 4.21 of the* SCM Agreement, paras. 5.10-5.236, WT/DS267/ARB/1 (Aug. 31, 2009), for a recent arbitral analysis of a request to cross-retaliate. In response to U.S. non-compliance in Brazil's challenge of U.S. cotton subsidies, Brazil sought authorization to suspend concessions under the Agreement on Trade-Related Aspects of Intellectual Property Right and the General Agreement on Trade in Services, arguing, as required under the DSU, that suspending concessions on goods alone was not "practicable or effective" and that the circumstances in the case were "serious enough" to permit it to do so. The arbitrator ultimately allowed Brazil to cross- retaliate, but required that a variable annual threshold tied to the level of U.S. imports into Brazil be exceeded before Brazil could exercise this option.

[14] As of December 1, 2009, "European Union" replaced "European Communities" as the official name of this WTO Member. The terms European Communities and EC still appear in older WTO materials, including panel and Appellate Body reports, bilateral procedural agreements in particular disputes, and communications to the WTO Dispute Settlement Body. Except for references to any such older WTO documents or other governmental materials using this name, this chapter uses "European Union" or the acronym "EU" in the report text or notes regardless of the time period being discussed. For further information, see *European Union or Communities?*, at http://www.wto.org/english/ thewto_e/countries_e /european_union_or_communitiesjopup.htm.

[15] *Canada—Continued Suspension of Obligations in the EC-Hormones Dispute*, WT/DS321.

[16] *European Communities—Measures Concerning Meat and Meat Products (Hormones),* WT/DS26 (complaint by United States); *European Communities—Measures Affecting Livestock and Meat (Hormones),* WT/DS48 (complaint by Canada).

[17] Panel Report, *United States - Continued Suspension of Obligations in the EC—Hormones Dispute*, WT/DS320/R (Mar. 31, 2008); Panel Report, *Canada - Continued Suspension of Obligations in the EC—Hormones Dispute*, WT/DS321/R (Mar. 31, 2008). At the request of the disputing parties, panel proceedings in the case were opened to the public via closed-circuit TV broadcast at the WTO, this being the first time that public access was permitted in a WTO dispute settlement proceeding. Disputing parties have also agreed to public access of this type in several subsequent disputes.

[18] Appellate Body Report, *United States—Continued Suspension of Obligations in the EC—Hormones Dispute*, WT/DS320/AB/R (Oct. 16, 2008); Appellate Body Report, *Canada—Continued Suspension of Obligations in the EC— Hormones Dispute*, WT/DS321/AB/R (Oct. 16, 2008).

[19] Press Release, European Commission, EU requests WTO consultations concerning WTO-compliance of its restrictions on hormone-treated beef and WTO inconsistency of continued US and Canadian trade sanctions (Dec. 22, 2008), at http://ec.europa.eu/trade/issues

[20] Press Release, Office of the USTR, USTR Announces Agreement with European Union in Beef Hormones Dispute (updated June 22, 2009), at http://www.ustr.gov/about-us/press-office/press-releases/2009/may/ustr-announcesagreement-european-union-beef European Commission, Memorandum on Beef Hormones dispute signed with the United States (May 14, 2009), at
http://ec.europa.eu/trade/issues

[21] At the time of the May 2009 agreement, some products had been removed from the list of covered items pursuant to the USTR's January 2009 announcement. While the Office of the USTR ultimately delayed the effective date of the additional duties on new products until September 19, 2009, the *removal* of items announced in January became effective as of March 23, 2009. Implementation of the U.S.-EC Beef Hormones Memorandum of Understanding, 74 Fed. Reg. 40864 (Aug. 13, 2009). The United States officially terminated the additional duties on new items on September 19, 2009, leaving in place the additional duties on the reduced list of products that had been in force since March 23, 2009. Implementation of the U.S.-EC Beef Hormones Memorandum of Understanding, 74 Fed. Reg. 48808 (Sept. 24, 2009).

[22] See Uruguay Round Agreements Act Statement of Administrative Action, H.Doc. 103-316, vol. 1, at 1032-33. Uruguay Round implementing legislation states that "[n]o provision of any of the Uruguay Round Agreements, nor the application of any such provision to any person or circumstance, that is inconsistent with any law of the United States shall have effect." Uruguay Round Agreements Act (URAA), P.L. 103-465, § 102(a)(1); see also H.Rept. 103-826, Pt. I, at 25.

[23] URAA, P.L. 103-465, § 102(b), (c).

[24] E.g., *Corus Staal BV v. Department of Commerce*, 395 F.3d 1343 (Fed. Cir. 2005), *cert. denied*, 126 S.Ct. 1023 (2006); see generally CRS Report RS22 154, *World Trade Organization (WTO) Decisions and Their Effect in U.S. Law*, by Jeanne J. Grimmett.

[25] Koyo Seiko Co. v. United States, 551 F.3d 1286, 1291 (Fed. Cir. 2008).

[26] Request for Consultations by the European Communities, *United States—Section 306 of the Trade Act of 1974 and Amendments Thereto*, WT/DS200/1 (June 13, 2000).

[27] Modification of Action Taken in Connection with WTO Dispute Settlement Proceedings on the European Communities' Ban on Imports of U.S. Beef and Beef Products, 74 Fed. Reg. 4265 (Jan. 23, 2009).

The continued imposition of the beef hormone sanctions as applicable to toasted bread products from Spain has been successfully challenged in the U.S. Court of International Trade, the specialized federal trade court located in New York City, on the ground that the sanctions expired by operation of law in late July 2007. Gilda Industries, Inc. v. United States, 625 F.Supp.2d 1377 (Ct. Int'l Trade 2009).

Section 307(c)(1) of the Trade Act of 1974, 19 U.S.C. § 2417(c)(1), provides that if "a particular action" has been taken by the USTR under Section 301 during any four-year period, e.g. the imposition of increased tariffs on the products of a foreign country, and neither the petitioner in the Section 301 case nor any representative of the domestic industry which benefits from the action has submitted to the USTR during the last 60 days of the four-year period a written request for the continuation of the action, the action is to terminate at the end of the four-year period. It was alleged in the case that the operative four-year period for the beef hormone sanctions began at the end of July 2003 and that no request was made to continue the sanctions during the final 60 days of this period. The court found that the retaliatory measures terminated by operation of law on July 29, 2007, absent a timely petitioner or industry request, neither of which had occurred. The court ordered the U.S. Department of Customs and Border Protection to refund to the plaintiff all retaliatory duties collected on its imported products between July 29, 2007, and March 23, 2009, the date these items were officially removed from the list of goods subject to the increased tariffs.

The United States has since appealed this decision to the U.S. Court of Appeals for the Federal Circuit. Gilda Industries v. United States, *appeal docketed*, No. 2009-1492 (Fed. Cir. Aug. 10, 2009). See generally *U.S. Faces Flood of Lawsuits after CIT Orders Refund of Duties*, INSIDE U.S. TRADE, Aug. 21, 2009, at 1.

[28] Press Release, European Commission, EU Prepares WTO action over US trade sanction law (Jan. 15, 2009), *at* http://ec.europa.eu/trade/issues. Article 22.4 of the DSU provides that "the level of the suspension of concessions or other obligations authorized by the DSB shall be equivalent to the level of the nullification or impairment." The "carousel" issue has also been raised by the EC in Doha Round dispute settlement negotiations. Dispute Settlement Body, Special Session, *Contribution of the European Communities and Its Member States to the Improvement of the WTO Dispute Settlement Understanding*, at 6, TN/DS/W/1 (Mar. 13, 2002).

[29] See *supra* note 21 and accompanying text.

[30] Panel Report, *United States—Sections 301-310 of the Trade Act of 1974*, WT/DS152/R (Dec. 22, 1999).

INDEX

D

E

F

S

T

U

V

W